Introduction to Algorithmic Government

Rajan Gupta · Saibal Kumar Pal

Introduction to Algorithmic Government

Rajan Gupta
Centre for Information Technologies
& Applied Mathematics
University of Nova Gorica
Nova Gorica, Slovenia

Saibal Kumar Pal
Defence Research
and Development Organisation
New Delhi, India

ISBN 978-981-16-0281-8   ISBN 978-981-16-0282-5   (eBook)
https://doi.org/10.1007/978-981-16-0282-5

This Palgrave Macmillan imprint is published by the registered company Springer Nature Singapore Pte Ltd.
The registered company address is: 152 Beach Road, #21-01/04 Gateway East, Singapore 189721, Singapore

Dedicated to

*My "**Gurumaa**" for holding my hand in Life,*
*My "**Parents**" for making me stand in Life,*
*My "**Nephew**" for making me strong in Life,*
*My "**Brother & His Wife**" for helping me progress in Life, and*
*My "**Wife**" for supporting and loving me unconditionally in Life!*

—Dr. Rajan Gupta

Dedicated to the memory of my parents.

—Dr. Saibal Kumar Pal

PREFACE

This book titled 'Introduction to Algorithmic Government' has got three significant things to offer—Background to Algorithmic Government, various Algorithmic Government applications around the World & India, and potential use cases of Algorithmic Government around the developing world in the near future.

Algorithmic Government or Government by Algorithm is an emerging concept introduced around the world. It involves using Data Science and Artificial Intelligence for decision making by the Government for various services and processes. In some nations, even digitization has not happened, but machines are ready to make decisions on behalf of humans in others. On the one hand, many governments struggle to score high on E-Governance Development Index by the United Nations. In contrast, on the other hand, some countries are even approving the electoral candidature of AI bots. This brings us to a position where we need to understand how automated decision making is taking place around the world.

The first chapter covers the background on the usage of technology for decision making. The second chapter discusses the core concepts of the Algorithmic Government, various models associated with it, along with the numerous advantages, disadvantages, challenges, limitations, concerns, and audits related to it. Chapter 3 presents the various technologies which are used for implementing Government by Algorithms around the world. The fourth chapter argues whether it is possible to replace humans with machines. Chapter 5 presents various progressive steps taken worldwide concerning the automation of decision making in the Public Sector. Chapter 6 showcases technological advancements and decision making in a developing country like India across multiple sectors. Chapter 7 presents various potential use cases that can be developed in different domains, specifically for developing and under-developed worlds. At the end of this book, multiple codes for prototypes of use cases from Chapter 7 are presented for technology enthusiasts.

This book will serve as introductory material for the readers from technology, public policy, and management fields. It will help develop understanding around different concepts present for automated decision making and usage of technology in the public sector as an advancement. The reader should differentiate E-Governance as the digitization of the Government processes, and Algorithmic Governance as the automated decision making on behalf of the Government.

Nova Gorica, Slovenia   Rajan Gupta
New Delhi, India   Saibal Kumar Pal

Acknowledgments

The authors of this book would like to gratefully and sincerely thank all the people who have supported them during the journey of writing this book, to only some of whom it is possible to mention here.

Primarily, the authors would like to thank their Ph.D. Supervisor—Prof. Sunil Kumar Muttoo, for his valuable guidance and research directions in the field of Computer Science & Data Science. Then the authors would like to thank current and former faculty members of the Department of Computer Science, University of Delhi—Prof. Vasudha Bhatnagar, Prof. Punam Bedi, Prof. Naveen Kumar, Prof. Neelima Gupta, Mr. P. K. Hazra, and Ms. Vidya Kulkarni. They helped provide infrastructure and resources related to Doctoral Research work, which was in Data Science and E-Governance. The doctoral work became the basis for this book.

The first author would also like to thank the Administrative and Teaching Unit of Deen Dayal Upadhyaya College, University of Delhi, under the guidance of Dr. Hemchand Jain, for providing their support toward the writing of this book. Also, the first author would like to acknowledge and thank Prof. Tanja Urbancic and Prof. Irina Cristea from Centre for Information Technologies & Applied Mathematics, University of Nova Gorica for their valuable support during the final submission of this book. The second author acknowledges the Defence Research & Development Organization (DRDO) for its valuable support.

This book would not have been possible without the valuable contributions from members of TCF Consultancy™—Mr. Shubham Gupta, Ms. Kanika Gupta, Mr. Gaurav Pandey, Ms. Shreya Khurana, Ms. Himani Girdhar, Mr. Hritik Kounsal, Ms. Iffat Aara, Ms. Muskaan Ratra, and Mr. Tarun Garg. They all helped in information collection and case studies validation using Python Programming.

Finally, this work would not have been possible without the invaluable support from the publishing team of Palgrave Macmillan, Springer, esp. Ms. Sandeep Kaur, Ms. Shreenidhi Natarajan, and Ms. Sagarika Ghosh. This book also recognizes incredible support from the book's endorsers, and the authors' guru, mentors, family, and friends. So the authors would like to thank them all from the bottom of their hearts.

CONTENTS

About the Authors

Dr. Rajan Gupta is a Research and Analytics Professional and has authored three books in the area of E-Governance and Data Science. He has done his Ph.D. in the field of Data Analytics for Improvement E-Governance in Developing Nations from the Department of Computer Science, University of Delhi. He completed his Master in Computer Application (M.C.A.) from the University of Delhi, Post-Graduate Program in Management (PGPM) from IMT Ghaziabad (CDL), and Executive Program in Business Intelligence and Analytics (EPBABI) from IIM-Ranchi. He is NET-JRF qualified under University Grant Commission, India, and holds a certificate in Consulting from Consultancy Development Centre (CDC), DSIR, Ministry of Science and Technology, Government of India. He is one of the few Certified Analytics Professional (CAP-INFORMS) around the world and is serving as ACB Member & CAP Ambassador in Asia Region. He has been accredited with GStat from American Statistical Association (ASA).

He has industrial working experience with firms like Samsung and TCF Consultancy™ in their research and analytics department. He is currently associated as Postdoctoral Research Fellow in Data Science and Data-driven Modeling at the Centre for Information Technologies and Applied Mathematics, University of Nova Gorica, Slovenia. He is also working as an Assistant with PhD at the School of Engineering and Management, University of Nova Gorica, where he is involved in pedagogical activities in computer science, data science and informatics. In the recent past he has worked as Assistant Professor with Deen Dayal Upadhyaya College, University of Delhi, India. He has also taught at the Department of Computer Science (Faculty of Mathematical Science), University of Delhi, India, and IMT—Ghaziabad, India to deliver lectures in Computer Science, Data Science, Analytics, IT, and Management. His area of interest includes Data Science, E-Governance, Algorithmic Government, Public Information Systems, and Information Security. He has ten years of combined experience in Research, Analytics, Consulting, and Teaching and has over 75 publications at various national and international forums in the form of books, chapters, journals, and conference papers.

He has recently contributed to the E-Governance Development Index report by the United Nations (EGDI-2020). He is a member of the reviewer panel of multiple international journals & conferences. He is also an invited public speaker and has conducted Workshops & Seminars on the usage of Data Science & Artificial Intelligence for Governments around the world. He has recently delivered a talk as a panelist on Data Science Application for E-Governance on an international forum sponsored by International Data Engineering and Science Association (IDEAS), USA, and conducted a Workshop on 'Inclusion of Marginalized Communities' through E-Governance at ICEGOV-2020 hosted by United Nations University.

Dr. Saibal Kumar Pal is a Senior Scientist at Defence Research & Development Organization (DRDO), Government of India, and has been awarded 'Scientist of the Year' for his significant contributions in the area of Information Security. He received his Ph.D. in Computer Science from the University of Delhi and is an Invited Faculty & Research Guide at several national institutions. His areas of interest are Information & Cyber Security, Computational Intelligence, Information Systems, and Electronic Governance. He has more than 300 publications in books, journals, and international conference proceedings. He has contributed to a number of significant projects & international collaborations and is a member of national advisory committees.

ABBREVIATIONS

ADM	Algorithmic Decision Making
ADRIN	Advanced Data Research Institute
AG	Algorithmic Government
AI	Artificial Intelligence
ANN	Artificial Neural Network
API	Application Programming Interface
AR	Augmented Reality
BIS	Bank for International Settlements
CAIR	Centre for Artificial Intelligence and Robotics
CEFR	Common European Framework of Reference
CHW	Community Health Workers
CSV	Comma Separated Values
CT	Computed Tomography
DL	Deep Learning
DRDO	Defence Research and Development Organization
E-Governance	Electronic Governance
E-Government	Electronic Government
G2B	Government to Business
G2C	Government to Citizens
G2E	Government to Employee
G2G	Government to Government
GAs	Genetic Algorithms
GDP	Gross Domestic Product
GLOFs	Glacial Lake Outburst Floods
GST	Goods & Services Tax
HART	Harm Assessment Risk Tool

IaaS	Infrastructure as a Service
ICT	Information and Communication Technologies
IoT	Internet of Things
ISRO	Indian Space Research Organization
IT	Information Technology
ITCZ	Intertropical Convergence Zone
ITF	International Transport Forum
KNN	k-Nearest Neighbors
M&E	Monitoring & Evaluation
ML	Machine Learning
MORTH	Ministry of Road Transport and Highways
NLP	Natural Language Processing
NN	Neural Network
NUSAP	Numeral Unit Spread Assessment Pedigree
OECD	Organization for Economic Cooperation and Development
OGD	Open Government Data
PaaS	Platform as a Service
PAIS	Punjab Artificial Intelligence System
ROI	Return on Investment
SaaS	Software as a Service
SGD	Stochastic Gradient Descent
SVM	Support Vector Machine
TF-IDF	Term Frequency–Inverse Document Frequency
TMH	TATA Memorial Hospital
UK	United Kingdom
UN	United Nations
UNESCO	United Nations Educational, Scientific and Cultural Organization
URL	Uniform Resource Locator
VR	Virtual Reality
WD	Western Disturbances
WHO	World Health Organization
YOLO	You Only Look Once

LIST OF FIGURES

LIST OF TABLES

CHAPTER 1

Role of Technology in Decision Making

Abstract The first chapter covers the background on the usage of technology for decision making. It presents the difficulties in the traditional decision-making system and argues how technology helps to plug the loopholes of the system. Also, the digitization of government services has been discussed, where developing nations like India have been doing well for the past few years. In many regions, authorities are adopting digital services for office work and interaction with citizens. And this has led to the rise in data generation at a massive level. Growing data leads to the adoption of technology for decision making in the public sector, which has been the whole premise for the usage of Artificial Intelligence in the Government set up.

Keywords Artificial Intelligence · Public sector · Automated decision making · Digitization · Government

1.1 Background

Technology is playing a significant role as a large number of tools are present to strategize and design the decision-making process, especially in the public sector. The Algorithmic Government is a technology-driven government process that transforms data into actionable information and

R. Gupta and S. K. Pal, *Introduction to Algorithmic Government*, https://doi.org/10.1007/978-981-16-0282-5_1

helps decision-makers understand the current state and make a decision (Engin & Treleaven, 2019). Time tracking and activity tracking, on the other hand, provides a way to collect data. Many public and private companies use Artificial Intelligence (AI) and machine learning (ML) algorithms as part of their decision-making process. AI improves the quality of decision making, thereby makes the process work more effective and efficient. AI and many other technologies like big data, the Internet of Things (IoT), blockchain, etc., have tremendous potential in transforming the government, as shown in Fig. 1.1.

Figure 1.1 shows that Algorithmic Government is implemented for the public sector automation like citizen services, supporting civil servants, national public records, national physical infrastructure, statutes and compliance, and public policy development. For automating these services, open data portals using IoT, AI, big data, behavioral/predictive analysis, and blockchain technologies are performing well worldwide to create a successful Algorithmic Government (Engin & Treleaven, 2019).

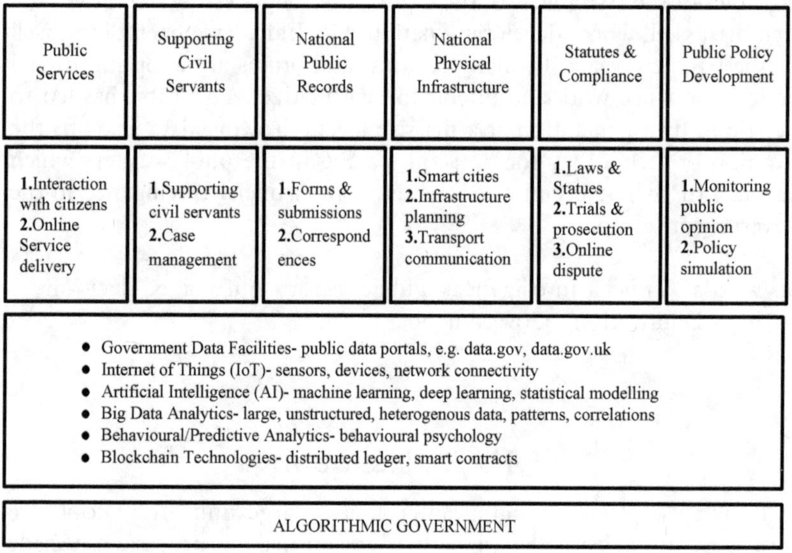

Public Services	Supporting Civil Servants	National Public Records	National Physical Infrastructure	Statutes & Compliance	Public Policy Development
1.Interaction with citizens 2.Online Service delivery	1.Supporting civil servants 2.Case management	1.Forms & submissions 2.Correspond ences	1.Smart cities 2.Infrastructure planning 3.Transport communication	1.Laws & Statues 2.Trials & prosecution 3.Online dispute	1.Monitoring public opinion 2.Policy simulation

- Government Data Facilities- public data portals, e.g. data.gov, data.gov.uk
- Internet of Things (IoT)- sensors, devices, network connectivity
- Artificial Intelligence (AI)- machine learning, deep learning, statistical modelling
- Big Data Analytics- large, unstructured, heterogenous data, patterns, correlations
- Behavioural/Predictive Analytics- behavioural psychology
- Blockchain Technologies- distributed ledger, smart contracts

ALGORITHMIC GOVERNMENT

Fig. 1.1 Algorithmic government service architecture (*Source* Engin and Treleaven [2019, https://ieeexplore.ieee.org])

1.2 Traditional Decision Making

Traditional decision making has always been dependent on the paper-based system. The paper-based system has many challenges that lead to the system's inefficiency, data loss, time loss, and more storage space requirement as a considerable amount of data is generated. Figure 1.2 shows an example of a traditional decision-making model for purchase by consumers (Xu & Chen, 2017).

Similarly, a lot of Government departments use paper-based decision making. Like, the Immigration department plays an essential role in maintaining the security of a country as they control the entry and departure of people across the nations. These agencies have to approve a wide variety of documents with applications ranging from identity cards, birth certificates, marriage registration, travel documents, and many others. Millions of application forms of multiple types are submitted to the agency for processing. In some countries like Hong Kong, agencies used a manual immigration process (Chun, 2007), which has been digitized over the years. The manual approach process starts with the applicant submitting a hardcopy of the application form along with the photocopies of relevant documents. The original records are verified at a later stage. The Authorization Officer reviews the case and assigns a suitable Case Officer who is familiar with handling that type of application. While considering the evidence, the Case Officer may ask for additional documents from

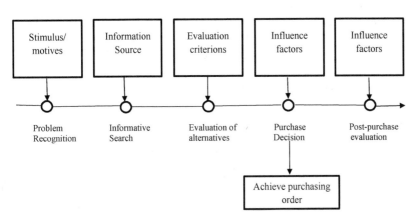

Fig. 1.2 Traditional decision-making model for purchase by a consumer (*Source* Xu and Chen [2017])

the applicant for verification. When all the other papers are submitted and verified, the Case Officer makes a final assessment reviewed by the Authorization Officer. The entire process may require the applicant to visit the agency several times. It may even take months to complete the process as it depends on the complexity of the process. The Case Officer plays a crucial role in applying their knowledge gained from the vast experience. Assessing a complex application can be very time-consuming and knowledge-intensive. Thus, AI can be used to capture the different types of knowledge required for the application assessment to make the process easier and less time-consuming.

In South Africa, the community health workers (CHW) program is organized under the Primary Health Care (PHCs) program (Neupane et al., 2014). Community health workers play a significant role in improving the health status of isolated communities. They provide preventive health services, promote access to essential healthcare services (Lewin et al., 2010), collect health-related data (Braun, Catalani, Wimbush, & Israelski, 2013), monitors the community health, and also acts as an interface between the community and the health system (Bhutta et al., 2010). CHW programs have monitoring and evaluation (M&E), supervision, and accountability, which serve as the key elements to ensure the effectiveness of the program (Lehmann & Sanders, 2007). Traditionally, CHWs used a paper-based M&E system, which led to similar problems like data loss, less storage space, inefficient filing system, lack of supervision of record-keeping, time-consuming, and difficulty in tracing the referrals made by the CHWs. The clients were also worried about the confidentiality of the information captured in the process. After a few years, mHealth was introduced to the use of mobile communication technology (Braun et al., 2013). This technology reduced many of the challenges faced during the paper-based system. mHealth has made the process very efficient and effective as through technology, health promotion, education, and awareness can be created among the people. However, only providing information through mobile or Internet is not categorized under Algorithmic Government. Instead, it includes digitization along with the decision-making powers within the machine.

1.3   DIGITIZATION OF GOVERNMENT SERVICES

Governments worldwide are increasingly using digitization and data analytics in the policymaking process, which is consequently leading to a more effective, efficient, and better quality of decision making. Humans generally rely on heuristics for day-to-day decision making, ignoring much of the available information (Kolkman, 2020). Algorithmic models are quantifying the policymaking. The range of quantification is vast, but algorithmic models are of particular interest as they provide evidence in decisions that allocate and save billion of government expenditure.

Figure 1.3 represents a policy-making cycle, an example of a heuristic framework of policymaking (Kolkman, 2020). There is a substantial increase in digital decision making across the central and local governments of various countries like the United Kingdom (UK). An investigation by the Guardian showed 140 of 408 councils are using privately developed algorithmic risk assessment tools to determine the eligibility for benefits and entitlements (Jones, 2020). The Data Justice Lab in 2018 showed that 56 out of 96 local's authorities and a quarter of police authorities are using algorithms for prediction, risk assessment, and assistance in decision making. Durham Police is using the Harm Assessment Risk Tool (HART) to predict reoffending.

Indian citizens are also taking a digital leap, making it one of the largest and fastest-growing space for government-citizen interactions. India had 560 million Internet subscribers in September 2018, second only to China (Kaka, 2020). Indians download more than 12.3 billion mobile applications in 2018, which is more than any country in the world except China.

Figure 1.4 shows that India is among the top two countries globally on many critical digital adoption dimensions. That is why the digitization of government services has a vast scope in India. Developing countries like India are now emerging healthy destinations for implementing technology-based solutions and helping the government make better and efficient decisions.

Figure 1.5 shows that countries like South Korea and Sweden are very high on the Digital Adoption Index score. Countries like Indonesia and India are digitizing faster than the other countries by relatively high

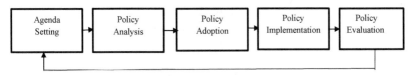

Fig. 1.3 Policymaking cycle (*Source* Kolkman [2020])

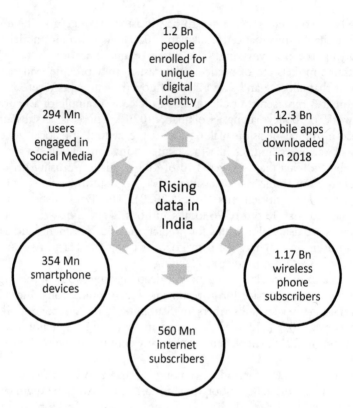

Fig. 1.4 Increasing digital services in India (*Source* Kaka [2020])

margins. The digital adoption index covers three elements, which are the digital foundation (cost, speed, reliability of Internet service), digital reach (data consumption, app downloads), and digital value (how much consumers engage online by chatting, tweeting, or shopping).

The public and private sectors are working very hard for the rapid digitization of various countries worldwide. Again, in a country like India, the Government's national biometric digital identity program (*Aadhar Program*) has played a significant role. It is considered to be the single most extensive digital ID program in the world. Almost 870 million bank accounts are linked to Aadhar in February 2018 compared to 399 million in April 2017 and 56 million in January 2014. Similarly, the

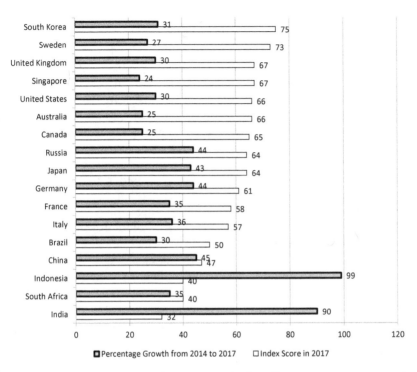

Fig. 1.5 Digital adoption index (*Source* Kaka [2020])

Goods and Services Tax (GST) network, initiated by the government in 2013, brought all transactions of 10.3 million indirect tax-paying businesses onto one digital platform (Kaka, 2020). At the same time, Reliance Jio from the private sector is also helping by providing Internet-enabled services to millions of consumers and made online usage more accessible. So, in short, many countries are now in the digital transformation stage, which is even evident by the E-Governance Development Index's progress by the United Nations. And digital transformations are making the way ahead for the implementation of Algorithmic models for decision making.

1.4   DATA GENERATION

The introduction of computers, smartphones, and other digital devices led to digital data generation (Kumar, Sood, Kaul, & Vasuja, 2020). Every piece of information generated and exchanged between human to human, machine to machine, and human to a machine, is treated as data. When these systems are combined, they make enormous amounts of information known as big data. Approximately 2.5 quintillion bytes of data get generated each day with the current pace. Over the last two years, 90% of data has been created globally (Marr, 2020). Twitter produced 1 Petabyte (100 Terabyte) of data daily, while Google processed 100 Petabyte data regularly, and YouTube added 72 h of video every minute (Ghotkar & Rokde, 2016). And these numbers are increasing rapidly.

Based on such a fast data generation, three significant features characterize big data, viz., Volume, Variety, and Velocity (Kumar et al., 2020). Volume relates to the quantity or size of the data, which is enormous. A substantial contributor to the ever-expanding digital universe is the Internet of Things worldwide in all devices, creating data at every second. Airplanes generate approximately 2.5 Terabytes of data each year from the sensors installed in the engine. The velocity is the speed at which the data is created, stored, analyzed, and visualized. In big data, the information is generated in real-time applications. With the availability of Internet-connected devices, wireless or wired, machines and devices can pass on their data when created. At every minute, we upload 100 hours of video on YouTube, around 20 million photos are viewed, and almost 2.5 million queries are performed on Google (Ghotkar & Rokde, 2016).

The data generated by organizations is unstructured. Today data comes in different formats like structured, semi-structured, and unstructured. The wide variety of data needs other techniques and approaches to store them. The diverse array of data, such as text, image, maps, network data, geographical information, etc., needs appropriate treatment. Even a standard text posted on platforms like Facebook or Twitter can give different insights, such as sentiment analysis on any concept.

Big data can be generated by humans, machines, or a combination of human machine. The information generated may be stored in structured or unstructured formats. Big data can be broadly categorized based on sources such as machine-generated, human-generated, and organization-generated. Machines are emerging as the largest source of big data. Human-generated data refers to the vast amount of social media data like a status update, posting tweets, uploading photos or videos, etc. Machine-generated data refers to data created from real-time sensors through industry, machines, or vehicles. Data comes from various sensors, cameras, satellites, log files, bioinformatics, healthcare tracker, and many other sensor data sources. People generate a large amount of data on social networking sites like Facebook, Twitter, LinkedIn, Instagram, and YouTube. Large-scale data arises through blogging sites, email, mobile text messages, and personal documents (Shelke, Abhang, & Shete, 2020).

The data generated through an organization is highly structured in nature and trustworthy. This type of data is stored in a relational database. Organizational information is private and is the smallest source in the global big data scenario. The corporate data, when combined with public domain data, provide meaningful insights to faster and better decisions. Through AI, trillions of dollars in value can be added to goods and services each year. AI could harness data about citizen's behavior to enable the government to work properly. Personalized public services can be developed and adapted according to individual circumstances. It also allows the government to make forecasts that are more accurate and help them to plan and predict future trends. The healthcare sector can also be inspected through this. The government can simulate complex systems ranging from military operations to private areas of a country, which will consequently enable the government to experiment with the different policy options and will be able to spot the consequence before committing to a measure (Araya, 2020).

1.5   Technology for Decision Making

Technology like Artificial Intelligence has different use cases ranging from developing autonomous vehicles, conducting facial recognition, creating chatbots, and conducting fraud detection. All of these applications of AI have a commonality and fall in one or more seven patterns (Walch, 2020). The seven patterns of AI are shown in Fig. 1.6 and are discussed below.

Hyper-personalization: Applying a machine-learning algorithm to develop a profile of each individual and then having that profile learn and adapt for a variety of purposes over time, e.g., recommend relevant products, displaying relevant content, and so on. It can be applied to different sectors and industries like healthcare for personalized fitness and wellness applications.

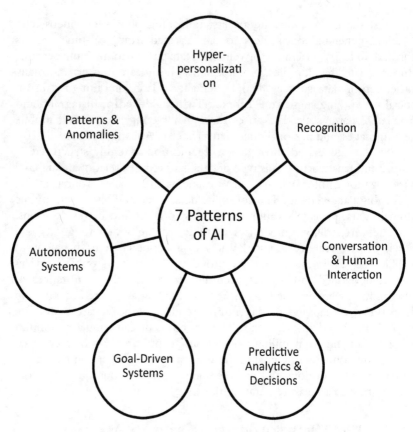

Fig. 1.6 Seven patterns of Artificial Intelligence (*Source* Walch [2020])

Autonomous Systems: Autonomous systems are physical and virtual software and hardware system which can accomplish a task or a goal with minimal human interaction. The autonomous patterns require a machine learning capability that can independently perceive the outside world, predict future behavior, and plan how to deal with the changes. The applications are autonomous machines and vehicles such as cars, trains, airplanes, etc.

Predictive Analytics: The objective of predictive analysis is to help humans make better decisions using machine learning and cognitive approaches to understand the actual behavior and predict future outcomes based on these patterns. This pattern is used in the assisted search, predicting behavior, optimization activities, giving advice, and intelligent navigation.

Conversational Pattern: The objective of this pattern is to enable machines to interact with humans; how humans interact with each other through conversational forms of texts like voice, text, and image. The application of this pattern is a chatbot, voice assistants, sentiment, mood, and intent analysis.

Patterns and Anomalies: The goal of pattern and anomalies pattern of AI is to use machine learning and cognitive approach to learn patterns in the data and the connection between the data points to check the existing model that it fits, or there is an outlier or anomaly. Fraud and risk detection can be an application of this pattern of AI.

Recognition pattern: The objective of this pattern is to have machine identify and understand things by using machine learning and deep learning to identify and determine objects within image, audio, text, etc. and improve the accuracy of the recognition-related tasks. Examples include object recognition, facial recognition, text recognition, audio, and video recognition.

Goal-driven system: Through reinforcement learning, the objective is to find the optimal solution to a problem. This pattern is not widely implemented, but it is gaining rapid adoption. Examples include game playing, resource optimization, real-time auctions, etc.

Technologies like AI are now used for decision making, which forms the basis for Algorithmic Decision Making for the Government. Figure 1.7 shows how Algorithmic Decision Making is carried out. The system is fed with historical data, and the machine generates the model. This model is applied to the real-time data, and decision making takes place by the engine. No human involvement is there throughout the system, and the machine learns from every real-time input and fine-tunes the model parameters after a set of iterations.

The International Transport Forum (ITF) at OECD is an intergovernmental organization covering all transport modes and currently working on transport policies through which people's lives can improve (ITF-OECD, 2020). ITF is working on Algorithmic Governance in Transport by automating the decision-making system. They found out that automated decision-making systems have a consequential impact on transport activity. AI and machine learning algorithms helped to accomplish the tasks which were previously difficult and time-consuming.

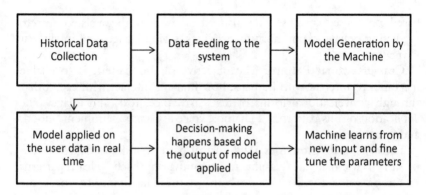

Fig. 1.7   Algorithmic decision making process (*Source* Author's Creation)

Beijing is saturated with sensors that can check the level of CO_2 and other pollutants in the atmosphere (Newcombe, 2020). The data generated from these sensors is enormous. Using AI, they combine the data with historical data patterns of weather and predict the pollution level. According to the result, they modestly dial back the industrial sector and traffic rather than shutting down the entire city.

1.6   Artificial Intelligence for Public Sector

Artificial Intelligence is a tremendous technological revolution of our time with the potential to disrupt all aspects of human existence. It enables the machines to act with a higher intelligence level with human capabilities of sense, comprehend, and work. Many countries worldwide are becoming aware of the potential economic and social benefits of developing and applying AI. Countries like China and the UK have estimated that 26% and 10% of their GDPs will be sourced from AI-related activities, respectively, by 2030 (Niti Aayog, 2020). Governments in countries like China, France, and Japan are helping their people to spend on AI technology development and adoption. They are setting up industrial and investment funds in AI startups and connecting large corporations with startups, and forming a national team.

Artificial Intelligence in a developing nation like India can also provide significant value to a wide range of sectors and is the critical source of competitive advantage for firms. AI in healthcare will remove the barriers to access healthcare facilities in rural areas who suffer from a limited supply of healthcare professionals. Through the use of AI-driven diagnostics, personalized treatments, imaging diagnostics, and early detection of potential pandemics will help to make the healthcare sector more effective, efficient, and available for everyone. AI in Agriculture will address the challenges such as lack of assured irrigation, overuse/misuse of pesticides, and fertilizers and will also meet the increasing demand for food. AI will improve the crop yield through real-time advisory, advanced detection of pest attacks, and predicting crop prices to inform sowing practices.

The potential use cases in smart mobility, including transports and logistics, are ride-sharing, semi-autonomous features like driver assist, predictive engine monitoring, and maintenance. It will also improve traffic management and inventory management. Through the adoption of AI in retail, there will be enhanced user experience by providing personalized suggestions, preference-based browsing, an image-based product search, and efficient delivery management.

Manufacturing is one of the biggest beneficiaries of AI-based solutions. It enables them to be flexible and adaptable technical systems to automate the process and respond to unexpected situations. Engineering, warehouse, supply chain management, and maintenance will have an impact. AI can also enable power storage in renewable energy systems through intelligent grids enabled by smart meters and improve photovoltaic energy's reliability and affordability. It will increase the efficiency in power balancing, and it can be deployed for predictive maintenance of grid infrastructure.

India's government has started a program for AI under Niti Aayog named #AIforALL, which aims to empower and enhance human capabilities to address the challenges of effective AI implementation. Through this strategy, there will be economic and social development of the country. Similarly, many other countries have started to look at AI as a potential source of decision making both at the public and private sector levels. This way, Algorithmic Government is rising at the world level, and a lot of countries, where either workload is very high, or there is a shortage of workforce, the government can still operate smoothly.

References

Araya, D. (2020). *Artificial intelligence and the end of government* [online] Forbes. Available at: https://www.forbes.com/sites/danielaraya/2019/01/04/artificial-intelligence-and-the-end-of-government/#2fb28873719b. Accessed 16 July 2020.

Bhutta, Z. A., Chopra, M., Axelson, H., Berman, P., Boerma, T., Bryce, J., ... & de Francisco, A. (2010). Countdown to 2015 decade report (2000–10): Taking stock of maternal, newborn, and child survival. *The Lancet, 375*(9730), 2032–2044.

Braun, R., Catalani, C., Wimbush, J., & Israelski, D. (2013). Community health workers and mobile technology: A systematic review of the literature. *PLoS ONE, 8*(6), e65772.

Chun, A. H. W. (2007, July). Using AI for e-Government automatic assessment of immigration application forms. In *AAAI* (pp. 1684–1691). Available at: https://www.aaai.org/Papers/AAAI/2007/AAAI07-273.pdf. Accessed 17 September 2020.

Engin, Z., & Treleaven, P. (2019). Algorithmic government: Automating public services and supporting civil servants in using data science technologies. *The Computer Journal, 62*(3), 448–460.

Ghotkar, M., & Rokde, P. (2016). Big data: How it is generated and its importance. *IOSR Journal of Computer Engineering* [Online] Available at: http://www.iosrjournals.org/iosr-jce/papers/conf.15013/Volume%202/1.%2001-05.pdf. Accessed 16 July 2020.

ITF-OECD. (2020). Governing transport in the algorithmic age [online] Available at: https://www.itf-oecd.org/sites/default/files/docs/governing-transport-algorithmic-age.pdf. Accessed 17 July 2020.

Jones, C. (2020). *The government's approach to algorithmic decision-making is broken: Here's how to fix it* [online]. NS Tech. Available at: https://tech.newstatesman.com/guest-opinion/algorithmic-decision-making. Accessed 16 July 2020.

Kaka, N. (2020). Digital India: Technology to transform a connected nation [online]. Available at: https://www.mckinsey.com/business-functions/mckinsey-digital/our-insights/digital-india-technology-to-transform-a-connected-nation. Accessed 16 July 2020.

Kolkman, D. (2020). The usefulness of algorithmic models in policy making. *Government Information Quarterly, 37*(3), 101488.

Kumar, Y., Sood, K., Kaul, S., & Vasuja, R. (2020). Big data analytics and its benefits in healthcare. In *Big data analytics in healthcare* (pp. 3–21). Cham: Springer.

Lehmann, U., & Sanders, D. (2007). Community health workers: What do we know about them. *The state of the evidence on programmes, activities, costs and* impact on health outcomes of using community health workers. Geneva: World Health Organization (pp. 1–42).

Lewin, S., Munabi-Babigumira, S., Glenton, C., Daniels, K., Bosch-Capblanch, X., Van Wyk, B. E., ... & Scheel, I. B. (2010). Lay health workers in primary and community health care for maternal and child health and the management of infectious diseases. Cochrane Database of Systematic Reviews (3). https://doi.org/10.1002/14651858.cd004015.pub3.

Marr, B. (2020). How much data do we create every day? The mind-blowing stats everyone should read [online]. Forbes. Available at: https://www.forbes.com/sites/bernardmarr/2018/05/21/how-much-data-do-we-create-every-day-the-mind-blowing-stats-everyone-should-read/#cb23bfd60ba9. Accessed 16 July 2020.

Neupane, S., Odendaal, W., Friedman, I., Jassat, W., Schneider, H., & Doherty, T. (2014). Comparing a paper based monitoring and evaluation system to a mHealth system to support the national community health worker programme, South Africa: an evaluation. BMC Medical Informatics and Decision Making, 14(1), 69.

Newcombe, T. (2020). Is government ready for AI? [online]. Govtech.com. Available at: https://www.govtech.com/products/Is-Government-Ready-for-AI.html [Accessed 17 July 2020].

Niti Aayog. (2020). National strategy for AI discussion [online]. Niti,gov.in Available at: https://niti.gov.in/writereaddata/files/document_publication/NationalStrategy-for-AI-Discussion-Paper.pdf. Accessed 17 July 2020.

Shelke, P., Abhang, N., & Shete, A. (2020). Social media data controlling and processing using big data. Journal of Innovative Thinking in Engineering, 1(1).

Walch, K. (2020). The seven patterns of AI [Online]. Forbes. Available at: https://www.forbes.com/sites/cognitiveworld/2019/09/17/the-seven-patterns-of-ai/#2652345612d0. Accessed 17 July 2020.

Xu, B., & Chen, J. (2017). Consumer purchase decision-making process based on the traditional clothing shopping form. Journal of Fashion Technology & Textile Engineering, 5(3), 1–12.

CHAPTER 2

Background of Algorithmic Government

Abstract The second chapter discusses the core concepts of the Algorithmic Government, various models associated with it, along with the numerous advantages, disadvantages, challenges, limitations, concerns, and audits related to it. The different types of Algorithmic Government systems, classified based on the degree of automation and transparency level, are also presented. Various ethical concerns like privacy, transparency, discrimination, and accountability related to the implementation of Algorithmic Government have been discussed, for which an audit framework named SMACTR has been presented at the end. This chapter also showcases the difference between Algorithmic Governance and Algorithmic Government and how a separate governance structure will be required to deal with Government by Algorithms.

Keywords Algorithmic ethics · Algorithmic bias · Algorithmic limitations · Governance structure · Algorithmic audit · SMACTR

2.1 Concept of Algorithmic Government

Algorithms are defined as the set of rules that are being designed to accomplish a particular task. These are step-wise procedures or solutions created using mathematical logic to process instructions and data

R. Gupta and S. K. Pal, *Introduction to Algorithmic Government*, https://doi.org/10.1007/978-981-16-0282-5_2

to achieve the desired result (Aaij et al., 2017). Algorithms possess the capability of completely replacing humans with their meta-functions. The decisions undertaken by the government bodies are algorithmic as decisions legislated by public governing bodies are an outcome of the exact guidelines that process various inputs and deliver precise results based on the auditable rules, i.e., laws and regulations. On the other hand, governance is defined as establishing policies and continuous monitoring of their proper application by the members of the governing body of an organization (Danaher et al., 2017). More precisely, governance is understood as a premeditated attempt to manage threats and opportunities to achieve a pre-determined goal (Black, De Carvalho, Khanna, Kim, & Yurtoglu, 2014). It is not essentially goal-directed or intentional-like regulation and comprises all sorts of social ordering independent of the set of governing rules (Hofmann, Katzenbach, & Gollatz, 2017).

Rouvroy and Berns, for the first time in 2009, conceptualized the term Algorithmic Government as a coordination contrivance different from the concept of social governance. And Algorithmic Government is authorizing software to undertake decisions independently without human intervention or control only certain aspects of everyday social activities according to some algorithmically defined policies (Just & Latzer, 2017). The main benefit of using algorithms in governance is that it becomes more powerful and prevalent. From the public authorities' perspective, there are three constitutive parts of using an Algorithmic Government framework; to regulate algorithmic systems to align it with the public policy outcomes, carry out their regulatory tasks, and replace traditional regulatory mechanisms. It is an emerging trend directed toward automating the governance process (Morozov, 2014). Algorithmic Government is chosen over algorithmic regulation because it deliberately holds social ordering methodically and physically decentralized and not state-centered. This concept's emergence reflects an interdisciplinary connection between technical, natural, and social systems and their corresponding controls (Wiener, 2019). Research works conducted in this context focus on the social interactions and cross-examines the role of algorithms and their collation effect in these specific contexts (Kitchin, 2017). Studies elaborate on how datasets and calculative procedures have led to the emergence of new algorithmic systems to solve social problems and spot disputed content, divergent behavior, and preferences. The Algorithmic Government intends to optimize the process of detecting patterns in data and translate social context into computable methods for maximizing the perceived organization benefits. The rapid advancements in AI and related technologies have the potential to reduce the cost of governing functions while simultaneously improving the decision-making quality and unbridle the power of managerial data making government performance more productive and proficient. The potential public areas that can be automated include the following.

1. Public Services: The process of interacting and distributing services to clients like answering queries, election processes, etc.
2. Supporting Civil Servants: Civil Servants can use intelligent tools like Robo-advisors for providing advisory support.
3. National Public Records: Automating the public services can be used for upkeeping the submissions and forms, messages, or citizen records.
4. National Physical Infrastructure: Automation of the public service sector can be used for maintaining the public infrastructure and infrastructure planning
5. Statutes & Compliance: Public sector automation can assist in upkeeping the laws & ordinances and managing the trials & prosecutions
6. Public Policy Development: Public sector automation can be used for evolving public policies using Robo-advisors

But the government's inability to properly manage this deployment can lead to an unsolicited imperviousness in public decision making and exaggerate concerns about illogical administration action and power.

2.2   MODELS OF ALGORITHMIC GOVERNMENT

Forms of Algorithmic Government

Different researchers have categorized Algorithmic Government into various types depending upon their technology in use. Doug Laney of Gartner in 2001 indicated the emergence of big data systems. Doug Laney of Gartner suggested that big data was massive from three different perspectives; volume, variety, and velocity (Kitchin & McArdle, 2016). Kitchen argues that there are seven diverse ways of measuring bigness, viz., exhaustivity, extensionality and scalability, determination and indexicality, relationality, and the three V's (Kitchin, 2014). These different ways of measuring the properties of big data help review the numerous challenges and opportunities it poses in the design of Algorithmic Government systems. The second part of the literature categorizes algorithms based on the search algorithms used; binary search, quick sort, selection sort, merge sort, and insertion sort. It is critically important to understand these different types of evaluating Algorithmic Government systems' normative and social properties. One of the most recent changes is in the Algorithmic Government's design from a top-down algorithmic approach to a bottom-up algorithmic approach. In the top-down approach, programmers define the set of rules, but in the bottom-up approach, the algorithms develop its own learning rule set in its counterpart. Moreover, the other part of the literature categorized the Algorithmic Government based on the various stages in the process of the Algorithmic Government; collection, processing, utilization, and feedback & learning (Pasquale, 2017). These different stages define how the information is acquired, processed, and analyzed in any governing system (Zarsky, 2016). According to this classification of the concept, Algorithmic Government is a loop that receives information, processes it, and uses the processed data as a feed by learning from all that it has already achieved or acquired (Zarsky, 2016). Thus, Algorithmic Government operates as an intelligent system.

The different types of Algorithmic Government systems are classified based on the degree of automation and transparency level, as shown in Fig. 2.1. Transparency is one of the most vital elements representing equality and self-determination. However, evaluating a particular type of Algorithmic Government differs from each other due to the existing difference in the supervisory bodies (Ananny & Crawford, 2017). Moreover, the degree of automation also matters a lot because governance's validity depends upon the responsibility and liability of the decision-making body. The level of human involvement further distinguishes between the two different types of Algorithmic Government systems. There is no human intervention level in the fully automated systems, whereas, in the recommender, humans approve or disapprove of a particular decision in the loop (Yeung, 2018). And the combination of all the four types of governance systems generates the ideal form of Algorithmic Government systems. The autonomous friendly systems are highly transparent, whereas trust-based systems operate with a low level of transparency. Furthermore, the licensed system is both transparent a well as

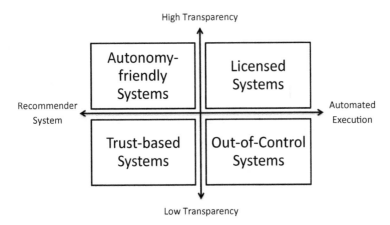

Fig. 2.1 Types of Algorithmic Government systems (*Source* Zarsky, 2016)

mechanized. And lastly, the out-of-control systems exhibit a low level of transparency but the decisions implemented are fully mechanized.

Layered Model of Governance

Modularity is one of the ways used for managing complexity and reducing interdependency between various modules. In layering, different parts of the modules leading to the outcome are organized in layers parallel to each other. The prominent layers are the social layer, the ethical layer, and the technical layer for the AI governance model, as shown in Fig. 2.2.

The social and legal layer of the AI governance model is responsible for creating rules and allocating responsibilities for regulating AI and establishing the AI certification process. The ethical layer applies to almost all types of AI systems. To ensure the proper functioning of the governing system, IEEE has defined specific principles for AI and other technical models. The algorithms are designed keeping in mind the principles defined by IEEE. Lastly, the technical layer of the AI governance model is the main foundation of the governing system (Gasser & Almeida, 2017).

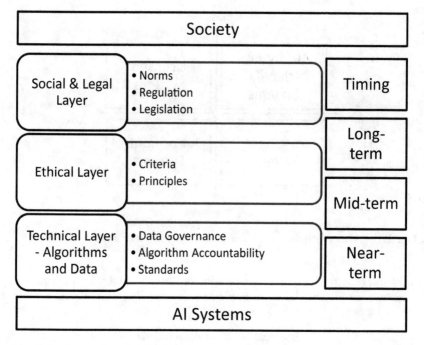

Fig. 2.2 Layered model for AI governance (*Source* Gasser & Almeida, 2017)

2.3   ADVANTAGES OF ALGORITHMIC GOVERNMENT

Artificial Intelligence technology has the ability to stimulate human-like reasoning capabilities. Integrating AI into the governance system, giving it Algorithmic capabilities, has the following benefits.

1. Using an Algorithmic Government system reduces the risk of human errors. AI-based governing systems implement decisions on the basis of the previously gathered information and particular data and ruleset. These rules remain consistent throughout the loop, reduce unnecessary mistakes and errors, and increase the level of precision achieved.
2. Algorithmic Government system possesses the ability to handle and manage risks like natural or human-made disasters.

3. The most significant advantage of using the Algorithmic Government is its 24 × 7 availability. Automated machines can run continuously, unlike humans.
4. Usage of AI in the governance system can help mechanize the repetitive mundane tasks for humans and increase creativity/efficiency.
5. Furthermore, the government can use AI applications for interacting with users or external partners, which saves the need to hire human professionals (customer care services).
6. Using AI and other related technologies are likely to improve the decision-making process's speed and implement quicker decisions.

Another part of the literature indicates other potential benefits of using the Algorithmic Government, including speed, productivity, comprehensiveness, and equality (Domingos, 2015). Algorithmic Decision Systems (ADS) provide several benefits from cost-cutting and increasing efficiency and reliability. The results generated by the Algorithmic Government are based on the patterns identified in the data collected and analyzed by the government. It is almost challenging for humans to interpret such large datasets. Moreover, the literature conducted in this context suggests that Algorithmic Government can handle a high level of complexity because it can accommodate a higher number of inputs.

Consequently, Algorithmic Government offers a new opportunity for involvement, social comprehensiveness, and democratic receptiveness (Schrape, 2019). Then, intelligent surveillance, biometric technologies, and other big data tools used in the governance system can enhance security and privacy issues. Cognitive systems can process a large amount of information that human brains cannot handle (Dawes, 1979). Furthermore, Fildes, Goodwin, and Lawrence (2006) suggested that algorithmic models' results create better results than human minds taking into account all the irregularities and analytics reasoning and judgments. The accuracy of the forecasts predicted by algorithmic models is far better and precise than the outcomes generated by human minds. Van Daalen, Dresen, and Janssen (2002) argued that Algorithmic Government could act as an eye-opener by bringing to notice one of the essential political agendas and supporting the management of a particular target system. Automated decision systems possess the ability to identify and recognize the potential impact of different policy alternatives and implement the one that is likely to affect positively. Zarsky (2016) suggested that algorithmic decision support systems are potentially opaque (due to innate complexity) and automated (limited human intervention). The data-driven government tapped with digital databases linking different datasets allows a much more flexible analysis improving the decision-making process at every stage (O'Hara, 2020).

2.4   DISADVANTAGES OF ALGORITHMIC GOVERNMENT

Alongside the numerous potential benefits of using algorithmic models, there are several disadvantages as well. The proprietorship and stewardship of data have progressively become a public concern. However, most of the algorithms are written to enhance efficiency and productivity without considering the societal impact of policy implementation. Then, security and privacy concerns are always linked to technological solutions. Furthermore, the lack of standards, scalability, storage, access, change management, and security against cyber-criminals are concerns with Algorithmic Government. There are numerous unplanned consequences of using the technological framework for managing the governing system.

1. The most significant disadvantage of using an algorithmic decision-making model is that it is a complicated procedure built using millions of datasets and codes. The model can also automatically change with passing the time, particularly when the machine witnesses the new data. It is challenging for developers to explain the process of implementing decisions. The operators control the data fed into the systems, thereby making it difficult to justify the appropriateness of the actual decision being implemented. The algorithms designed based on the historical data might reflect historical biases or shall be incomplete.

   - Different modules of algorithms perform various tasks functions, generating a unique outcome. Each module is easy to manage when handled separately but becomes even more complicated when combined.
   - Iterative algorithms recurrently run a sequence of steps until the algorithm unites to a constant outcome. A single pass through these steps may provide insight into the process but does not explain the final decision. The convergence criteria may give insight into overall goals but may be independent of individual outcomes.

2. Another aspect of the Algorithmic Government that poses a challenge is its capacity to implement many decisions. Here, in this case, a flawed algorithmic system can cause potential harm, making it difficult to respond adequately or efficiently, damaging the governing system's performance at a larger scale (New & Castro, 2018).

3. Then, the availability of data is also a significant concern in implementing Algorithmic Government. The available dataset may not be of exact standards or optimum quality. There are high chances that the data fed into the system is inconsistent or obsolete, thereby generating outdated policy imperatives.

4. Skill shortage is another concern. Many countries planning to use Algorithmic Government do not have well-experienced or trained staff to deploy and operate AI solutions making it difficult for faster integration of AI into governance.

5. Cost is yet another major problem restricting the government from integrating AI into its existing processes. Due to the complexity involved, both implementation and ongoing maintenance are an additional expense for the government.

6. Software programs require to be upgraded regularly to adjust to the changing business needs and requirements. And several risks associated with this may also change. Not only restoration wastes a considerable amount of time, but there is also a risk of losing a specific piece of information while altering the governance processes. In this context, continuous learning poses a severe problem.

7. Polonetsky and Tene (2014) highlighted privacy and data protection issues related to surveillance systems that are functioning using Algorithmic Government. Danaher (2016) emphasized problems related to opacity and transparency algorithmic data. Apart from this, several other researchers have highlighted concerns about the inaccuracies, inadequacies, and unintended consequences of these systems undermining the Algorithmic Government's legality.

Zarsky (2016) classified problems related to the algorithmic decision-making process into two broader categories, as shown in Fig. 2.3. They

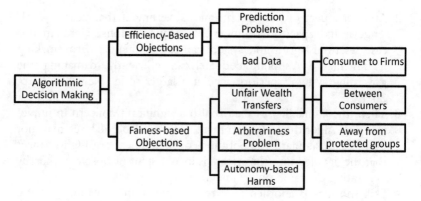

Fig. 2.3 Zarsky's classification of protestations to Algorithmic Government (*Source* Zarsky [2016])

are efficiency-based objections and fairness-based objections. Efficiency-based objections argue that the decisions implemented might be incorrect, and fairness-based objections suggest that the decisions implemented might mistreat people.

2.5   Limitations with Algorithmic Government

Some of the significant limitations with the Algorithmic Government are as follows.

1. Humanity and human agency are lost: With the emergence of logic-driven society, humans, rational beings are being ignored and avoided, passing away the decision-making process to the robots. The automation of the human system for improving efficiencies and productivity can lead to the dehumanization of humans. Thus, the system may see decreased human involvement.
2. Furthermore, algorithms written using mathematical procedures are insufficient to apprehend the richness of people's lives and the diversity of their understandings and know-hows. Owing to algorithms' very nature, it will reflect the biased thinking of people leading to results that are more effective and efficient but will lack the appropriateness, correctness, and fairness.

3. Restricted Work: AI machines work on programming. These machines can only be programmed to undertake specific categories of work. Thus, relying on computers to completely replace or alter the governance system is not possible.
4. Software Malfunction: Code-driven decision-making body relies on machines and algorithms, which can also breakdown. Automating the decision-making process will make it even more confusing to identify the main reason behind the malfunction.
5. Commercial and Public Interests: The conflicting goals of private and public entities make it difficult for the developer to formulate policies that align with the needs and expectations of the two governing authorities.
6. Technological uncertainty: This was considered another barrier to the effective implementation of the Algorithmic Government. Both the government officials and the developers lack clarity regarding algorithm development (Danaher et al., 2017) and the technologies which would be useful, scalable, and efficient.

2.6 Practical Concerns with Algorithmic Government

The literature about Algorithmic Government shows that AI changes the perspective of society and its people. AI increased the amount of data collected by the government for its analysis, or detailed surveillance helps quantify the relevance of different policy implementations (Rieder & Simon, 2016). The datafication process offers social sorting opportunities and poses threats to human rights like privacy, the fairness of speech, etc. Furthermore, Algorithmic Government has led to an effect on the human agents, making it challenging to establish connotations between humans and machines. Kemper and Kolkman (2019) argues that it is practically impossible or infeasible to achieve absolute fairness and transparency in computer codes. Another critical concern is that of algorithmic bias. Automated decision making by algorithmic systems routinely favors people and collectives that are already privileged while discriminating against marginalized people (Noble, 2018). While this constitutes a significant concern to tackle the increasing automation of humans' life, biased datasets and decision rules also create discrimination. Yet, there is a need to implement a governance system driven by datasets for countries to stay ahead in the digital competition and change how the state is operated. However, it is impossible to implement effective and precise policy decisions without collecting an adequate amount of non-personal information. The government should design their unique & customized algorithm structures rather than relying on private contractors to eliminate the conflicting roles or public and private governing bodies and formulate unique algorithms dedicated to shared goals and missions. The involvement of the private sector has worn out transparency and responsibility.

2.7   Ethics with Algorithmic Government

Despite the increasing adoption of an Algorithmic decision-making model, the government cannot address several ethical concerns. The legal and ethical criteria are not suitable enough to handle the ethical considerations of the automated systems. This can further lead to the potential misuse of an essential piece of information. The four major ethical issues concerning the usage of Algorithmic Government systems are as follows.

1. **Privacy:** The users of the AI machines face an extensive threat to privacy. The data collected by the automated machines for future policy implementation or government applications tracking online user activities is an invasion of the user's personal space.
2. **Lack of Transparency**: AI-based governing models are so much complex that even the developers fail to explain their functioning. This makes it difficult to trust the validity of the outcomes and the results. The policies are implemented based on the data fed into the system and the complex processing of algorithms. Hence, it is difficult to confirm the validity of the policies implemented.
3. **Bias and discrimination:** Real-world biasness or creators can alter the algorithms according to their preferences and viewpoints.
4. **Lack of governance and accountability:** This is one of the critical issues with AI governing systems and models. It becomes challenging to identify who should be held responsible for some misconduct or wrong implementation of an algorithm. There is no one specific governing authority who takes accountability for the storage and the dataset (Kraemer, van Overveld, & Peterson, 2011).

To address the ethical issues with Algorithmic Government, the government needs to establish an algorithmic risk management process to manage the associated technical, social, and legal risks. Additionally, the government should create explainable AI-based algorithms to improve the level of transparency and increase the level of trust in the decisions implemented using Algorithmic Government processes. The government must then establish procedures or use cases in conjugation with suggestions from both external and internal parties. The designed algorithms must include all the relevant designs in the applications. Moreover, the designers must develop datasets and algorithms in accordance with data ethics and AI ethics, respectively (GovtTech, 2020).

2.8   AUDITS AND REGULATIONS WITH ALGORITHMIC GOVERNMENT

With increased access to AI tools and related technologies, accountability is done to assess and review the potential impacts and behavioral responses toward these technological systems. Due to algorithms' very nature, the person or the governing authority designing the algorithms are held responsible. AI system is reliable only when the implemented technical system meets the quality assurance pipeline's principles. However, a separate governance structure is required to keep a check on whether the system meets the declared ethical expectations or not. Audits are tools that are being used to check whether or not algorithms are designed to comply with industry standards and regulations (Raji et al., 2020).

SMACTR *(Scoping, Mapping, Artifact Collection, Testing, and Reflection)* is a formal audit framework used to check whether Algorithmic Government complies with the set ethical principles or not (Raji et al., 2020). The gray area in Fig. 2.4 indicates a process, and colored areas reflect the documents which are being checked. Orange materials are reports generated by the audit teams, and blue records are produced by production teams, whereas the green ones are developed by both the teams together.

- **The Scoping Stage:** This stage clarifies the objective of the audit procedure. Here, risk analysis is done to propose suitable changes in the development process. This stage's output is a product requirement document explaining how the algorithms should be designed

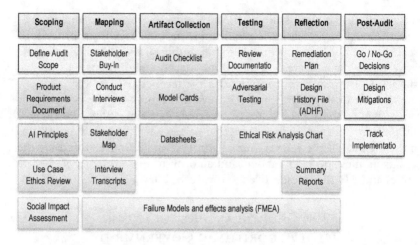

Scoping	Mapping	Artifact Collection	Testing	Reflection	Post-Audit
Define Audit Scope	Stakeholder Buy-in	Audit Checklist	Review Documentatio	Remediation Plan	Go / No-Go Decisions
Product Requirements Document	Conduct Interviews	Model Cards	Adversarial Testing	Design History File (ADHF)	Design Mitigations
AI Principles	Stakeholder Map	Datasheets	Ethical Risk Analysis Chart		Track Implementatio
Use Case Ethics Review	Interview Transcripts			Summary Reports	
Social Impact Assessment	Failure Models and effects analysis (FMEA)				

Fig. 2.4 Audit framework (*Source* Raji et al. [2020])

to implement the right governing decisions. This articraft developed at this stage is an ethical review of the system use cases and social impact assessment.

- **Mapping Stage**: At this stage, the perspectives of different internal teams involved in the audited system are considered. Here, the needs of the internal stakeholders and collaborators are fed into the system for its execution. This stage primarily produces a stakeholder map, a collaborator contact list, a system map for product development, and multiple models.
- **Articraft Collection Stage**: This stage identifies and collects the required documentation to prioritize areas that need to be tested. The audit-check list is generated at this stage to initiate the audit process. This stage ensures that full documentation is completed before the actual audit process commences. Furthermore, data-sheets and model cards are also prepared at this stage, which is essential for developing the Algorithmic Government model.
- **Testing Stage**: At this stage, the algorithms generated are tested as use cases to gauge the system's accuracy. Auditors review the document collection and assess system failures' likelihood to check whether the plan complies with declared principles. Adversarial testing is done at this stage to find possible vulnerabilities, both pre-

and post-launch of the technology, for instance, any specific security or privacy concerns that are likely to emerge.

- **Reflection Stage**: The audit phase results are further analyzed at this stage compared to the ethical prospects explained at the scoping stage. A mitigation or action plan is developed at this stage, encapsulating the probable risks and test failures for the design team to identify areas for future developments.

2.9 GOVERNANCE STRUCTURE FOR ALGORITHMIC GOVERNMENT

Government and Governance

Both Government and Governance are irreplaceable terms. Governance is not the same as the Government, even though the Government can still be a subset or a constituent element of the governance process. The governance concept corresponds to a multi-stakeholder approach that focuses on one particular theme, territory, or practice. The governance process provides a more holistic view of an organization or a society that directs itself. It is more precisely understood as a set of rules and laws formed by the Government and implemented through state representatives. In simpler words, governance is everything that the Government does (Peters & Pierre, 1998). The governance body works toward achieving good results by following a set pattern of rules. In contrast to the traditional public power pattern in which authority is granted the control to plan and implement decisions, governance mechanisms operate on the command and control model. Unlike in the context of the Government, wherein the Prime Minister controls and regulates other ministers, which further dominates civil servants and local government officials (Richards and Smith 2004), the governance mechanism cannot bring about the desired changes as the power is dispersed among different administrations. On the other hand, the term Government is used for governing while the Government is an office or the authority of governing. It is a body of elected members that is headed and controlled by a single leader. These people are responsible for implementing policies and regulations for maintaining law and order in the country and resolve grievances that emerge. The governing body comprises of both temporary as well as permanent members. The bureaucracy that runs and works in different ministries and government departments in the background is permanent. On the other hand, the Council of Ministers is elected by the people and serves for a fixed period. They can be replaced after their term as their position is temporary. Among a narrower set of participants, the Government describes a stricter and more limited set of activities (Meehan, 2003). Governments have a range of tools at their disposal, but they tend to concentrate only on a couple of familiar ones that demand their direct involvement.

Algorithmic Government and Algorithmic Governance

To address the challenges imposed by continually evolving technologies and keeping pace with the competitive environment, governing bodies are always looking out ways to explore and utilize technologies to shape and guide society's behavior and governance. Moreover, the growth and spread of AI-related technologies have created immense pressure on the Government to use AI and associated best practices to envoy decision-making processes to computers. Governance is a term that has been deployed to define coordination between actors based on rules. It is neither intentional nor goal-directed (Katzenbach & Ulbricht, 2019). Instead, it requires unintentional collaboration (Hofmann et al., 2017). However, governance excludes all modes of social ordering that are solely occasional and do not depend on any rule; governance implies a minimum degree of stability required to create perceptions by actors that are a precondition for cooperation (Hobbes, 2001).

On the other hand, Algorithmic Governance is a term used to present an idea that highlights the fact that governing administrations use algorithms and inter-connected mathematical models to undertake complex decisions using computing capabilities. Compared to the governance mechanism, which is being controlled and managed by the traditional manual form of administration structure, a mathematical computational-based algorithmic model is more powerful and pervasive and consequently becomes more comprehensive, receptive, and allows for more social diversity (Danaher et al., 2017). Among all the proposed benefits of algorithmic governance systems, including speed, effectiveness, extensiveness, and fairness, algorithmic systems can reinforce social, ethical, legal problems (Domingos, 2015).

Separate Governance Structure

Both public and private sectors are increasingly adopting Algorithmic systems for effectively implementing decisions at various levels with potentially visible consequences for individuals, societies, and individuals. There is an emergent need to have an appropriate governance mechanism to ensure that the risks and benefits are equally distributed to generate positive and influential outcomes for society. Unless proper governance mechanisms are effectively put in place, there are higher chances that algorithmic systems' opacity could lead to circumstances where people are negatively affected. As with the governance of another aspect of society, Algorithmic accountability is essential for confirming fruitful results for different social sectors. Transparency of algorithmic governance system corresponds to the legitimacy of its data, goal, outcome, compliance, influence, or the automated decision-making systems. However, maintaining transparency is extremely crucial for ensuring accountability.

Principles vs. rule-based approaches are the two available fundamental approaches to governance. The rule-based governance system provides certainty to the governance system, whereas the principle-based act as a guideline that offers flexibility, enabling the regulatory regime to have some durability in the rapidly changing complex business environment. However, most regulatory systems operate by using an appropriate mix of principles and rules. Rules are clearly defined boundaries indicating the governance mechanism's scope, whereas principles are universal guidelines provided to enhance the regulatory regime's overall competitiveness. The emerging problem of applying current regulatory structures to processes is a lack of clarification on modern algorithmic components that have changed significantly. The system's degree of effect on people when a product integrates algorithmic behavior cannot be determined. Vacuum cleaners, for example, have historically been recognized as posing such health hazards by electrocution and potential dispersion of fine matter particles, all of which are checked as part of the CE certification that before being sold inside the EEA, the vacuum cleaner must pass. By incorporating autonomous navigation, camera image processing, and communication algorithms, i.e., turning it into a robot vacuum, how 'upgrading' a vacuum cleaner product line alters the potential for the product's negative impact. There are parallels between the regulatory problems posed by the use of algorithmic decision making as part of goods or services and the effect of switching to the provision of online digital services. To uphold the 'online and offline equivalence' concept for legal and moral rights/responsibilities, an urgent need for revising the existing legislation, rules, and international agreements has been observed in the digital environment. Similar updates may be needed to ensure a level playing field, where algorithmic services that do or do not integrate upholding decisions using algorithmic models to be equally liable for effects that discriminate, limit and weaken freedom and destabilize the moral rights of the consumers (Koene, Clifton, Hatada, Webb, & Richardson, 2019).

References

Aaij, R., Adeva, B., Adinolfi, M., Ajaltouni, Z., Akar, S., Albrecht, J., ... & Cartelle, P. A. (2017). New algorithms for identifying the flavour of B-0 mesons using pions and protons. *The European Physical Journal C, 77*(4), 238.

Ananny, M., & Crawford, K. (2015). A Liminal press: Situating news app designers within a field of networked news production. *Digital Journalism, 3*(2), 192–208.

Black, B., De Carvalho, A. G., Khanna, V., Kim, W., & Yurtoglu, B. (2014). Methods for multicountry studies of corporate governance: Evidence from the BRIKT countries. *Journal of Econometrics, 183*(2), 230–240.

Danaher, J., Hogan, M. J., Noone, C., Kennedy, R., Behan, A., De Paor, A., ... & Murphy, M. H. (2017). Algorithmic governance: Developing a research agenda through the power of collective intelligence. *Big Data & Society, 4*(2), 2053951717726554.

Dawes, R. M. (1979). The robust beauty of improper linear models in decision making. *American Psychologist, 34*(7), 571.

Domingos, P. (2015). *The master algorithm: How the quest for ultimate machine learning will remake our world*. New York, NY: Basic Books.

Fildes, R., Goodwin, P., & Lawrence, M. (2006). The design features of forecasting support systems and their effectiveness. *Decision Support Systems, 42*(1), 351–361.

Gasser, U., & Almeida, V. A. (2017). A layered model for AI governance. *IEEE Internet Computing, 21*(6), 58–62.

GovtTech, (2020). Ethics in the balance: AI's implications for government. Available from https://www.govtech.com/policy/Ethics-in-the-Balance-AIs-Implications-for-Government.html. Accessed on 2nd August 2020.

Hobbes, T. (2001). *Of man, being the first part of Leviathan*. Vol. XXXIV, Part 5. The Harvard Classics. New York: PF Collier & Son, 1909–14; Bartleby. com.

Hofmann, J., Katzenbach, C., & Gollatz, K. (2017). Between coordination and regulation: Finding the governance in Internet governance. *New Media & Society, 19*(9), 1406–1423.

Just, N., & Latzer, M. (2017). Governance by algorithms: Reality construction by algorithmic selection on the Internet. *Media, Culture & Society, 39*(2), 238–258.

Katzenbach, C., & Ulbricht, L. (2019). Algorithmic governance. *Internet Policy Review, 8*(4), 1–18.

Kemper, J., & Kolkman, D. (2019). Transparent to whom? No algorithmic accountability without a critical audience. *Information, Communication & Society, 22*(14), 2081–2096.

Kitchin, R. (2014). Big Data, new epistemologies and paradigm shifts. *Big Data & Society, 1*(1). https://doi.org/10.1177/2053951714528481.

Kitchin, R. (2017). Thinking critically about and researching algorithms. *Information, Communication & Society, 20*(1), 14–29.

Kitchin, R., & McArdle, G. (2016). What makes Big Data, Big Data? Exploring the ontological characteristics of 26 datasets. *Big Data & Society, 3*(1). https://doi.org/10.1177/2053951716631130.

Koene, A., Clifton, C., Hatada, Y., Webb, H., & Richardson, R. (2019). *A governance framework for algorithmic accountability and transparency.* Available from https://nottingham-repository.worktribe.com/preview/3979926/EPRS_STU%282019%29624262_EN.pdf. Accessed on 23rd November 2020.

Kraemer, F., van Overveld, K., & Peterson, M. (2011). Is there an ethics of algorithms? *Ethics and Information Technology, 13*(3), 251–260.

Meehan, E. M. (2003). *From government to governance, civic participation and 'new politics': The context of potential opportunities for the better representation of women.* Centre for Advancement of Women in Politics, Queen's University Belfast.

Morozov, E. (2014). The rise of data and the death of politics. *The Guardian, 20*(07), 2014.

New, J., & Castro, D. (2018). How policymakers can foster algorithmic accountability. *Center for Data Innovation.* Available from http://www2.itif.org/2018-new-algorithmic-accountability.pdf. Accessed on 3rd November 2020.

Noble, S. U. (2018). *Algorithms of oppression: How search engines reinforce racism.* nyu Press. Teachers College Record. https://www.tcrecord.org. ID Number: 22663.

O'Hara, K. (2020). Data-driven government: The triumph of thatcherism or the revenge of society?. In *Thatcherism in the 21st Century* (pp. 55–73). Cham: Palgrave Macmillan.

O'hara, K., & Hildebrandt, M. (2020). Introduction: Life and the law in the era of data-driven agency.

Pasquale, F. (2017). Toward a fourth law of robotics: Preserving attribution, responsibility, and explainability in an algorithmic society. *Ohio State Law Journal, 78*, 1243.

Peters, B. G., & Pierre, J. (1998). Governance without Government? Rethinking public administration. *Journal of Public Administration Research and Theory, 8*(2), 223–243.

Polonetsky, J., & Tene, O. (2014). The ethics of student privacy: Building trust for ed tech. Available from https://papers.ssrn.com/sol3/papers.cfm?abstract_id=2628902. Accessed on 3rd November 2020.

Raji, I. D., Smart, A., White, R. N., Mitchell, M., Gebru, T., Hutchinson, B., ... & Barnes, P. (2020, January). Closing the AI accountability gap: Defining an end-to-end framework for internal algorithmic auditing. In *Proceedings of the 2020 Conference on Fairness, Accountability, and Transparency* (pp. 33–44).

Richards, D., & Smith, M. J. (2004). The hybrid state: Labour's response to the challenge of governance. *Governing as New Labour: Policy and Politics Under Blair* (pp. 106–125).

Rieder, G., & Simon, J. (2016). Datatrust: Or, the political quest for numerical evidence and the epistemologies of big data. *Big Data & Society, 3*(1), 1–6.

Schrape, J. F. (2019). The promise of technological decentralization: A brief reconstruction. *Society, 56*(1), 31–37.

Thornton, P., & Danaher, J. (2018). *On the wisdom of algorithmic markets: Governance by algorithmic price.* Available at SSRN 3314078.

Van Daalen, C. E., Dresen, L., & Janssen, M. A. (2002). The roles of computer models in the environmental policy life cycle. *Environmental Science & Policy, 5*(3), 221–231.

Wiener, N. (2019). *Cybernetics or control and communication in the animal and the machine.* MIT press.

Yeung, K. (2018). Algorithmic regulation: A critical interrogation. *Regulation & Governance, 12*(4), 505–523.

Zarsky, T. (2016). The trouble with algorithmic decisions: An analytic road map to examine efficiency and fairness in automated and opaque decision making. *Science, Technology and Human Values, 41*(1), 118–132.

CHAPTER 3

Techniques and Technologies

Abstract This chapter presents the various technologies which are used for implementing Government by Algorithms. They are Artificial Intelligence, machine learning, deep learning, blockchain, augmented reality, virtual reality, big data, cloud computing, data lakes, Digital Twin, edge computing, granular computing, and Fog of Things. There are different aspects like data handling, data storage, data processing, service mapping, security, computations, and advancements required to successfully implement automated decision making through Algorithmic Government. Other emerging areas in technology will also be beneficial for the Government to adopt automated systems.

Keywords Artificial Intelligence · Machine learning · Deep learning · Blockchain · Big data · Cloud computing · Data lakes · Digital Twin · Edge computing

3.1 Artificial Intelligence

Artificial Intelligence refers to machines' ability to replicate human functions, the ability to learn and solve problems. In computer science, we call them 'Intelligent bots.' The goal of AI is to tackle complex issues, in a similar way humans do, through different tasks as shown in Fig. 3.1.

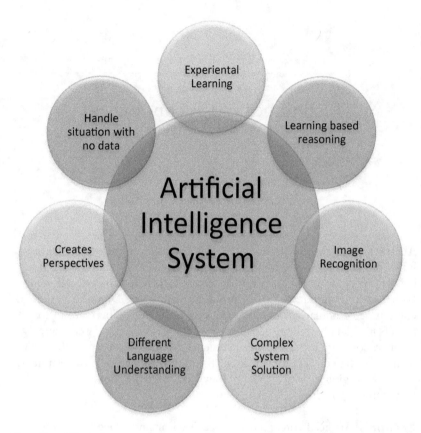

Fig. 3.1 What does an artificial intelligence system must do (*Source* Author Creation)

Today there are three spectrum levels in AI. Assisted Intelligence, which refers to the automation of primary tasks like assembly lines machines. Augmented Intelligence, where AI learns from human input and can make more accurate decisions based on information. Autonomous Intelligence refers to intelligence where there is no human interaction like that for the self-driven cars (Chen, 2009).

AI is a combination of Algorithmic Decision Making (ADM) and big data. Big data refers to a massive amount of unstructured data from various sources. The term big data gained popularity in the 2010s. An

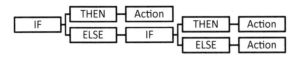

Fig. 3.2 Set of rules in the form of a decision tree (*Source* Author Creation)

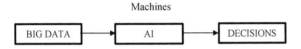

Fig. 3.3 Decision-making model using AI (*Source* Author Creation)

algorithm is a set of rules or instructions to solve a problem. ADM means the result of algorithms is put into action without the human loop. As shown in Fig. 3.2, a simple algorithm displays the set of rules in the form of a decision tree.

In today's world, connected devices capture an incredible amount of data. It may be money transactions, gestures, likings, dislikings, and much more. All this information is used to make better decisions. A decision-making model that used data is shown in Fig. 3.3, where AI is used to create a business decision based on the user's data collected from connected devices.

Artificial Intelligence can provide considerable incremental value to various sectors (Kuziemski & Misuraca, 2020), especially in a developing country like India. It will be a crucial source of competitive advantage. Some common uses of AI are as follows.

AI in manufacturing: The Volvo industry is making fair use of AI and IoT devices to maintain passengers' safety. In 2015, the automation industry fitted sensors to 1000 vehicles to gather their data in a hazardous condition. The collected data predicts the early warning signs and prevents accidents, failure in cars, and passengers' safety.

AI in financial services: In financial services, there is always a risk of accepting fraudulent applications and enduring losses. To decrease such fraud, many departments and institutions analyze the data from credit bureau data sources, which allows accessing the credit risk assessment of an individual consumer where the system uses advanced pattern recognition to find good and bad loan applications.

AI in healthcare: The application of Artificial Intelligence can help address health issues in rural areas. It can be achieved through the early identification of potential pandemics, image diagnostics, and AI-driven personalized treatment.

AI in education: The Potential use of AI is in enhancing the learning experience of individuals by personalized training and skilling, reducing the dropouts, enhancing classroom studies.

AI in smart cities: With the rise in the urban population, smart cities are a new concept. To enhance the quality of life, AI can help to meet the demands. In traffic management, to reduce congestions, provide more security and threat alerts systems are potential use cases of AI in smart cities (Yigitcanlar, Desouza, Butler, & Roozkhosh, 2020).

The Indian Government has launched the National Artificial Intelligence portal, which is managed by National Association of Software and Service Companies (Nasscom) and backend by e-Governance division of Ministry of Electronics and Information Technology (MeitY), with an objective of one platform for AI advancement in India (https://indiaa i.in/). The portal provides information on the entire ecosystem of AI and serves as a platform for AI resources. Similarly, many countries are now adopting AI in various sectors for decision making by the Government.

3.2   Machine Learning & Deep Learning

Machine learning is a process in which the computer is capable of learning by themselves (Alpaydin, 2020). It is part of an emerging artificial intelligence technology over the past years, which automates complex problems. Machine learning models are broadly divided into supervised and unsupervised learning. In a nutshell, identifying the patterns in training data and estimating the correct outcomes in newly input data is covered under machine learning. In the government sphere, supervised learning is most relevant. In supervised learning, the task is to learn from specific examples and predict future events. Supervised learning has classification and regression techniques. In unsupervised learning, the information which is used for modeling comprises unstructured data. The system doesn't figure out the right output, but it explores the data and can draw inferences from datasets to describe hidden structures from unstructured data. Unsupervised learning includes various clustering techniques. Figure 3.4 shows the workflow of the machine learning modeling process.

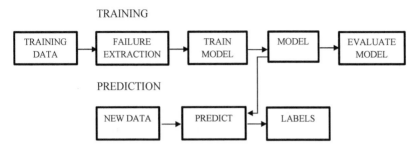

Fig. 3.4 Machine learning modeling process (*Source* Author Creation)

Deep learning is a class of machine learning that is concerned with algorithms inspired by the human brain's function, also called an artificial neural network. It helps to make the decision more accurate and insightful. In deep learning, the computer model learns from the text, images, videos, and audios, which helps achieve high accuracy. These models are trained using large datasets and neural network layers. The term 'deep' in deep learning refers to hidden layers that help to achieve high accuracy.

It is a sub-component of AI function that tries to mimic a human brain's procedure for processing the information it receives, recognizing speech patterns, and ultimately making final decisions. It can do all this without the need for humans to supervise or control them. Before the launch of this concept, AI-computation capabilities were restricted to processing natural data that too in the raw form. However, deep learning approaches are representation-based learning methods with multiple representation levels obtained by writing non-linear but straightforward modules (LeCun, Bengio, & Hinton, 2015). Deep learning is an advanced computational technique of AI capable of recognizing intricate structures in the high-dimensional data fed into the system. The degree of deep learning's opacity depends upon the number of deep learning layers and connections among the layers. If the layer's level of contact is small, the deep learning technology is more easily interpretable and vice-versa (Knight, 2017). Its architecture is a multi-layer stack of simple modules, all or most of which are subject to learning. Each of the stack modules transforms the input to maximize both selectivity and the inconsistency of the representation. For several non-linear layers, say with a depth of

5 to 20, the device can perform too complex input functions that are simultaneously sensitive to the minute information.

Moreover, deep learning techniques are beyond the control of humans. Coglianese and Lehr (2016) argue that human experts retain very substantive and limited control over the situation. It is an optimization process of the algorithm and a trial-and-error approach in which the algorithm is directed and nudged by humans (Kim, 2020). Deep learning is used for various use cases in multiple industries. In the automation industry, companies are using them to detect the traffic signs and traffic lights, which helps the self-driving vehicles to recognize the signs and respond according to it automatically. In industries with the help of deep learning, we can detect the person and help to warn if they are unsafe, which will help avoid accidents and increase safety measures. Both machine learning and Deep Learning are prominently used for solving complex decision-making problems around the world.

3.3   BLOCKCHAIN

Blockchain refers to a digital ledger where blocks store the information of transactions or a list of records linked using cryptography and maintained across several computers connected in a peer-to-peer network (Deloitte, 2018). The block contains the hash of the previous block, transaction details, and timestamp. The blocks are made up of digital pieces that store information. The blocks hold the transition details like time, date, amount, who participates in the transactions, and name, distinguishing them from others just like out names. The blockchain executes operation quicker and enhanced customer experience and ensure transparency to the customer. There are three types of blockchains public, private, and permissioned blockchain. Public blockchain means a fully transparent transaction based on a decentralized architecture, where anyone can read and participate. No one has control over that network. Private blockchain is centralized, and only permitted entities can join the network. In a private blockchain, the write permission is only given to trusted entities, and the read permission is given to all the participants. Permission blockchain provides read and write permission to only a few restricted entities (Zyskind & Nathan, 2015).

Blockchain technology has the potential to revolutionize interactions between governments, businesses, and citizens (Cerf, Matz, & Berg, 2020). In 2008, a technical paper was released, which described the new electronic cash system called 'Bitcoin.' The report proposed that we introduce the transaction cryptographically, where the participants will be able to execute a transaction without the need for a trusted third party. And it became a reality in the next few years. A report by the Committee on Payments and Market Infrastructure set up by Bank for International Settlements (BIS) characterized this technology as:

- Electronic means they are easy to use and easily accessible.
- Not liable to anyone means they do not require third party trust between transactions.
- Peer-to-peer exchange means it is a decentralized structure.

In India, blockchain saw an early adoption in 2016 by the banks and financial institutions, but India has also seen blockchain adoption in the government sectors. As per the reports, NITI Aayog is working to make the country's largest blockchain network, speed up contract transactions, reduce fraud, and increase transparency. Land registration and records used blockchain technology exhaustively around the world. As we know, the land is the costliest asset and epic center of land fights and frauds. In the absence of an efficient system of records maintenance, the Government has made multiple attempts to digitalize it. The land registration process is costly and time-consuming because it involves manual paper-work, verification, and authentications from various bodies. The blockchain technology will bring a sound and robust solution to digitize the entire registration process where all the stakeholders will be present at a single platform.

Figure 3.5 depicts the solution of land registration using blockchain technology. A prototype was developed and showcased. Necessary stakeholders were brought on board, citizens to manage their land transfer (including uploading essential documents, payments) through a single user-friendly portal and viewing their transaction's current status. In the future, blockchain technology will be heavily used in implementing Algorithmic Governance and Decision Making (Batubara, Ubacht, & Janssen, 2018; Hyvärinen, Risius, & Friis, 2017).

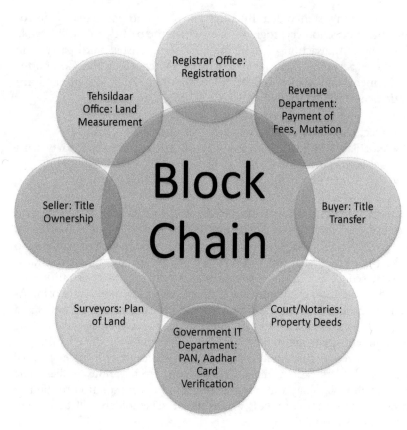

Fig. 3.5 Blockchain-based process flow (*Source* Deloitte, 2018)

3.4 Augmented Reality & Virtual Reality (AR & VR)

Earlier AR & VR only existed in science fiction. But in the twenty-first century, augmented reality and virtual reality have gained a lot much attention (Briggs, Dul, Dobner, Mariani, & Kishnani, 2018). They are regarded as world-changing technologies. Augmented reality is a blend of the digital world and physical elements to create an artificial environment. AR has characteristics like synchronized real and virtual objects running in real-time 3D. In recent years, the scope of AR has expanded in fields of research, science, medicine, and education. AR toolkit is an open-source available for the creation of AR applications. Virtual reality projects the image into a whole new environment with a headset user can experience the entire new 360-degree environment around him. AR and VR have various applications in different industries. A few of them are listed down.

Gaming & Entertainment: In 2016, an application called Pokémon Go created a storm in the world, which was an AR-based game. The player had to collect coins by walking around in the real world while holding their smartphones. With the help of a camera, they can catch virtual Pokémon's. It has 65 million players by April 2017.

Social Media: Snapchat jumped to AR/VR technology early to provide its user-interactive photo filters. Recently, they have started releasing wearable shoppable, where the users can try different brand products.

Education: With the VR technology, there will be a significant change in the teaching style, learning from printed books to simulation study. Instead of reading the boring history from the books, VR technology can change the whole concept where students can participate in the event and interact also. Google Expeditions Pioneer Program, Alchemy VR, Discovery VR, and EON Reality are major contributors to the education field.

Travel & Tourism: AR has the potential to redefine travel and tourism (Nayyar, Mahapatra, Le, & Suseendran, 2018). The innovative use of AR is increasing day by day in travel app development, and it is growing continuously. AR offers services as a 360 tour of the hotel room, lobby, and bathroom, which will provide the information in a more interactive way than 2D pictures. With the AR-based app development, governments can enhance their infrastructure by providing more interactive methods to explore historical places. Especially in India, with so many historical sites all around the country, it will be the best opportunity for the government to increase the tourist attraction with the use of emerging technologies like AR/VR.

There are currently many AR applications available like Google sky map, Spot crime, Ray-Ban virtual mirror, and Nokia Lumia. Many companies are now working on advanced wearable technology platforms, which will enhance the AR/VR utility. And this can certainly be tapped by the Government Sector for strengthening the decision making. Evidence[1] has

[1] Deloitte—https://www2.deloitte.com/us/en/insights/industry/public-sector/augmented-virtual-reality-government-services.html.

now been found where Governments are considering the usage of AR and VR in their decision-making process (Doolin, Holden, & Zinsou, 2013; Eggers, Schatsky, & Viechnicki, 2017; Yusuf et al., 2020).

3.5   Big Data

Big data can be defined in several ways as per various researchers (Jeble, Kumari, & Patil, 2017; Kim, Choi, & Byun, 2019; Munné, 2016; Shamim, Zeng, Shariq, & Khan, 2019) with potential applications in Government sector. Big data has a massive volume of structured and unstructured data, which is established as the ocean of information. Big data is large unstructured dataset which is gathered and require new technology to process them. Only data volumes are not relevant in big data, but also what different organizations do with that data matter's the most. Every day we create around 2.5 quintillion bytes of data, and with the help of this, we can predict the amount in upcoming years. Approximately 90% of the data generated is unstructured or raw data, but it offers considerable value and creation and discovery opportunities. In the early 2000s, big data's mainstream definition is defined into 3 V's—volume, velocity, and variety, but after further refinement, it now has 5 V's—volume, velocity, variety, veracity, and value. Volume means a large amount of data in terabytes or petabytes. Velocity represents the rate of data accumulation is increasing day by day at a quick pace. Variety means multiple sources of data sources like enterprise systems, social media, text, video, audio, email, and other digital devices. Veracity means the quality of data is essential for the accuracy of the decision. And Value means an outcome that can be inferred from heterogeneous data. There are different sources from where the big data originates, such as transactional data, social media data, electronic items, and Internet applications. Big data analytics is a tool used for decision making. It has made it easier to analyze the data. Analytics is used in making decisions in e-commerce, E-Government, health, security, and public safety through database segmentation, graph mining, social network analysis, text analytics, and web analytics.

The growing use of big data analytics has built pressure on governments to adopt new technologies to transform all data into actionable information to provide citizens with valuable services. Big data analytics help in the effective decision-making process by understanding the data patterns and their relationship. Figure 3.6 shows the framework of big data and decision making.

Fig. 3.6 Conceptual framework of big data and decision making (*Source* Author Creation)

Big data analytics will help survey the needs of the country's people and enable the government to provide them with what they want. More data about citizens will help find the citizens' interests and likings and identify their weaknesses, which were not possible earlier. The data generated through other government applications will also help train the models and apply the intelligence for automated decision making.

3.6   Cloud Computing

Cloud computing is defined as the delivery of computing services, including servers, storage, databases, networking, software, analytics, and intelligence over the Internet. It is a new way of delivering IT resource services. Cloud computing is a shift in business thinking in IT resources. It is very beneficial for the organization to shift to cloud infrastructure (Martens & Teuteberg, 2012). Some factors are listed below.

Cost: Cloud computing eliminates the capital expense of buying hardware and software and setting up or running on-site datacenters. The flexible pricing model of clouds allows for just paying the number of resources that you have used.

Broad network access: The cloud can be accessed from anywhere worldwide as it just requires Internet connectivity.

Unlimited Storage: Storing information in the cloud gives almost unlimited storage capacity.

Performance: Cloud computing provides services worldwide and has data centers which are updated regularly to fast and efficient computing infrastructure.

Reliability: It provides data backups and recovery if any mishap happens. The data can be mirrored at different redundant sites on the cloud provider's network.

Cloud computing is divided into four deployment models. The public cloud is owned and operated by third party providers and provides services like servers and storage over the Internet, for example—Microsoft Azure. The private cloud, where all the resources are held and managed by a single organization. A private cloud is one in which the services and infrastructure are maintained on a private network. The hybrid cloud is a mix of both private and public clouds. This type of cloud provides greater flexibility, more deployment options, and security. The community cloud is a cloud infrastructure that is shared by several organizations and supports specific concerns.

The cloud architecture can be categorized as Infrastructure as a Service (IaaS), Platform as a Service (PaaS), and Software as a Service (SaaS). Due to cloud computing advantages, governments have launched many E-Governances services on cloud technology in many countries (Jun & Jun, 2011; Rastogi, 2010; Tadili & Semma, 2015). In a country like India, cloud computing technology will help build a new modern, prosperous India (Husain & Khanum, 2017). It will transform the nation into an information Society. The cloud will help provide Government services faster and cheaper, thereby accelerating IT adoption and use for Algorithmic Governance.

3.7   DATA LAKES

A data lake is a central storage location in an entity, corporation, or institution, to which data of any size and at any rate can be copied, with the help of various import methods (initial, batch, streaming) in either native or raw format. This might be any of the following forms; streams of sensors, user contact logs, social media capture, feeds, repositories for photos or recordings, or snapshots of databases from the enterprise's IT structures (ERP, CRM, etc.). The purpose is to extract meaningful information by exploring the data to be used in services and applications, train mathematical models, and transform it. A manufacturer of home appliances, for example, could equip devices with sensors that monitor client usage patterns. It will give the captured sensor data back to the producer, connecting with the consumer data. The manufacturer can then implement a predictive maintenance algorithm on the unified collected data to extract meaningful information for promotional campaigns, which could help the marketers provide customer-tailored added services. By consolidating data into the lake, data can be connected with other sources without crossing system or organizational boundaries (Klettke, Awolin, Störl, Müller, & Scherzinger, 2017). The data scientist collaborates with other divisions like IT, marketing, or the R&D department to provide the required information/data. The data lake needs to help data scientists to analyze the data, and it also shares results by posting or granting access to the data warehouse. The notion of processing data of any type and size using any import method (initial, batch, streaming) presents challenges to the storage infrastructure. Thus, additional storage space in the form of cloud storage must deal with performance issues arising on account of varying file sizes. Since information is stored on the lake in its original format, data scientists face a challenge with data integration. Before extracting analytical results, the data scientist needs to profile the information to understand the structure, consistency, and data schema. The next step is to have relevant data extracted and converted from the raw data into a format that correlates with other knowledge. Data scientist follows three steps to extract meaningful information from the data—data preparation, data analytics, and result provisioning. Data lakes have also been criticized for rapidly transforming into 'Data Swamps.' The danger stems from the potential lack of data control, pipelines, software, and users for processing. The absence of control might have legal insinuations (Burk & Miner, 2020). Going ahead with the implementation of Algorithmic Governance, the Government would require various data lakes in different departments for decision-making purposes.

3.8   Digital Twin Technology

The concept of Digital Twin was introduced in the year 2002. Since the inception of this technology, it has become essential to system engineering. At the forefront of the Industry 4.0 transition, Digital Twin is facilitated by advanced data processing and access to the Internet of Things (IoT). The amount of data available from manufacturing, healthcare, and smart city environments has increased with IoT. By developing a linked physical and virtual twin (Digital Twin), the Digital Twin will tackle the challenge of seamless integration between IoT and data analytics. A Digital Twin environment makes it possible to analyze rapidly and make real-time decisions through accurate analytics. To put it simpler, it is a complex model of a device, process, or service that is virtual. Thus an object, a factory, or even a business service can consist of Digital Twins. A Digital Twin's vision includes incorporating the business, contextual, and sensor data from physical systems or processes into the virtual network (Madni, Madni, & Lucero, 2019).

The Digital Twin model allows real-time monitoring of systems and processes to promote research and develop educated technology roadmaps. It pursues timely data review to fix issues before they occur and plan thoroughly to reduce preventive maintenance by combining the virtual and physical worlds. The usage of Digital Twins has increased drastically in smarter cities, for planning and developing them along with increasing the amount of connectivity. Moreover, manufacturers can use this technology to keep track of the products for saving time and money and provide real-time suggestions on machine performance and feedback on the production line. Digital Twins coupled AI algorithms can generate greater accuracy as the computer can carry vast data required for arrangement and prediction analysis. The Digital Twin will enable the manufacturer to test the product and the device in actual context to generate a more considerable valuable asset.

Moreover, the Digital Twin can be profoundly used by healthcare operators to provide real-time analysis of the body and propose smarter predictions and decisions in real-time. It can also be used to support predictive maintenance and continuing repair of medical device facilities. The Digital Twin in the Medical World has the power to make life-saving decisions with AI centered on real-time data (Fuller, Fan, & Day, 2019). Digital twinning is a potential technology for many government areas while making decisions.

3.9   Edge Computing

With the rapid advancement and development of mobile Internet and Internet of Things (IoT) applications, traditional centralized cloud computing faces severe challenges such as high latency, low spectral efficiency, and non-adaptive form of communication. To solve these challenges, modern technology is driving a trend that moves centralized cloud computing to the edge of network devices. Several cutting-edge computing technologies from various backgrounds have emerged to reduce latency, boost spectral efficiency, and support the massive form of machine communication. In edge computing, extensive data generated by different types of IoT devices can be processed at the edge of the network instead of being transmitted to the centralized cloud infrastructure due to bandwidth and energy consumption concerns. Edge computing can offer a quicker response and better quality services compared to cloud computing. Edge computing is more suitable for IoT to provide useful and safe services for many end-users. Edge computing-based architecture can be the future IoT infrastructure (Ai, Peng, & Zhang, 2018). End-to-end responsiveness between the mobile and associated cloud is the biggest challenge of cloud computing. The cloudlet, a mobility-enhanced small-scale cloud Data Center (DC) located at the edge of the Internet, is proposed to resolve this problem. A cloudlet is a trusted, resource-rich server or computer cluster that is well connected to the Internet and accessible to nearby mobile devices for use. The benefits of using cloudlets are as follows.

- In comparison with the cloud, in its provisioning, a cloudlet needs to be even more agile because the relationship with mobile devices is highly dynamic due to consumer mobility and can be used to achieve a higher degree of latency, a higher bandwidth.
- A VM handoff technology must be used to help user mobility to automatically migrate the offloaded services to the second cloudlet on the first cloudlet as a user moves away from the currently associated cloudlet.
- It can be used as a first point contact for IoT sensor data, thereby enforcing privacy policies to release the data into the cloud.
- Also, during network failures, if cloud services become unavailable, the cloud service or denial-of-service attack can temporarily cover the loss (Satyanarayanan, 2017).

In cloud computing, users program their code, whereas, in edge computing, a series of computational functions are applied to the data along the data propagation path. Thus, the infrastructure is not transparent to the user. Most computation can be performed at the edge rather than at the edge of the Cloud Centric. In this case, the computation stream will assist in deciding which functions/computing should be used and how the data is propagated. Moreover, the number of applications running on top-node edge computing can be huge (Shi, Cao, Zhang, Li, & Xu, 2016). Algorithmic Government would require the functionality of edge computing as data will be massive, and latency issues will arise for computations.

3.10   GRANULAR COMPUTING

In recent years, the emergence of ubiquitous computing has led to a drastic rise in data collection, data generation, and automated data processing, including both non-personal and personal data. These data are frequently used and reused by various stakeholders in their original and updated form and are released online or on the Internet. Under the resulting dynamic data flow environments, it is becoming increasingly difficult for people to manage data from concerted data flows. Granular computing was first coined in the year 1997 to propose a new computational technique for performing human-data interaction (HDI), which suggests 'placing the human being at the center of data flows and providing mechanisms for citizens to communicate explicitly with these systems and data' (Mortier, Haddadi, Henderson, McAuley, & Crowcroft, 2014). In a given semantic context, information granulation includes the ability to discern necessary from unnecessary detail, and when used for interaction with data structures, often the ability to determine the motives of individuals, i.e., the pragmatics of a given piece of information. Both are exceedingly complex activities (Noy et al., 2013). The task requires the computers to detect and process the information in a manner that competes with human reasoning abilities.

Moreover, it offers tools and techniques for granularly representing and reasoning and the theoretical foundations to integrate the various granular modules. This integration's primary goal is to amplify human intelligence capabilities by using algorithmic processing and networking competencies for enabling interactive human feedback. For realizing such a kind of man-machine relationship, processing such kind of granular information is necessary. It provides an accurate representation of the social and natural system, which are organized into various levels. Different levels concentrate on different levels of granularities, which are distinguished by varying sizes of grain. The redundant, irrelevant information is removed, and the emphasis is placed on the proper level of abstraction to support and augment the collaborative planning process and iteratively updated visualization of user suggestions. Ideas are automatically generated in the form of a floor plan that expresses common ideas of the persons involved and immediately reacts with feedback. The automatically generated floor map helps participants immediately recognize flaws in their ideas, visually discover commonalities of and differences between ideas, and possibilities and opportunities that would otherwise not be obvious to them. For the generation of the floor plan, a granular spatial planning tool is used, whose data structure is based on the granular geometry (Yao, 2005). For citizen-centric services and processes, granular computing will be helpful for the implementation of Algorithmic Government.

3.11   FOG OF THINGS (FoT)

The fog computing paradigm is one of the kinds of IoT-based platforms that provide computing, storage, and networking capabilities between devices and overcome traditional cloud services' limitations. This platform's main characteristic features are wireless access, widespread geographical distribution, mobility, location awareness and low latency, real-time applications, heterogeneity support, etc. The most significant advantage of using Fog of Things is that systems don't need Internet connectivity. Moreover, it is capable of improvising bandwidth capacity. Furthermore, it can extend cloud computing competence to the edge of the network even without Internet connectivity. In Fog computing, small servers locally perform the data processing by using all the network edge processing capacity and further distributing the IoT services in the network edge through a message and service-oriented middleware.

The Fog of Things platform comprises the FoT device, FoT Gateway, FoT Server, FoT profile, Applications, and FoT profiles. FoT-Devices are the essential components of the system paradigm of FoT that performs the most basic functionality of the FoT-based platform. It transforms the raw data into structured content, which is then passed through the FoT gateway for easy access to other devices. All the FoT devices do not require an Internet connection. FoT gateways act as 'small local servers' and can be distributed across diverse geographical areas, offering FoT scalability and enhancing the overall response time.

Furthermore, FoT-based servers act as a storage platform with enhanced management capabilities. FoT profiles are included to foster and optimize the management of the distributed characteristics of the FoT paradigm (Prazeres & Serrano, 2016). Using this paradigm, FoT services provide a homogeneous interface enabling all the functionality required to interact with resources present in the cloud. This feature helps to implement many Algorithmic decision-making models.

References

Ai, Y., Peng, M., & Zhang, K. (2018). Edge computing technologies for Internet of Things: A primer. *Digital Communications and Networks, 4*(2), 77–86.

Alpaydin, E. (2020). *Introduction to machine learning.* MIT press.

Batubara, F. R., Ubacht, J., & Janssen, M. (2018, May). Challenges of blockchain technology adoption for e-government: a systematic literature review. In *Proceedings of the 19th annual international conference on digital government research: Governance in the data age* (pp. 1–9).

Briggs, R., Dul, J., Dobner, E., Mariani, J., & Kishnani, P. (2018). Digital reality in government. How AR and VR can enhance government services. *Deloitte Insights.* Available from https://www2.deloitte.com/us/en/insights/ind ustry/public-sector/augmented-virtual-reality-government-services.html on 16/07/2020. Accessed on 15 November 2020.

Burk, S., & Miner, G. D. (2020). *It's all analytics!: The foundations of AI, Big Data and Data Science landscape for professionals in healthcare, business, and government.* Boca Raton: CRC Press.

Cerf, M., Matz, S., & Berg, A. (2020). Using blockchain to improve decision making that benefits the public good. *Frontiers in Blockchain, 3,* 13.

Chen, H. (2009). AI, e-government, and politics 2.0. *IEEE Intelligent Systems, 24*(5), 64–86.

Coglianese, C., & Lehr, D. (2016). Improving the administrative state with machine learning. *Administrative and Regulatory Law News, 42,* 7.

Deloitte. (2018, January). *Blockchain in public sector: Transforming government services through exponential technologies.* https://www2.deloitte.com/con tent/dam/Deloitte/in/Documents/public-sector/in-ps-blockchain-noexp. pdf.

Doolin, C., Holden, A., & Zinsou, V. (2013). Augmented government: Transforming government service through augmented reality. *Deloitte Consulting LLP.* Available from http://www.deloitte.com/assets/Dcom-UnitedStates/ Local%20Assets/Documents/Federal/us_fed_augmented_government_0606 >,13.

Eggers, W. D., Schatsky, D., & Viechnicki, P. (2017). *AI-augmented government. Using cognitive technologies to redesign public sector work.* Deloitte Center for Government Insights.

Fuller, A., Fan, Z., & Day, C. (2019). *Digital twin: Enabling technology, challenges and open research.* arXiv preprint arXiv:1911.01276.

Husain, M. S., & Khanum, M. A. (2017). Cloud computing in E-governance: Indian perspective. In *Securing government information and data in developing countries* (pp. 104–114). IGI Global.

Hyvärinen, H., Risius, M., & Friis, G. (2017). A blockchain-based approach towards overcoming financial fraud in public sector services. *Business & Information Systems Engineering, 59*(6), 441–456.

Jeble, S., Kumari, S., & Patil, Y. (2017). Role of big data in decision making. *Operations and Supply Chain Management: an International Journal, 11*(1), 36–44.

Jun, L., & Jun, W. (2011). Cloud computing based solution to decision making. *Procedia Engineering, 15*, 1822–1826.

Kim, E. S. (2020). Deep learning and principal–agent problems of algorithmic governance: The new materialism perspective. *Technology in Society, 63*, 101378.

Kim, E. S., Choi, Y., & Byun, J. (2019). Big Data analytics in government: Improving decision making for R&D investment in Korean SMEs. *Sustainability, 12*(1), 1–14.

Klettke, M., Awolin, H., Störl, U., Müller, D., & Scherzinger, S. (2017, December). Uncovering the evolution history of data lakes. In *2017 IEEE international conference on big data (Big Data)* (pp. 2462–2471). IEEE.

Knight, W. (2017). The dark secret at the heart of al. *Technology Review, 120*(3), 54–61.

Kuziemski, M., & Misuraca, G. (2020). AI governance in the public sector: Three tales from the frontiers of automated decision-making in democratic settings. *Telecommunications Policy,* 101976.

LeCun, Y., Bengio, Y., & Hinton, G. (2015). Deep learning. *Nature, 521*(7553), 436–444.

Madni, A. M., Madni, C. C., & Lucero, S. D. (2019). Leveraging digital twin technology in model-based systems engineering. *Systems, 7*(1), 7.

Martens, B., & Teuteberg, F. (2012). Decision-making in cloud computing environments: A cost and risk based approach. *Information Systems Frontiers, 14*(4), 871–893.

Mortier, R., Haddadi, H., Henderson, T., McAuley, D., & Crowcroft, J. (2014). *Human-data interaction: The human face of the data-driven society.* Available at SSRN 2508051.

Munné, R. (2016). Big data in the public sector. In *New horizons for a data-driven economy* (pp. 195–208). Cham: Springer.

Nayyar, A., Mahapatra, B., Le, D., & Suseendran, G. (2018). Virtual Reality (VR) & Augmented Reality (AR) technologies for tourism and hospitality industry. *International Journal of Engineering & Technology, 7*(2.21), 156–160.

Noy, N., McGuinness, D., Amir, E., Baral, C., Beetz, M., Bechhofer, S., ... & Finin, T. (2013). *Research challenges and opportunities in knowledge representation.* Available from https://corescholar.libraries.wright.edu/cgi/viewcontent.cgi?referer=https://scholar.google.com/&httpsredir=1&article=1217&context=cse. Accessed on 20 November 2020.

Prazeres, C., & Serrano, M. (2016, March). Soft-iot: Self-organizing fog of things. In *2016 30th international conference on advanced information networking and applications workshops (WAINA)* (pp. 803–808). IEEE.

Rastogi, A. (2010). A model based approach to implement cloud computing in e-Governance. *International Journal of Computer Applications, 9*(7), 15–18.

Satyanarayanan, M. (2017). The emergence of edge computing. *Computer, 50*(1), 30–39.

Shamim, S., Zeng, J., Shariq, S. M., & Khan, Z. (2019). Role of big data management in enhancing big data decision-making capability and quality among Chinese firms: A dynamic capabilities view. *Information & Management, 56*(6), 103135.

Shi, W., Cao, J., Zhang, Q., Li, Y., & Xu, L. (2016). Edge computing: Vision and challenges. *IEEE Internet of Things Journal, 3*(5), 637–646.

Tadili, H., & Semma, A. (2015). How governments can benefit from cloud computing. *International Journal of Computer Science Issues (IJCSI), 12*(5), 170.

Yao, Y. (2005, July). Perspectives of granular computing. In *2005 IEEE international conference on granular computing* (Vol. 1, pp. 85–90). IEEE.

Yigitcanlar, T., Desouza, K. C., Butler, L., & Roozkhosh, F. (2020). Contributions and risks of artificial intelligence (AI) in building smarter cities: Insights from a systematic review of the literature. *Energies, 13*(6), 1473.

Yusuf, M., Sophan, M. K., Muntasa, A., Alamsyah, N., Nakkas, H., & Sari, P. P. (2020). E-government learning media through augmented reality technology. *Bulletin of Social Informatics Theory and Application, 4*(1), 12–20.

Zyskind, G., & Nathan, O. (2015, May). Decentralizing privacy: Using blockchain to protect personal data. In *2015 IEEE security and privacy workshops* (pp. 180–184). IEEE.

CHAPTER 4

Can AI Replace Government for Decision Making

Abstract This chapter argues whether it is possible to replace humans with machines for specific services. With the rising market potential of Artificial Intelligence and its related technologies, policy-makers and government bodies identify areas where it can be put to improve governments' functioning and deliver considerable benefit to society. AI can be useful for the Government as it enhances capabilities like sensing, thinking, and acting. It also reduces paperwork, backlogs, and improves predictions. But the biggest challenge is Algorithmic Bias, which identifies systematic and repeatable errors that result in unequal results, such as the privilege of one arbitrary group of users over the others.

Keywords Algorithmic bias · AI benefits · AI-driven government · Human decision making

4.1 ARTIFICIAL INTELLIGENCE AND THE FUTURE OF HUMANS

Modern AI technologies, algorithms, and computer systems have strongly influenced the world in the twenty-first century. The increasing integration of AI has threatened the prominence of human skills and proficiencies in different tasks. Both humans and *robonoids* work with cognitive function skills to perform the job assigned to them like problem-solving, learning, planning, thinking, and observing. Various experts argue that AI-based technologies will threaten human effectiveness and portend human agency, capabilities, and human autonomy. These algorithms driven computer programs will exceed human skills and intelligence, such as complex decision making, sophisticated analytics, pattern recognition, speech analytics, natural language processing.

Despite the positive consequential benefits of AI automation, there are fundamental differences in the human psyche and Artificial Intelligence systems that cannot be replaced by machines completely. The human mind is far more capable of performing more straightforward tasks than AI-based machines. The human brain possesses the ability to integrate emotional intelligence into the decision-making process and is better aware of facts, figures, and the surrounding environment. Moreover, humans' experiences during their lives also assist the decision-making process, thereby enhancing the decision's validity and conformity. On the contrary, decisions implemented through AI systems are an outcome of the data fed into the system and its processing, which needs to be designed by human beings to perform diversified tasks. AI is the creation of human brains, and thus, AI cannot completely replace humans (Eglash et al., 2020). The machine can only assist the decision-making body, but the power to make decisions or introduce changes still is concentrated on human beings.

However, there is a new need to have laws and practices to ensure that the computer science, computer programming, and AI development process is under the control of humans so that AI robotic machines do not harm humans. AI should be used to increase the effectiveness of human work rather than replace human jobs to avoid the unemployment crisis soon (Fitzpatrick, 2018). Though AI developments can significantly contribute to society, it can also lead to unemployment problems in the country, giving rise to numerous other issues like a truncated standard of living, health problems, growing poverty, social impediments, etc. (Jakimovski, 2010). AI machines are indebted to solve the stated issues by recompensing taxes just like humans to curb this problem. The fees received by smart devices or robots can be used for improving the social status of the society b arranging for vocational training programs and up-skilling initiatives for people who might have lost their jobs to smart machines (Paul, 2018).

The advancement and progression in AI development activities have created an entirely new range of human careers replaced by smart machines. This synthesizes the need to have new social skills to fill up these technical positions in the era of computers and robots, such as design mindset, cross-cultural competence, virtual collaboration, adaptive thinking, computational thinking, and intelligent management skills. Müller and Bostrom (2016) suggested that the human workforce should be regularly retained or re-educated to successfully meet the talent need for the changing demand of the working place in modern workplaces. In a nutshell, a new educational system has required redesigning its academic curriculum to equip new skills and knowledge for automated workplaces of the future (Rainie & Anderson, 2017).

Thus, a collaborative intelligence method is much more appropriate. Humans and machines work together, enhancing and uplifting each other competencies, utilizing each other's strengths and capabilities to generate long-term gains. Thus, the governing body needs to understand how humans can complement machines' work and how devices can enhance what humans do best.

4.2 Artificial Intelligence for Government & Politics

With the rising market potential of Artificial Intelligence and its related technologies, policy-makers and government bodies identify areas where it can be put to improve governments' functioning and deliver considerable benefit to society. Policy-makers most commonly use the following two approaches for successfully integrating any new application into its existing processes.

- **Preemptive approach**: In this approach, the government prohibits the use of an old-fashioned application that poses a potential threat to the social order
- **Permission-less innovation**: In this kind of approach, the government prioritize experimenting with new technologies as a default measure for solving problems as they arise

The AI-based data-driven policy is the most effective solution which the government can utilize for the same. Before the launch of AI, the decision-making process was solely based on assumptions, beliefs, and personal experiences. Consequently, there was no means by which the accuracy of the policies implemented could be confirmed. But the emergence of data-driven technologies enabled the government to process a large number of datasets to be more responsive to citizens and cut down the distortions associated with assumptions-based decision-making processes (Thierer, Castillo O'Sullivan, & Russell, 2017).

Remunerations for Using AI in Politics

1. The data-based decision-making process possesses the capability to detect corruptions made in the system.
2. AI-enabled systems and methods can better evaluate any candidate based on his past work experience, education qualifications, leadership behavior and skills, and behavioral responses to different situations.
3. AI and related technologies can improve system productivity and performance by critically analyzing the system's existing ambiguities.
4. AI-based techniques can help the government in reducing high cost which is wasted in political campaigning.
5. Also, AI-enabled systems can be put to use for removing all fake news and false agendas.

AI-Driven Digital Government: The Engagement Model

The AI-based Engagement model determines decisions based on people's engagement over social media platforms. The main benefit of using the Engagement model is that it enables the government to improve citizens' decision-making process and improve the e-voting procedures. The government authorities can use the Engagement model of the decision-making process to identify areas that are not performing well and places where they are best-performing. Based on the information sourced, government bodies can formulate strategies for improving the lives of the citizens of their respective nations and resolve the problems as they arise. Despite the enormous advantageous benefits of the Engagement model, surveillance of every step is an invasion of personal privacy, which distorts individual freedom of thinking and could lead to arousal of ethical questions relating to the use of someone's data. Additionally, replacing human forces with machines is yet another problem for public entities as it is likely to deteriorate the nation's employment status (Butterworth, 2018; Kaya, 2019).

AI Applications for Government

The following is the list of potential areas where the government uses the potential benefits of AI-based technologies to improve its performances and efficiency.

1. The government can allocate public servants and bureaucrats with better quality work using the AI-enabled systems to uplift their workers' satisfaction level.
2. Also, the government can make use of AI technologies for automating the repetitive tasks and saving human costs and time.
3. Using AI techniques, the government could re-employ staff and upskill them to improve the administration's functioning.
4. The government can offer jobs in the areas that are much more recompensing and involve creative thinking and empathy, which AI and other related technologies cannot replace (Kumawat, 2020).

4.3   How AI Can Benefit the Government

1. Sensing: AI can substitute human sensual capabilities, speed up the more straightforward tasks such as visual detection. For instance, AI technologies can inevitably examine street traffic with the help of cameras in real-time, which the government can use to make the best use of public transport facilities for reducing pollution and managing the ever-increasing flow of traffic. Also, the government can use bots for robotic process automation to simplify jobs and speed up the various tasks that were earlier handled by human forces. Some examples include form filling, moving files and folders, copying and pasting, managing historical files, scrapping the data over the web, etc., as shown in Fig. 4.1.
2. Thinking: Machine learning, natural language processing, and other AI-based technologies can analyze a large chunk of data much quicker and efficiently than humans. Consequently, the government can use these novice forms of techniques to improve the delivery

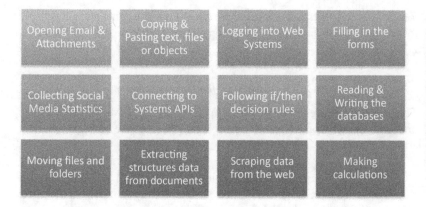

Opening Email & Attachments	Copying & Pasting text, files or objects	Logging into Web Systems	Filling in the forms
Collecting Social Media Statistics	Connecting to Systems APIs	Following if/then decision rules	Reading & Writing the databases
Moving files and folders	Extracting structures data from documents	Scraping data from the web	Making calculations

Fig. 4.1 Some functions that can be replaced by bots (*Source* Author Creation)

outcomes of teaching and learning process by simplifying the daily-routine-based administration tasks or modifying learning content according to the learner's need.

3. Acting: AI and its applicative devices and technologies such as chatbots or virtual assistants can simplify humans' decision-making process. These supportive technologies free up a significant amount of time, enabling the front-line workers to focus on activities that require their thorough attention to improve the quality of services delivered. For instance, in the Winter Olympics conducted in South Korea, many robots fortified with AI-powered translation software were castoff to provide info to visitors and players (Atalla, 2019).

4. Slashing Paperwork Burdens: By automating the daily tasks, most of the paperwork will be mechanized. Before this, government officials waste a considerable amount of time in completing paperwork. Instead, according to the estimates suggested by the federal government, *documenting and recording information consumes a half-billion staff hours each year, at the cost of more than $16 billion in wages alone,* which can be significantly reduced by deploying AI technologies.

5. Reducing Backlogs: Government officials can use AI technologies for reducing the turn around time or delays. Long waiting times are both frustrating for the customers and citizens and employee forces. The Social Security Administration has more than one million cases

unresolved at the end of fiscal 2016, worsening the problematic situation. Even the US Patent and Trademark Office has more than 558,091 patent applications pending by the end of the fiscal year 2019, hampering the startups' success and work. These large data backlogs can be easily removed.

6. Improving Prediction: Natural language processing and machine learning technologies can expose patterns and provide probable solutions to problems. For example, the Army's Medical Department uses a machine learning algorithm to evaluate the seriousness of wounds for assisting the medical department in arranging treatment or emigration (Deloitte, 2020).

4.4   Impact of AI on the Nature of the Government

Even though AI is anticipated to exceed human capabilities and functions, it is also forecasted to expand human labor. The finance sector is already witnessing the potential benefits of AI technologies in improved investment strategies proposed by the financial advisors. Moreover, AI diagnostic systems in the field of medicines are much more reliable and accurate than assumptions made by doctors while scrutinizing the patients' problems. Instead, according to McKinsey's estimates on some 400 cases, AI has helped in delivering a significant value of $6 trillion to almost 19 industries across different sectors by improving their human tasks. Even the government functions have started using AI to provide better customer services and automating simple tasks wherever possible. For instance, China has already started using robots to retrieve case histories and verdicts to reduce the lawyers' workloads. AI-enabled systems have enabled Chinese courts to track messages and comments made on social media, which can be used as evidence in the court. Even the traffic police in China are using facial recognition systems for identifying and convicting offenders. Despite the best of intentions, human systems are vulnerable to preconception and suffer from insentient biases. On the other hand, algorithm-based decisions are based on evidence, thereby reducing the risks associated with subjective decision making of discrete judges (World Government Summit, 2018).

The government's digitization movement is led by the need to have a system in place for a legal settlement and detecting fraud. AI-based systems are vital for renovating the public sector and reducing backlogs while simultaneously lowering costs. Progressing democracies into the age of big data is critical for reducing the public sector's dysfunctional areas and underpinning government lapses and errors. AI-enabled systems integrated into the government system have committed to improving service deliveries for inhabitants and reducing civil servants' work. With the elimination of some government functions, AI can foster open government development, supplementing its democratic operations (Forbes, 2019).

On the other hand, the survey results organized by the Center for the Governance of Change at IE University in Spain explained the negative consequences of replacing politicians with machines. The biggest problem of AI is its inability to think and respond rationally. First and foremost is that the devices are not as objective and rational as humans. Moreover, the algorithm-based systems are primarily controlled by humans, and thus, there are high chances that human biases can sneak into automated decision-making systems. Furthermore, if the data fed into the system is problematic, the commendations generated are also expected to be challenging. Moreover, computer systems are not proficient enough to capture the factors at work in human society and how they interact. And even if one particular model generates an accurate result in a specific instance, the results are likely to differ from varying places and time-zones (Samuel, 2019).

4.5   BIASNESS DUE TO AI

According to recent estimates, humanity today generates a trillion amounts of data every day, which, if printed, will waste a considerable duration of time on the earth. A large percentage share of the information is personal data, including health-related information, banking transactions. Moreover, a growing share of personal data flowing across businesses and Government, the risk of data breach increases. People involved in these transactions have minimal awareness of the collected data or fed into the algorithmic software. Moreover, to detect patterns and determine behavior based on the patterns identified in the data, algorithmic decision-making and assisting systems are being used. For instance, banks will use algorithms to identify possible fraud transactions based on past fraudulent conduct patterns and use algorithms to segment their customers into distinct categories according to their needs and preferences. Algorithmic bias is defined as a concept that is used to discriminate between the results obtained from the analysis of discrete datasets. Discrimination can be described as an unwarranted difference between individuals, based on their membership, or perceived membership, in a specific party or category. To extract meaningful information, algorithms must differentiate between individuals or groups to provide sufficient estimation of someone's creditworthiness. An algorithm is considered well-calibrated only when risk scores reflect the real scenarios of the people who give this score. To be more specific, algorithmic bias identifies systematic and repeatable errors that result in unequal results, such as the privilege of one arbitrary group of users over the others. For example, a credit score algorithm can refuse a loan without being unreasonable if it is consistent in weighing the relevant financial requirements (Rovatsos, Mittelstadt, & Koene, 2019). To remove the element of biasness from the algorithmic decision making, corporations must conduct episodic audits.

- **Conduct Audit**: Frequent audits should be conducted to delete the biasness from the datasets.
- **Get Feedback from Users**: It is imperative to seek feedback from the customers to discover content that was inappropriately marketed to the customers using conversational and virtual chatbots and wide-ranging other virtual AI assistants.
- **Ensure that AI resources are straightforward and explainable**: It is imperative to avoid the black box effect. For any automated activity, developers must explain why an algorithm engages in a particular course of action.

Some recent examples faced Algorithmic bias due to which replacing Government completely with AI looks tough.

- Amazon, the world-leading e-commerce retailer, recently discontinued the usage of recruiting algorithms to deal with gender biases and include an equal composition of males and females. Before this, the algorithm was automatically programmed to identify word patterns in resumes rather than specific skill sets, and these data were benchmarked against the company's overwhelmingly male to assess the suitability of the applicant.

- New York City uses an AI-based algorithmic decision model to keep track of kids, track when the neighborhood requires a fire-station, help the government process large datasets, process DNA samples at crime scenes to identify the victim. The court uses this algorithm to forecast whether the suspect should be imprisoned or unconfined on bail pending trial, etc. Recently, a man was wrongly convicted for a crime never done by him. (Brookings, 2020).

4.6   CHALLENGES FOR GOVERNMENT WHILE ADOPTING AI

1. **Effective use of data**: The main problem is that both private and public institutions are not designed in a fashion to handle and exploit the advantage of the large volume of datasets. The majority of these institutions have a basic understanding of these datasets. Moreover, organizations lack the required capability to understand and manage the data.
2. **Data and AI skills**: Organizations do not have the appropriate skills required to manage AI solutions within an enterprise. Specifically, public agencies lack the core AI skills to deploy as well as operate AI solutions.
3. **The AI environment**: The AI landscape is very dynamic and ever-changing. There are a few well-known players in more developed technology markets, so customers know where to go. For example, the cloud environment is dominated by Alibaba, Amazon, Google, and Microsoft, which account for about 84% of the global public cloud market. A large number of potential buyers are unaware of the advancements taking place in the field of AI.
4. **Legacy-culture**: Both organizations are faced with difficulties in the implementation of emerging technologies. However, public agencies appear to be less flexible than their peers in the private sector. The employees present in the public sector are less motivated to experiment and adopt a transformative technology AI (Weforum, 2020).

REFERENCES

Atalla. (2019). *AI has the potential to overcome the biggest challenges governments face and dramatically improve life for citizens.* Available from https://www.worldgovernmentsummit.org/observer/articles/could-an-ai-ever-replace-a-judge-in-court. Accessed on 5 August 2020.

Brookings. (2020). *Algorithmic bias detection and mitigation: Best practices and policies to reduce consumer harms.* Available from https://www.brookings.edu/research/algorithmic-bias-detection-and-mitigation-best-practices-and-policies-to-reduce-consumer-harms/. Accessed on 23 November 2020.

Butterworth, M. (2018). The ICO and artificial intelligence: The role of fairness in the GDPR framework. *Computer Law & Security Review, 34*(2), 257–268.

Deloitte. (2020). *Using cognitive technologies to redesign public sector work.* Available from https://www2.deloitte.com/content/dam/insights/us/articles/3832_AI-augmented-government/DUP_AI-augmented-government.pdf. Accessed on 5 August 2020.

Eglash, R., Robert, L., Bennett, A., Robinson, K. P., Lachney, M., & Babbitt, W. (2020). Automation for the artisanal economy: Enhancing the economic and environmental sustainability of crafting professions with human–machine collaboration. *AI & Society, 35*(3), 595–609.

Fitzpatrick, G. (2018, October). Mind the gap: Modelling the human in human-centric computing. In *2018 IEEE Symposium on Visual Languages and Human-Centric Computing (VL/HCC)* (pp. 3–3). IEEE Computer Society.

Forbes. (2019). *How Artificial Intelligence (AI) can be used in Politics & Government?* Available from https://www.forbes.com/sites/danielaraya/2019/01/04/artificial-intelligence-and-the-end-of-government/#3d9ffeed719b. Accessed on 5 August 2020.

Jakimovski, J. (2010). Unemployment as a complex and serious personal and social issue. *Škola biznisa,* 73–79.

Kaya, T. (2019, October). Artificial intelligence driven e-government: the engage model to improve e-decision making. In *ECDG 2019 19th European Conference on Digital Government* (p. 43). Academic Conferences and publishing limited.

Kumawat, D. (2020). *How Artificial Intelligence (AI) can be used in Politics & Government?* Available from https://www.analyticssteps.com/blogs/how-artificial-intelligence-ai-can-be-used-politics-government. Accessed on 5 August 2020.

Müller, V. C., & Bostrom, N. (2016). Future progress in artificial intelligence: A survey of expert opinion. In *Fundamental issues of artificial intelligence* (pp. 555–572). Cham: Springer.

Paul, K. (2018). Why robots should pay taxes. *Market Watch, viewed,* 22.

Rainie, L., & Anderson, J. (2017). *The future of jobs and jobs training.* Pew Research Center.

Rovatsos, M., Mittelstadt, B., & Koene, A. (2019). *Landscape summary: bias in algorithmic decision-making.* Center for Data Ethics and Innovation.

Samuel, S. (2019). *A quarter of Europeans want AI to replace politicians. That's a terrible idea.* Available from https://www.vox.com/future-perfect/2019/3/27/18283992/ai-replace-politicians-europe-survey. Accessed on 5 August 2020.

The matter of AI takeover: Will artificial intelligence replace human beings? Available from https://towardsdatascience.com/the-matter-of-ai-takeover-will-artificial-intelligence-replace-human-beings-79d2c788f358. Accessed on 9 August 2020.

Thierer, A. D., Castillo O'Sullivan, A., & Russell, R. (2017). *Artificial intelligence and public policy.* Mercatus Research Paper.

Weforum. (2020). *5 challenges for government adoption of AI.* Available from https://www.weforum.org/agenda/2019/08/artificial-intelligence-government-public-sector/. Accessed on 23 November 2020.

World Government Summit. (2018). *Could an AI ever replace a judge in court?* Available from https://www.worldgovernmentsummit.org/observer/articles/could-an-ai-ever-replace-a-judge-in-court. Accessed on 5 August 2020.

CHAPTER 5

Applications of Algorithmic Government Around the World

Abstract This chapter presents different progressive steps taken worldwide concerning the automation of decision making in the public sector. During the COVID-19 pandemic, more than 100 nations used contact tracing apps that used the Artificial Intelligence technique to manage the spread of infection. In general, a lot of experimentation is going on around the world. The postal services in America, digital farming technology in Japan, Lawbots in China, AI-based electoral candidates in New Zealand, military surveillance in Australia, AI-based healthcare in Africa, and Roads & transportation improvement in Europe are some of the prominent areas around the world which are thriving on the usage of Artificial Intelligence technology in the public sector for automated decision making. Many countries are investing huge amounts in technology adoption in the near future.

Keywords Contact tracing apps · Lawbots · AI elections · AI investment policy

Decision making actively governs the policies of the Government in the interest of the citizens. With the upcoming and emerging technology, the human workforce can be replaced by future technological advancements, which ease the automaton process in the interests of the public. During

R. Gupta and S. K. Pal, *Introduction to Algorithmic Government*, https://doi.org/10.1007/978-981-16-0282-5_5

69

the COVID-19 pandemic, almost 100 nations used contact tracing apps[1] that used Artificial Intelligence techniques to manage the spread of infection. But in general, a lot of experimentation is going on around the world.[2] The following are the case studies of few countries depicting their algorithmic decision-making process in the public sector.

5.1   AMERICA

The postal services in America handle quite a large number of volumes. Postal service is the country's basic functionality and is used by the majority of sectors, including education, personal, business, legal, etc. The postal service in the past has not provided efficient and reliable services in all the areas of the sectors, which could have been beneficial to both rural and urban areas alike. Although it has been used in majorly, all sectors yet the postal services have not been able to deliver. They have not been able to cope up with the revenues, and operating costs are just increasing. The postal services have been in loss for more than a decade, and there is a net loss of 3.9 billion dollars. The postal services have a budget around the fuel cost, and the postal services vehicles have been involved in so many road accidents. Due to the uncertain nature of the financial status, postal services in America are at a halt. The postal service sector is also designated as a high-risk sector due to the postal delivery persons and vehicles' deaths and accidents. To overcome this issue, the government has started to build autonomous cars for postal services and mails and parcels using AI technology.

Autonomous vehicles designed are based on technology that uses high tech cameras, and the use of radar and lidar makes it easy to navigate. Artificial Intelligence uses the data that is collected from cameras, radars, and the driving vehicle system makes further analysis. It combines the sensors' information with the detailed digital maps that provide the layout, traffic signs, speed limits, and other necessary information related to the roads. The complex vehicle system can also communicate with surrounded vehicles to coordinate with others and avoid collisions and road accidents. The vehicles' level till now is seen as they use the autopilot for navigation, i.e.,

---

[1] Contact Tracing Apps around the World—https://www.technologyreview.com/2020/05/07/1000961/launching-mittr-covid-tracing-tracker/.

[2] AI Policy around the world—https://www.holoniq.com/wp-content/uploads/2020/02/HolonIQ-2020-AI-Strategy-Landscape.pdf.

they require a physical driver to intervene in some hazardous situation if it arises. With the increase of AI technology, it is seen as shortly autonomous vehicles will be made to deliver postal service emails, parcels, etc. There is no setup of framework architecture for all the legal implications, so that remains unclear. The AI system also learns driving patterns from the humans and mistakes performed by them. Based on the vehicle's level, they can then provide the physical driver if the requirement demands. Manufacturers are already in the race to build autonomous cars, and based on the investment, it seems that the postal service sector is committed to integrating autonomous vehicles into the delivery model.

The AI technology in the postal services industry will be beneficial as well as cost-effective. Since the autonomous vehicles are based on electricity, the fuel cost is saved. AI technology to implement autonomous vehicles will help the workers as they will not suffer from fatal accidents and deaths since the vehicle's system will communicate with other cars, so chances of collision and accidents are minimal. The autonomous vehicles will make administrative work easier and faster. Though the technology seems to be near, many problems may arise as the project implementations come closer. The workers who are already in the job might lose their jobs, the delivery of packages and parcels is a topic yet to be discussed. If done well, the postal services in America will become efficient and faster. If the technology is not implemented in the correct order, this also threatens to displace human labor. It also raises the questions of data privacy and many such problems. Yet, it seems it will solve many issues shortly.

Apart from the postal services department, many use cases across multiple levels are being planned up in the United States. As per a report[3] on US federal agency (Engstrom, Ho, Sharkey, & Cuéllar, 2020), there are 12 use cases either identified or implemented for the Office of Justice Programs, 10 for Securities and Exchange Commission, 9 for National Aeronautics and Space Administration, 8 each for Food and Drug Administration and Geological Survey, 7 for Social Security Administrations, 6 for Patens and Trademark Office, 5 for Bureau of Labor Statistics, and 4 for Customs and Border Protection.

---

[3] Government by Algorithm—https://law.stanford.edu/publications/government-by-algorithm-a-review-and-an-agenda/.

5.2   Asia

There are various growing concerns around the world. One of them is agricultural sustainability, which also includes a shortage of water in Japan's countryside (Doan & Kosaka, 2020). Sustainable development is the world's demand at the current moment. Using and developing agriculture is such a way that we meet the present generations' needs without compromising the needs of the future generation. In the agricultural sector, future generations must take care of the land to provide them food and productivity in the farming sector. Using agricultural land for the sake of our current needs will be very difficult for the prospect. As we know, the fertilizers used up deteriorate the soil's quality and make it less productive as the years progress. The world is also facing a water shortage, and providing water to agricultural land is an emergent issue. The inexperienced farmers do not know how to maintain the land's productivity and keep the current generation's needs. The choice of their fertilizers makes the soil suitable for one or two seasons, and later the quality of the land is degraded. There is less production with the ground's degradation, and meeting the current needs will be a difficult task.

Following this issue, digital farming technology has been developed in Japan. This technology, with the use of IoT devices and AI-enabled devices, collects the data from the farming practices and the surrounding environment. This data is analyzed, and it tells the inexperienced farmers to use the techniques followed by experienced farmers for sustainable development. The knowledge provided by these experienced farmers is used for sustainable development in the agricultural sector. This digital technology can help in better decision making by analyzing the current situation and environmental surroundings and will suggest better farming techniques that can hold up the soil for better productivity in the future as well. These technologies can help those farmers where the supply of water is limited. This technology is capable of bringing a massive change in the sustainable development of the agricultural sector. Inexperienced growers generally use more fertilizers and water, so using experienced cultivators can help control the quality of crops and maintain a sustainable development environment. AI analyzes the soil and plant data and uses the knowledge to find the minimum amount of water required to serve the purpose. Using digital farming, the IoT sensors collect information and send data for AI devices that analyze and suggest better farming methods for sustainable development.

Digital farming in Japan is already being used and is highly praised. As we know the problem of water shortage, this technique of farming can primarily reduce this problem. This technique is inexpensive and highly efficient. Implementing this technique has brought a change in agriculture, where the use of water had no limits. Still, the usage of new technology manages how much water is sufficient for the land to grow a particular crop type. This technique will raise the value of farming and save both land and water for future generations. This technology has made sustainable development possible in the field of the agricultural sector. It will give the experience to those farmers as well who are new in the farming sector. It will help the newcomers adapt to the farming techniques while using less water and fewer fertilizers that will increase the soil's age. This technique will maintain the productivity of the land. This technique is also helpful in solving the problem of water shortage in the world. This technology uses extensive experiences from experienced farmers and uses the knowledge to develop sustainable agricultural sector techniques. This technique has already shown Japan's results and is moving toward other nations like Taiwan, Vietnam, and China.

Apart from farming, Japan also allowed an AI bot[4] to participate in elections for mayor's post, and it was even claimed to be World's first AI Mayoral candidate. It was built on the dataset of the region and answered most of the queries. A similar thing happened in New Zealand[5] as well. In the Chinese territory, AI is extensively used for managing the repetitive work of people in the Judiciary,[6] and soon we may see Lawbots giving judgments. Also, China is using AI aggressively in the Social Credit Systems of its citizens for better trust and worthiness assessment.

5.3 AUSTRALIA

In this twenty-first century, Governments worldwide are funding the technological sector for increased productivity and efficiency. Governance in Australia is expanding its IT sectors and technologies for decision making

---

[4] AI Mayoral Candidate—https://law.stanford.edu/publications/government-by-algorithm-a-review-and-an-agenda/.

[5] AI Candidate in NZ Elections—https://analyticsindiamag.com/worlds-first-ai-powered-virtual-politician-sam-joins-the-electoral-race-in-new-zealand/.

[6] AI in Chinese Judiciary—https://english.bjinternetcourt.gov.cn/2019-07/01/c_190.htm.

(Management Advisory Committee, 2002). Artificial Intelligence is introduced in the management to replicate humans' work, and the task can be
done repeatedly, faster, and efficiently. The use of Artificial Intelligence
in the Defence sector is a new beginning to this era. The problem earlier
was unable to detect weapons, vehicles, and other military-related stuff.
The section had to rely on the data observed and collected by humans,
resulting in errors and mistakes. Managing a large amount of data and
complex maintenance are the issues in the military workforce.

The military has faced this issue for ages, but now the introduction of
AI has brought a new change to this industry, making it much easier to
perform these tasks. Government agencies are using AI to recognize gun
truck's military tanks, and many more. Using cognitive automation has
brought this change. To reduce the human workforce, AI assistants can
be used to increase the military's readiness and the effectiveness of the
operations in more constrained environments where humans can barely
reach. AI assistants have accelerated the speed of work and reduce human
errors. This also creates a broader perspective in the training of other
military persons in wider aspects of the field. The training of AI and
machine learning systems is done for military vehicles. Moreover, new
trucks and tanks are being designed using AI technology to help in better
and faster decision making in the real-time war situation. Monitoring and
processing of data collected by the machines for military surveillance. The
Australian defense has also brought in augmented reality to maintain these
systems to close the skill gaps between humans and automated systems.
The government is also initializing facial recognition methods, solving
logistics problems, and much more in the military tasks. Support games
for military training and creating life-like war situations can be used to
visualize such cases. Better solutions can be designed using the use of
AI technology. The NSW business OCIUS technology claims using AI
technology, using cameras to detect electronic hearing, and much more.
These things work 24*7 and provide continuous coverage at a low cost
without affecting a single human life. Automation of combat weapons will
be a lifeline for the human workforce. In contrast, speed weapon development and identifying targets by the AI technology will play a crucial
role in security surveillance activities.

The impact of the solution will define the future trends of military
services around the world. The AI technology-based decision making has
been so useful in the early stages of its implementation. When this AI
technology is fully implemented can make life so easy for the defense of

the country. The detection of weapons, military trucks, under the sea monitoring all this has been possible due to the introduction of AI technology. The Australian government has already approved 29.9 million dollars to increase the capability of Artificial Intelligence and machine learning in the country. The AI technology-based decision making in the military has proven to be faster, less of errors, and least damage to human life. AI technology is creating real like war situations, and the troops' training had been better after that. Implementation of AI technology can help use the human workforce in those areas where AI technology is least developed. More efficient and capable systems in the defense forces strengthen and provide a computation of data faster and predict the results much quicker.

5.4   AFRICA

In Africa, AI helps the continent with some of the root problems, including poverty, education, sustainable development, delivering healthcare, and eradicating diseases (Besaw & Filitz, 2019). Many Governments have given access to innovative and productivity-boosting technologies that can help the continent grow. Healthcare systems in Africa face many challenges on a day-to-day basis. The governments face many structural problems. There is a shortage of quality and equipped professionals and services. The healthcare system of the countries in Africa does not match the standards set up by the WHO. There is a lack of services provided to the patients. Lack of awareness in the health sector is one reason patients do not get the necessary treatment and care. There are lesser health services policies framed. Even though the staff and medicines are available, affordability comes into play. Poverty does not allow the needed services to be in the reach of the patients. AI can plug and reduce these gaps in the health sector. Many startups in the continent are building AI-enabled technologies to focus on healthcare scenarios in the continent.

AI-enabled devices for healthcare can train the individuals in better treatment and supplement themselves as staff for the healthcare department. With high technology penetration, the professionals can focus on more patients and give more time to the patients. AI technology can help formulate better health policies, and these machines can better understand the patterns in the spread of the disease. These devices can build better solutions to tackle these situations. These devices can make the healthcare system more active. The conditions which are not taken seriously advance analysis techniques of AI can quickly figure out the problem and, in advance, better tailor the treatment. AI technology can prevent a disease from becoming a health crisis. The government is now looking at these technologies to simplify the problem of healthcare on the continent. With AI, technology health services will be much cheaper, readily available, and results in better treatment of the patient. AI technology is for analysis and diagnosis. Using AI services in the sector has already resulted in a faster and better understanding of the tests. It helps the working professionals in finding out complex problems and their solutions. AI tools as the online conversation and machine monitoring have extended the services to millions and remote areas. AI technologies can be useful in accurately predicting and prescribing treatment for people in remote areas. AI technology can make life-saving decisions much quicker than humans because it analyzes powers and capabilities with higher accuracy.

The government has started to incorporate AI technology in the health sector. With an increase in population and the number of diseases increasing, it is necessary to find a solution faster with higher accuracy. AI technology has a massive impact on providing services to millions, even in remote areas. The AI technology has helped in better prediction of results and treatment. It proactively selects a therapy based on analysis and prevents the disease from spreading. The AI technology has helped find patterns in a particular condition and get better results faster with high accuracy. AI technology in the African continent is a blessing in the health sector. The AI technology better understands the disease and can bring up the cause and ways to further spread the disease. AI offers vast opportunities for how we know the condition and how we can improve health. Using this technology, the healthcare system will provide better delivery of services to the continent's citizens.

5.5   EUROPE

There has always been a rapid increase in deaths due to road accidents. Millions of lives are lost due to road accidents around the world. Even with the variety of safety measures such as seat belts, helmets, and many more, there has been an increase in road accidents. Pedestrians and cyclists are on unprotected vehicles; hence, the injuries caused to them are fatal. Every mistake on the road can have deadly consequences and vulnerable. Life is lost; thus, something needs to be done to avoid these accidents. Currently, the government is applying this AI technology in autonomous driving and cameras to prevent accidents. Accidents can be avoided either the virtual assistants and self-driving cars manage themselves and avoid accidents. AI technology here plays a significant role. The German government has urged car manufacturers to use AI technology and knowledge gathered from these devices to prevent road accidents and fatal deaths every day. AI technology is new to Germany; hence the developments are still in the research phase, and later implementation of these technologies is meant to be done. Road accidents are a matter of grave concern, and if AI technology can help the world solve this issue, this will be an excellent achievement for humans. The AI technology in Germany has a goal of zero road accidents, and to achieve this, Artificial intelligence technology is a must.

Artificial Intelligence will enable vehicles to make decisions that could save lives. The sensors and cameras will detect the person on the road either on a cycle or walking by. The AI technology will perform the task based on the detection of critical points of human eyes, nose ears, and detect the full body of the person. These points will help to discover the posture and movement of the body. Using the detection analysis will be made about how far the individual is and how they can be saved from an accident. The system can detect if the person instantaneously comes in front of the vehicle; the driver can get late in recognizing the danger and applying breaks. Simultaneously, the AI-enabled technology will handle this situation and inform the driver about it. AI technology can detect pedestrians, cyclists and even avoid other cars coming in front of it. For this, the vehicles must coordinate with other vehicles and find ways to avoid collisions with each other. The German government has funded the car manufacturing industry to use AI-enabled technology and integrate this into the vehicles. However, to achieve this, we must grow toward the world of autonomous driving. The government of Germany has already stated its goals in this particular field. Once implemented, millions of road accidents can be prevented using AI technology. AI technology can be a boon to human life and make such decisions that could be lifesaving. All this processing and analysis that is done should be computed exceptionally fast because there will be no time to think and analyze in a real-time scenario. AI technology is in the country's early stages, so it will take time to implement this when we see this happening in real-time.

AI technology-based decision making will have a considerable impact on the vehicle manufacturing industry and humans as well. AI technology, if utilized and implemented correctly, can turn out to be a life-saving machine. Trials are in process in the country. The AI technology in vehicles and to avoid road accidents is possible shortly. When the car can detect people, other vehicles, and other things, the device will avoid collisions. The car will collect the data from sensors and cameras; using this data, the processing needs to be done, and detecting the person and avoiding collision will be done through the AI-enabled system. AI technology can make decision making in real-time situations easy and free of errors.

The European region seems to be the most advanced in terms of the adoption of the Algorithmic Government. A survey by IE Center for the Governance of Change[7] suggested that a quarter of Europeans favor technology-based decisions at the Government level. 43% of the respondents from the Netherlands, 31% each from Germany and the United Kingdom, 29% from Ireland, 28% from Italy, 26% from Spain, 25% from France, and 19% from Portugal, responded affirmatively in favor of usage of Algorithmic Decision Making at Government level. In fact, Estonia is one of the most advanced regions in Europe with a robust E-Governance infrastructure through schemes like E-Estonia. And now, it is moving toward implementing AI in judicial systems[8] just like the Chinese System.

5.6   Policy Level Progress Around the World

By 2030, China purposes to become the world's leading AI innovator. For this purpose, the country has published a national AI-based strategy and has announced plans to invest a massive amount toward developing AI-based skills. Beijing announced a US$2.1 billion AI-centric technology park, and Tianjin plans to set up a US$16 billion AI fund. Money is flowing from the private sector, too. In 2017, Chinese AI startups received 48 percent of global AI venture funding, outpacing the United States for the first time. China is recorded to be the second-highest number of AI companies globally, behind the United States—and is home to the most highly regarded AI corporation in the world (Deloitte, 2020).

---

[7] European Tech Insights—https://docs.ie.edu/cgc/European-Tech-Insights-2019.pdf.

[8] AI in Judicial System of Estonia—https://www.wired.com/story/can-ai-be-fair-judge-court-estonia-thinks-so/.

India, the fastest-growing economy with the second largest population globally has substantial stakes in the AI revolution. Recognizing AI's ability to turn economies and India's need to strategize its future, Hon'ble Finance Minister, mandated in his 2018–2019 budget address, set up the AI National Program. In line with the above, NITI Aayog has adopted a three-pronged approach—conducting exploratory proof-of-concept AI projects in different regions, creating a national strategy for developing a vibrant AI ecosystem in India, and working with various experts and stakeholders. Since the beginning of this year, NITI Aayog has collaborated with several leading AI technology-based companies (NITI, 2020).

Europe is well equipped to take advantage of AI's potential, not only as a user but also as a developer and a creator. It has outstanding research centers, creative start-ups and is a global leader. It has placed robotics in the competitive manufacturing and services industries, ranging from automobile to health, energy, financial services, and agriculture. Europe has developed a robust computing infrastructure (e.g., high-performance computers) that is important to the functioning of AI. In April 2018, the EU Commission adopted the Correspondence on Artificial Intelligence, a 20-page paper setting explaining the EU approach to AI. The goal of the EU Commission is to increase the EU's technical and industrial ability and the involvement of the public and private sectors in the AI, to prepare Europeans for the socio-economic changes brought about by AI, and to ensure that an adequate ethical and legal structure is in place (Salami, 2020).

In May 2017, Finland's Minister of Economic Affairs Mika Lintilä appointed a steering group to investigate how Finland can become one of the world's leading countries in the field of AI technology. While the group will not issue its final report until April 2019, two preliminary reports have already been published. The Finnish government has started to integrate the group's findings into government policy. The first report, Finland's age of AI, explains Finland's strengths and weaknesses in AI and provides recommendations to turn Finland into a global leader of AI. The second document, the Work in the Age of AI, corresponds to a 28 pager policy document on AI, which discussed the ethics and culture while working with Artificial Intelligence.

5.7   Prominent Global Projects

There are many global projects which are using the concepts of Government by Algorithms. They are either running successfully or are in progress for their execution. Many departments are successfully working toward adopting AI in their work processes and moving toward Algorithmic methods. Table 5.1 shows the list of such projects and departments.

Table 5.1   List of prominent global projects under Algorithmic Government

S.No.	Name of the project or department	Scenario
1.	US Citizenship and Immigration Services (USCIS)	In 2015, the (USCIS) started using chatbots; Emma managed the visitors who inquired on the website and handled more than 14 million immigration calls. This software automatically routes the user to the required human agent for real-time interaction. The chatbot uses natural language processing to feed thousands of instant messages, including various usual migration issues and service requests, such as a request for a visa application status. It is all managed by Algorithms
2.	Canada's AI Investment in Research and Talent	Canada was the first nation to invest a considerable amount to increase the number of AI graduates and establish a national research community based on AI. It currently has the following three institutes; the Alberta Machine Intelligence Institute (AMII) in Edmonton, the Vector Institute in Toronto, and MILA in Montreal, working toward building a community that possesses the required AI-based skills and competencies
3.	Infocomm Development Authority of Singapore	The Government of Singapore recently collaborated with Microsoft to create an interactive interface for fulfilling its plan of building a Smart Nation. The project primarily aims to expose online public service websites to all the cities and all age groups

(continued)

Table 5.1 (continued)

S. No.	Name of the project or department	Scenario
4.	Denmark's Digital Growth	Denmark launched a digital growth strategy in 2018 to make progress on AI-related technologies and transform digital businesses of the city for Danish people
5.	Atlanta Fire Rescue Department	Georgia Institute of Technology, Emory University, and the University of California, Irvine worked with the Atlanta Fire Rescue Department (AFRD) to strengthen predictive analytics software to forecast fire risk scores for 5000 buildings and mitigate the impact of the same
6.	China's Next Generation Artificial Intelligence Development Plan	China launched a next-generation AI development plan to support and foster AI development strategies, to further build an AI-based industry worth 1 trillion RMB by 2030
7.	City of Pittsburgh Traffic Improvement	The City of Pittsburgh partnered with Rapid Flow Technologies for building SURTRAC (Scalable Urban Traffic Control), automated traffic optimization, and controller software that can be used to oversee traffic, decrease travel time and haul-time
8.	India	Under NITI Aayog, the government has adopted an AI strategy to enable Indians to develop competencies and skills for securing quality jobs, putting resources and scaling AI-usage across sectors to amplify the level of development happening across the world
9.	Singapore Armed Defense	To deal with labor deficiencies, SAF is using AI-based technologies for combating the need for soldiers and replacing them with sensors and cameras, and other autonomous weapons wherever possible
10.	New York City Department of Social Services (DSS)	DSS is using AI for digitizing and automating the process of the online experience for the visitors

References

Besaw, C., & Filitz, J. (2019). AI & global governance: AI in Africa is a double-edged sword. *United Nations University Centre for Policy Research.* Available from https://cpr.unu.edu/ai-in-africa-is-a-double-edged-sword.html. Accessed on 16th July 2020.

Deloitte. (2020). *Future in the balance? How countries are pursuing an AI advantage: Insights from Deloitte's state of AI in the enterprise,* 2nd ed.. Available from https://www2.deloitte.com/content/dam/Deloitte/lu/Documents/public-sector/lu-global-ai-survey.pdf. Accessed on 23rd November 2020.

Doan, M. C., & Kosaka, M. (2020). Agricultural business innovation with new ICT: Case studies of Fujitsu, spread and MimosaTEK. In *Business innovation with new ICT in the Asia-Pacific: Case studies* (pp. 177–208). Singapore: Springer.

Engstrom, D. F., Ho, D. E., Sharkey, C. M., & Cuéllar, M. F. (2020). *Government by algorithm: Artificial Intelligence in Federal Administrative Agencies.* Available at SSRN 3551505.

Koshizuka, N., Haller, S., & Sakamura, K. (2018). CPaaS. io: An EU-Japan collaboration on open smart-city platforms. *Computer, 51*(12), 50–58.

Management Advisory Committee. (2002). Australian Government use of information and communication technology. *Commonwealth of Australia.* Available from https://www.apsc.gov.au/australian-government-use-information-and-communication-technology. Accessed on 2nd September 2020.

NITI. (2020). *National strategy for AI discussion.* Available from https://niti.gov.in/writereaddata/files/document_publication/NationalStrategy-for-AI-Discussion-Paper.pdf. Accessed on 23rd November 2020.

Salami, E. (2020, July 8). Europe's readiness for the AI takeover: Some salient points and comments from the EC's white paper on AI. *26 Computer and Telecommunications Law Review (C.T.L.R.)* (5), 124–125. Available at SSRN: https://ssrn.com/abstract=3646098 or https://doi.org/10.2139/ssrn.3646098.

CHAPTER 6

Applications of Algorithmic Government in Different Sectors

Abstract This chapter showcases technological advancements and decision making in a developing country like India across multiple sectors. The evolution of technology, a new stage of its adoption worldwide, provided India an opportunity to define its brand of AI leadership #AIforALL, where all AI prospects are applied to the country's needs and aspirations. Different sectors discussed in this chapter are Healthcare, Agriculture, Education, Mobility & Transportation, Law Enforcement, and Defense. Some common challenges faced in every sector across different regions are lack of data, low intensity of AI research, low availability of AI workforce, unavailability of computing infrastructure, high resource cost, privacy, and security.

Keywords Healthcare · Agriculture · Education · Mobility & Transportation · Law Enforcement · Defense

6.1 Introduction

Artificial Intelligence (AI) is the ability of machines/systems to perform human-like tasks such as learning, problem-solving, and decision making. With advancements in data collection, processing, and computation, AI can take over various schemes to enable connectivity and enhance productivity. The evolution of technology, a new stage of its adoption worldwide, provided India an opportunity to define its brand of AI leadership #AIforALL, where all the prospects of AI are applied to the country's needs and aspirations. AI is a collection of technologies that enable machines to act like humans with higher levels of intelligence, as shown in Fig. 6.1. Computer vision and audio processing techniques can recognize the world around them by processing images and sound. Natural language processing and inference engines enable AI systems to analyze the collected information. These capabilities are attained by their ability to learn from experiences and adapting over time. Every application starts with extensive training data.

AI framework is a combination of the following three distinct but inter-related components.

- Opportunity: AI can overcome the physical limitations of capital and labor by enabling—

  (a) Intelligent automation, i.e., automating complex physical tasks that need adaptability.

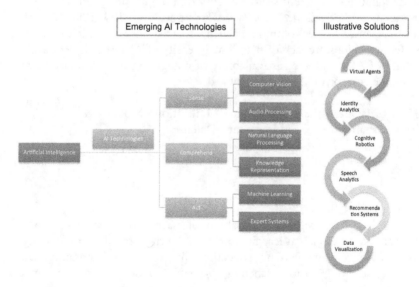

Fig. 6.1 Artificial intelligence technologies (*Source* www.accenture.com)

(b) Labor and capital augmentation, i.e., to let humans focus on their role that adds more value, complementing their capabilities and improving capital.

(c) Innovation diffusion, i.e., as the industry sectors are inter-dependent, innovation in one industry can have positive effects on another.

- AI for a greater good: AI can help in social development and inclusive growth. It can support access to health facilities, real-time advisory to farmers, and building smart cities effectively.
- AI garage for 40% of the world: AI helps institutions develop solutions that can be implemented in the rest of the world. For example, the Government can send AI-based answers, to diagnose tuberculosis, once created in India to other countries like Africa.

Some of the vital sectors, along with the use cases, are presented in the following sub-sections. They are majorly presented with respect to developing nations like India.

6.2   HEALTHCARE

AI and Robotics can be useful in many areas in healthcare, as shown in Fig. 6.2. AI in healthcare (Mahajan et al., 2019) can help solve barriers to healthcare facilities, mainly in rural areas that suffer from poor connectivity and a limited number of professionals. The healthcare sector faces the following challenges.

- Shortage of qualified professionals and services: There is a shortage of qualified doctors, nurses, technicians, and infrastructure. It is evident through numbers like 0.76 doctors, 2.09 nurses, and 1.3 hospital beds per 1000 population, whereas WHO recommends 1 doctor, 2.5 nurses, and 3.5 hospital beds per 1000 population, respectively.
- Non-uniform accessibility to healthcare: Physical access is the primary barrier to health services, which creates an imbalance between rural and urban India. There are 34% of the urban population and 66% of the rural population. Simultaneously, there are 33% of doctors in rural areas and 67% of doctors in urban areas.

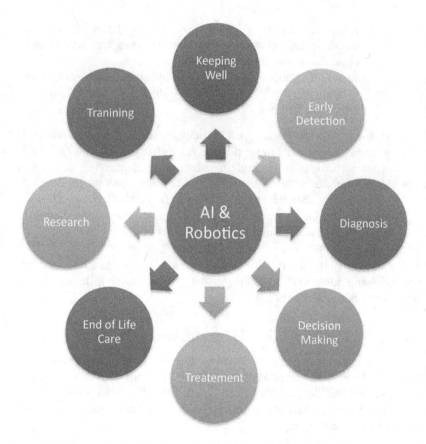

Fig. 6.2 Areas for application of artificial intelligence in healthcare (*Source* www.PWC.com)

- Affordability: Loans and sales make a portion of hospital costs in rural areas (around 47%) and urban (around 31%) of assets. Poor people suffer the most. According to the Government, 63 million people face poverty every year due to their healthcare expenditures.
- Approach to essential healthcare: Due to lack of awareness, access to healthcare services, and some behavioral factors, most people go to the hospital when a disease reaches an advanced stage, which increases the cost and reduces the chances of cure.

Case Study

Tata Memorial Hospital (TMH) is one of the best cancer hospitals in Mumbai, India. It registered more than 67,000 new patients for treatment in 2015, covering 23% of the patients from Maharashtra and 21.7% of patients from different states like Uttar Pradesh, Bihar, Jharkhand, and West Bengal to TMH. Patients had to go more than 18,000 km on average for the treatment due to a lack of healthcare access. Patients were stressed due to the financial expenses of traveling a long way. Therefore, most of the patients chose to move to TMH when cancer develops to an advanced stage, reducing the chances of cure. Early detection of cancer can be crucial across the country. Machine learning solutions that aim to assist a pathologist in making a diagnosis can help fill the healthcare gap. For the implementation of this solution, quality pathology datasets should be available. NITI Aayog is at an advanced stage for releasing a program to develop a national repository of pathology images. Components of this repository are 'Digital Pathology,' which requires all glass slides generated at high resolution and magnification, followed by accurate, comprehensive, and precise interpretation of the scanned images using various data sources and information available from patient care. Another project which is under discussion is Imaging Biobank for cancer. Human cancer can be visualized by using imaging modalities. Certain image-based features correlate to molecular and clinical features like mutation (KRAS, etc.), prognostic power, receptor status, gene expression patterns, intra-tumor heterogeneity, etc. Reports show an association between radiographic imaging and tumor stage, metabolism, and gene/protein profiles. These correlations, if established, may have a significant impact as imaging is regularly used in clinics. This provides an opportunity to use AI to improve decision making in cancer treatment at a low cost.

Aptaal glasses for blind and visually impaired people: Aptaal designed by Aptagrim's helps the user capture images sent to machine learning models deployed on smart glasses. When the photos are processed, speech is addressed to Aptaal glass, which the user hears via a built-in speaker on the glass. It uses facial recognition Tensor flow model, image captioning using CNN, and supports navigations with a voice to guide using Google Maps. It helps visually impaired people to overcome environmental and social challenges.

6.3   AGRICULTURE

AI can help meet the increased demand for food and can address challenges like inadequate demand prediction, lack of irrigation, misuse of pesticides and fertilizers (Dharmaraj & Vijayanand, 2018). Some use cases are advanced detection of pest attacks and prediction of crop prices. India is purely an agrarian economy where the agriculture sector has 49% of India's workforce, contributes 16% of GDP (Gross Domestic Product), and provides food security to almost 1.3 billion people. India's unsustainable agricultural practices are reflected by land degradation, increased dependence on inorganic fertilizers, reduced soil fertility, and rapid drop of water tables. Fluctuation in agriculture growth, changes in monsoonal rainfall, and inefficient markets cause income variability of farmers. Access and availability of services in the agriculture chain is a challenge. Various concerns are shown in Fig. 6.3.

Case Study

Microsoft developed a sowing app using AI in collaboration with ICRISAT powered by Microsoft Cortana Intelligence Suite with Machine Learning and Power BI. This app sends sowing advice to farmers on an optimal day to sow. All they require is a phone which can receive text

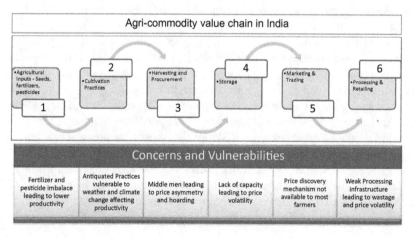

Fig. 6.3 Agri-commodity value chain in India (*Source* www.niti.gov.in)

messages. The advisories have information like optimal sowing date, farm-yard manure application, soil test-based fertilizer, seed treatment, and sowing depth in 2017. The program reached more than **3000** farmers across Andhra Pradesh and Karnataka during the Kharif crop season for crops like ragi, maize, rice, and cotton. The app increased the yield from 10 to 30%.

Blue river technology is designed using computer vision and machine learning technology, making farmers use herbicides by spraying only the areas where weeds are present. This reduces the use of inputs for farming.

NITI Ayog and IBM developed a crop yield prediction model to provide advice to farmers for Precision Farming. It improves crop productivity, soil yield, early warning on the pest, and agricultural control inputs. It is implemented in 10 districts across the Indian states of Assam, Jharkhand, Bihar, Maharashtra, Madhya Pradesh, Uttar Pradesh, and Rajasthan.

6.4 Education

AI can solve access issues and quality issues in the education sector (Tewari, 2020). Some use cases enhance the learning experience using personalized learning, automating administrative tasks, or recommending vocational training. The education sector mainly faces the following challenges.

- Multi-level classrooms: In small areas, it is not possible to have separate classes for different grades. Teachers must handle heterogeneous groups of children (different ages, abilities) in the same classroom.
- Lack of attention: Several factors like inadequate infrastructure in the school, language barriers, significant learning gaps concerning grades, family circumstances, poor health, and poor teachers may lead children to the risk of dropout.
- Less adoption of technologies: This is due to a lack of teacher training. According to a survey, 83% of teachers use computers just to promote student practice.

Case Study

Creating smart content: Content Technologies Inc. (CTI) is an AI research and development company that creates customized educational content. This technology uses deep learning to analyze existing materials and textbooks and creates custom learning materials, including books, chapter summaries, and multiple-choice tests.

Predicting dropouts: Andhra Pradesh government has tied up with Microsoft to make particular efforts to lower the school dropout rate. The application, powered by Azure machine learning, processed all the students' data based on gender, academic performance, teacher skills, and school infrastructure to find predictive patterns. With these predictions, education officials can help students who are most likely to dropout using different programs and counseling sessions.

Write-to-learn: Pearson's software uses natural language processing and gives personalized feedback to students, hints, and tips to improve their writing skills. Software rate essays and then provides suggestions for their improvement. Used by teachers as essay grading becomes a less time-consuming process. A teacher can spend more time teaching.

6.5   MOBILITY & TRANSPORTATION

Various use cases are autonomous fleets for ride-sharing, predictive engine maintenance, traffic management, autonomous delivery, etc. (Mathur & Modani, 2016). Various issues faced by the transportation sector are as follows.

- Congestion and road accidents: This sector is underdeveloped and leads to an inefficient economy. The government shows the following growth pattern of vehicles.
- High number of traffic deaths: According to the Ministry of Road Transport and Highways (MORTH), the total number of road accidents during 2015 was 501,423. This count keeps on increasing with years, as the number of vehicles is rising, as visible in Fig. 6.4.

Case Study

From the last few years, most of the investments in AI have been made in autonomous vehicles. Due to congestion and traffic conditions in India,

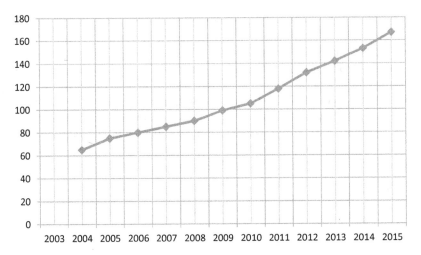

Fig. 6.4 Registered vehicles per 1000 population (*Source* www.niti.gov.in)

algorithms trained on India's data have been robust. Error rates of object classification fell from 28.5 to 2.5% since 2010. Therefore, India can use present-day techniques in this sector.

Intelligent transportation system: System includes sensors, CCTV cameras, speed recognition cameras, automatic number plate recognition cameras, and stop line violation detection system can be used for toll pricing and enforcing traffic regulations through smart ticketing.

6.6 Law Enforcement

Technologies used by law enforcement are facial recognition, speech recognition, drones, and predictive analytics.

Case Study

Predictive Analytics: Researchers have worked in big data for processing data to generate predictive policing models. National Crime Records Bureau has worked with Advanced Data Research Institute (ADRIN) to develop this technology. The system is used for crime mapping, analytics, and the predictive system, which helps police officials with personal digital assistants access the information at crime scenes, which reduces the burden of filing reports. This software accesses data from Delhi's police dial 100 helpline and ISRO's satellite imagery to locate hotspots using clustering algorithms. This helps Delhi police to predict when and where crime might occur. Currently, crime mapping is done every 15 days. Then neighborhood analysis is done through algorithmic evaluation of geo-spatial data. The proximity analysis is done, enabling the review of data of criminals, witnesses, victims, and people near the crime location.

Speech and facial recognition: Punjab police, along with an AI startup—Staqu, commissioned the Punjab Artificial Intelligence System (PAIS), which loads criminal records and automates research using facial recognition features. When an officer finds the suspect, he clicks the picture; the picture is entered in the app, which compares this image with stored images. This app then sends the suspect's criminal background within a few minutes to the officer's phone.

Robo-Cops: In Hyderabad, H-Bots robotics invented a robot that is still in progress that can handle law and order and enhance traffic management. If implemented, it can maintain security at malls and airports.

6.7   DEFENSE

Defense: In defense, AI is used for intelligence, surveillance, robot soldiers, risk terrain analysis, cybersecurity, and intelligent weapon systems (Ray, 2018).

Case Study

Intelligence, Surveillance, and Reconnaissance: Indian army uses autonomous vehicles to detect naval mines in waters and territorial waters to detect adversaries. Rustom-2 can operate in both manual and autonomous modes. The DRDO (Defence Research and Development Organization) has made a robot known as Daksh, which can be used with a robot range of 500 meters (DRDO Robotics, 2020).

Robot soldiers: The Centre for Artificial Intelligence and Robotics (CAIR) with DRDO has developed a Multi-Agent Robotics Framework (MARF). It uses multi-layered AI architecture to create robots that can work together as a team like real soldiers. Robots built are Wheeled robots with Passive suspension, robot sentry, and snake robot.

Risk terrain analysis/GIS: According to a report by Defence Research and Development Organization, the applications include: (i) Military Geospatial Information system which helps in generating terrain trafficability maps (Going maps- GMs) using soil, slope, moisture, landform, and land use which are then integrated; (ii) Terrain Feature extraction system helps determine land use using multilayer perceptron training, which generates multiple themes; (iii) Terrain Reasoner system which allows decision-makers to find alternative routes for completing a mission; (iv) Terrain Matching systems which integrate complex case-based reasoning into a whole.

Intelligent Weapon systems: Defence Research and Development Organization indicated that a Pilotless Target Aircraft (PTA), Lakshya-II, was tested for many rounds. It is India's first armed drone. It has a precision of 20 meters and has completed nine flights successfully.

Eugenie, device failure detector: It generates alerts for a device failure or its reducing efficiency. It helped to reduce the maintenance costs of electronics and other devices. It is given equipment data for several years and a strategy to use the data. It applies a digital transformation blueprint to the data using IOT sensors. It helped the defense sector to transform from preventive to predictive maintenance. It achieved more than 92% accuracy.

6.8 Others

Andhra Pradesh's government developed the Kaizala app with Microsoft. It is used to crowdsource citizen feedback from social media accounts and verifies the feedback by linking it to citizens' mobile numbers. Information is then processed using an automated Application Programming Interface (API). It is also used to send automated messages to citizens. For example, Microsoft reports that ration-shop owners are warned if they have not distributed ration portions on time. The weather department uses this messaging system to send warnings for the weather.

CamfyVision's FacEAI_ PRO to enhance student's safety and to detect mishandling: CamfyVision provides solutions to ensure the safety of kids by searching for kids missing from class, monitoring the premises of the school, etc. This product works using AI, ML, Deep learning, and computer vision techniques. CamfyVision has an automated children and staff management system with real-time monitoring. It improves discipline, quality of education and enhances the user experience, which helps take India's education system to the international level. It works as follows if a kid is missing for more than 15 minutes, it alerts several times. And if the child doesn't return within 30 minutes, alerts are sent, so the school authorities take that action. When the child boards and deboards the school vehicle, parents, school safety staff are sent 'entry and exit' notifications.

Tara app to improve teachers' English proficiency: If a teacher does not have a good command of English, there will be poor learning outcomes for the children. Children fail to understand the language, which leads to poor performance. Learning matters' Tara helps to increase teachers' vocabulary, which improves their communication skills. It works on Amazon's Echo dot, Google Home, and smartphones. It has four components of learning—listening, speaking, reading, and writing (LSRW). Tara mimics the user by listening, responding to the user's utterances, giving feedback, correcting the grammatical mistakes, and conversing with the user repeatedly. It creates a non-judgmental environment so that learners can speak confidently without any fear. In the start, an assessment is taken to rate LSRW skills on a scale of 5, which is designed to show the Common European Framework of Reference (CEFR) guidelines. Assessment is made after three months of starting the course and at the end of the year, i.e., after six months. They are rated based on grammar, comprehension, vocabulary, pronunciation, fluency, and expression. A monthly performance report is created every time.

Different sectors face different challenges, but all of them face some common challenges.

- Lack of data: The key challenge faced is the unavailability of good quality and domain-specific public datasets. Open Government Data (OGD) platform supports available data of the Government of India. There are more data sources, but the quality of data needs to be improved. The issues faced are data unreliability, insufficient standardization, and limited data.
- The low intensity of AI research in fundamental technologies.
- Evolution of core research into market applications.
- Low availability of AI expertise, workforce, and skills: The researchers seem to prefer foreign universities, and even the undergraduate students are interested in pursuing research outside India. So, there is a lack of expertise in India.

- Computing infrastructure: Researchers require access to specialized hardware for research purposes. The unavailability of high-performance systems limits the ability of the researchers.
- High resource costs.
- Low awareness for the adoption of AI in businesses: Many people are unaware of the benefits of adopting AI in their businesses.
- Privacy, security, and ethical regulations are unclear.

The developing nations worldwide have similar use cases in various sectors, and Indian datasets can provide a template for other countries to test their model and applications (Chakrabarti & Sanyal, 2020).

REFERENCES

Chakrabarti, R., & Sanyal, K. (2020). Towards a 'responsible AI': Can India take the lead? *South Asia Economic Journal.* https://doi.org/10.1177/139 1561420908728.

Dharmaraj, V., & Vijayanand, C. (2018). Artificial intelligence (AI) in agriculture. *International Journal of Current Microbiology and Applied Sciences, 7*(12), 2122–2128.

DRDO Robotics. (2020). *Robotics, defence research & development organization.* Retrieved from https://www.drdo.gov.in/robotics on 15 June 2020.

Mahajan, A., Vaidya, T., Gupta, A., Rane, S., & Gupta, S. (2019). Artificial intelligence in healthcare in developing nations: The beginning of a transformative journey. *Cancer Research, Statistics, and Treatment, 2*(2), 182.

Mathur, S., & Modani, U. S. (2016, March). Smart City—A gateway for artificial intelligence in India. In *2016 IEEE Students' Conference on Electrical, Electronics and Computer Science (SCEECS)* (pp. 1–3). IEEE.

Ray, T. (2018). Slow and steady: India's tentative steps into the AI race. *The Diplomat, 14.*

Tewari, A. (2020, July). Sustainable education in India through artificial intelligence: Challenges and opportunities. In *12th ACM Conference on Web Science Companion* (pp. 41–47).

CHAPTER 7

Potential Use Cases of Algorithmic Government

Abstract This chapter presents various potential use cases that can be developed in different domains, specifically for developing and under-developed nations. Multiple codes for prototypes of use cases from this chapter are presented for technology enthusiasts. The problem of fake news in media, managing floods in disaster management, assessment in the education system, the online admission process for schools and colleges, loan fraud issues in finance industry, and online reputation management are some of the use cases discussed in the chapter which can be automated for the Government sector. Although these are the early stages of algorithmic implementation in various regions, with the amount of data increasing, governance can be made more robust and flexible.

Keywords Education · Media · Disaster management · Reputation management · Finance industry

7.1 MEDIA

The Problem of Fake News

Fake news depicts sensationalism, which presents misinformation or hoaxes that spread through traditional media and popular online social media. The rapid increase in social media has changed the way of acquiring information. More news is consumed through social media, providing information timely and comprehensively on the events world-wide. As compared to traditional communication (newspapers or television), visualized info like images and videos explain better and attract attention from the viewers or the readers. With misleading words, social network users get easily affected by fake news, which leads to tremendous effects on offline society. Reading a story on social media is becoming easier and accessible, due to which fake news becomes a significant issue for the public and the government. Fake news misleads readers and spreads, which negatively affects or manipulates public events. Fake news creates a lot of hurdles for the government at every level. During this pandemic, authorities are found busy in clarifying people to protect them from rumors.

The reasons for people switching from traditional to online news consumption, i.e., advantages of online use of news are that it is less expensive as compared to conventional media; requires less time than on traditional media; and it is easy to share content in the form of videos, blogs, or pots with other users or comment on social media. There is also a disadvantage of social media, i.e., the quality of news on social media is lower than the traditional news. As it is cheaper, faster, and easier to provide news online, much fake news is produced for many reasons, such as financial and political gain. This gives ease to publishers to publish their articles in collaborative environments. People believe that the information received from social media sites is reliable. It is analyzed that people are unable to recognize deception, which affects the news ecosystem.

There are various psychological factors due to which people believe in fake news: (i) social credibility, i.e., people think the source is credible if others find the source if credible, especially when there is not enough information about the source; (ii) frequency heuristic, i.e., people favor information that they frequently hear even if it is fake. Many malicious accounts on social media become sources of fake news. There are mainly five types of fake news—first, Deliberate Misinformation, which is information that is spread in a way to deceive target users. Second, Clickbait grabs the user's attention so that the user clicks on the fake news. Third, Parody or Satirical articles use absurdity and exaggeration to comment on events that unease the readers. Fourth, False headlines use to draw the attention of the reader. The title may not match the context of the article. This type is untrue and misleading. The fifth is Hoaxes, which deceives the reader by causing harm and material loss to the user.

Why Fake News Spread Is a Concern?

The spread of fake news has a severe negative impact on society. Firstly, fake news destroys the authenticity balance of the news ecosystem. For example, it can be seen that fake news is more widely spread than popular authentic news. Secondly, fake news makes people accept false beliefs. Lastly, fake news changes how people interpret and respond to the real story. For example, some fake news is created just to trigger people's trust and confuse them, hinder their ability to differentiate between what is right and what is not valid. Fake news many times leads to communal riots. For example, some lawbreakers spread a video a few years ago on WhatsApp and other social media platforms, which lead to the enormous communal violence that led to the destruction of belongings to different communities.

The spread of fake news containing forged or misinterpreted images can cause many adverse effects like manipulating important events. For example, recently, there was a piece of fake news that depicted an entire community of people as a disease source (COVID-19). A few people in mid-March at a religious place in Delhi led to many positive cases in India. Many fake videos depicted the group as 'Corona Villains.' A video was spread that claimed some foreign country people intentionally licked kitchen utensils to spread the novel coronavirus. The footage was fact-checked, which proved that a group of humble people consumed food from those utensils to ensure that no grain of food was left and wasted. During this pandemic, authorities are found busy in clarifying people to protect them from rumors.

According to a statistical report, 47% of the population acquires news from online mediums like social media, and others receive from TV, newspapers, and radio. The most trusted news source in 2018 was newspapers. The primary source of news for people is an online search engine, and 45% of the population believes the story is accessed via search engines. Top networks used to access reports are Facebook and WhatsApp by 52% of the community. 41.8% of fake news data in the election is due to social media, which is higher than shares of both traditional mediums (TV/radio/print) and online search engines.

Therefore, it is essential to help reduce the adverse effects caused due to fake news such that it benefits both the public and the news ecosystem.

How Algorithms Can Provide Solution

The steps performed in the implementation of Fake News Detection are mainly data preprocessing, data visualization, feature extraction, and applying models. The following are the steps.

1. Create a column 'label' in the data frame, which is our target feature denoting whether the news is True or Fake.
2. Combine the columns 'title,' 'text,' and 'subject' into one feature column called 'article.'
3. Create the final data frame with only 'article' and 'label' features.
4. Start with data preprocessing, i.e., transform the raw data into a useful and efficient format like removing null values, punctuation, stop words, and then perform lemmatization.
5. Search for the null values and removing them from the data frame if present.
6. Convert every word in the 'article' feature to lower case.
7. Remove the punctuation from the data, i.e., full stop, colon, comma, brackets, etc.
8. Remove the stop words, i.e., useless words in the data like 'a,' 'an,' 'the,' 'in,' etc.
9. Perform lemmatization, i.e., the process of grouping together different forms of a word to its root form such that they can be analyzed as a single item.
10. Then perform the data visualization, i.e., bar plots, pie charts, word cloud, etc.
11. The next important step is feature extraction, i.e., attribute reduction in the dataset.
12. Create a bag of words (BOW), i.e., text (sentence or document) is represented as a bag (multiset) of words, ignoring grammar but keeps count of word occurrences.
13. Create TF–IDF (Term Frequency–Inverse Document Frequency) vectorizer, i.e., mathematical statistic that reflects how important a word is to a document and contains information on both more essential and less important words. It converts the collection of data into a matrix of TF–IDF features.

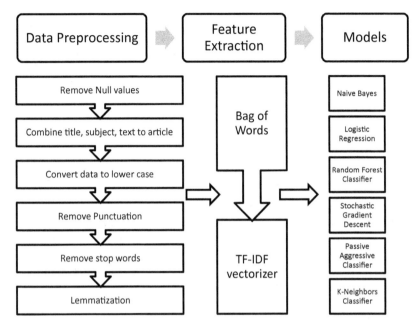

Fig. 7.1 Block diagram representation of fake news detection architecture (*Source* Author creation)

14. Then comes the final phase, which comprises of applying various models like Passive-Aggressive Classifier, Naïve Bayes, Stochastic Gradient Descent (SGD), Logistic Regression, Random Forest Classifier, K-nearest neighbors classifier, etc.
15. Applying the classification model has initialized the model, trains the classifier, predicts the target, and then finally evaluates the classifier model.

The block diagram of the process is shown in Fig. 7.1.

Which Analytical Techniques Can Help?

The text classification problem requires to define three sets. First, is training dataset $D = \{d_1, d_2, \ldots, d_n\}$, second is the class label $C = \{c_1, c_2, \ldots, c_n\}$ and last, is the test dataset $T = \{d_1, d_2, \ldots, d_n\}$. Each data

d_i of the training dataset is labeled with the class label c_i from the class label set C, and each data of the test dataset is unlabeled. The classifier's main aim is to construct a model from training data by relating features to one of the target class labels. After the classification model is trained, it can predict the class labels of test data. The formula for both training and testing is given in Eq. 7.1 and 7.2.

$$f : D \rightarrow C \tag{7.1}$$

$$f(d) = c \tag{7.2}$$

Preprocessing generally involves steps such as stop-word removal, punctuation removal, lemmatization, etc. Feature extraction is a data representation process that includes several activities to scale down data complexity and carry out the classification process in an accessible manner. It involves the calculation of TF (Term Frequency) and IDF (Inverse Document Frequency) from tokenized data. Finally, the data is normalized to unit length to perform classification efficiently.

F. Sebastiani surveyed the different classifications and discussed the specific role of machine learning algorithms in classification. Colas et al. compared SVM's performance with KNN and Naïve Bayes classification algorithms on Reuters 21,570 dataset. The performance metrics were calculated for each classifier. The overall performance of the SVM classifier worked well. If the preprocessing and internal parameters are adjusted well, then KNN and Naïve Bayes perform well too.

In logistic regression, the probabilities of the outcomes are modeled using a logistic function. This model is designed mainly for classification and helps understand the effect of independent variables on the dependent or outcome variable. It works only when the predicted variable is binary and assumes there are no missing values.

Naïve Bayes classifier is a probabilistic classifier that works well in real-world situations like document classification and spam filtering. It requires a small amount of training data to predict. This classifier is extremely fast as compared to others. There are two variants: the Multivariate Bernoulli model (B_NB) and Multinomial model (M_NB). Bernoulli works well on binary data. The multinomial model works on frequencies of attributes available in vector space representation of data.

Stochastic Gradient Descent is an efficient and straightforward classifier to fit linear models. It is helpful when the number of samples (data) is large enough. It is sensitive to feature scaling.

K-nearest neighbors (KNN) is a lazy learning model, stores instances of training data. Classification is done from a majority vote of k-nearest neighbors at each point. It is simple to implement, robust to noisy training data, and effective when the number of samples or data is large but has high computation costs.

Random forest classifier fits the number of decision trees on subsamples of datasets (size of subsamples is the same as original input sample size; these samples are drawn with replacement) and uses an average to improve the prediction accuracy. It is more accurate than a decision tree and removes overfitting, but it is complex and challenging to implement the algorithm.

Passive-Aggressive algorithm remains passive when the classification outcome is correct but becomes aggressive when miscalculation (updating and adjusting).

These classifiers' efficiency is measured by performance metrics like accuracy, precision, recall, F1 score, etc. The highest accuracy for the dataset used in this book (Appendix A) is of Passive-Aggressive classifier, which is 99.5%, and next is that of Stochastic Gradient Descent, which is 99.1%. Passive-Aggressive classifier has the highest F1 score. Therefore, the classifier which can best fit the data is the Passive-Aggressive classifier. The prototype code with algorithmic implementation is shown in Appendix A.

Conclusion

The extensive spread of fake news has plenty of negative impacts on society. The false news detection system can help mitigate the adverse effects of fake news on both the community and the news ecosystem. The solution can maintain the authenticity balance of the news ecosystem. It can help people accept false beliefs and differentiate between what is right and what is not. Fake news is not a problem; the rise of this fake news on social media makes it sturdy and challenging. The rate of production of counterfeit digital news is large and rapid. Thus it is challenging for machine learning to detect fake news effectively. False news detection can help to reduce misinformation risk and communal riots.

Using fake news detection, alert systems can be created that can alert users whether the news or the page is fake or not. Also, the alerts can be sent to the media so that they can inform the public. Various detection systems can be created as an extension of this. Also, intervention systems can be designed that can intervene to offload the page if it is fake. Malicious accounts containing false news can be removed so that the spread is reduced. The primary source of the news can be determined, and that source can be further blocked to stop the spread. Users with certain news can be immunized rather than fake ones. It can help minimize the spread scope and reduce fake news that created unnecessary tension in the polity. It can reduce public chaos and censorship over the media. It is a tool that can help editors and journalists to pace up the verification procedure for the content that has been generated from social media. And the quality of the news can be improved.

7.2   Disaster Management

The Problem of Floods as Natural Disaster

A country like India is a sub-continent located in the core of the summer monsoon belt. India has many major river systems, such as the Himalayan Indus Ganga Brahmaputra system and the peninsular Godavari, Mahanadi, Krishna, Kaveri on the east coast, and Narmada and Tapi on the west coast. After Bangladesh, India is most prone to floods. The most vulnerable states are the coastal regions which are Gujarat, Maharashtra, Goa, Karnataka, Kerala, Tamil Nadu, Andhra Pradesh, Orissa, and West Bengal. It receives more than 80% of rainfall from June to September, during which most floods occur. India faces floods almost every year with varying magnitudes. Tide is the most persistent disaster. Floods are mainly caused by riverbanks' low capacity to control high flow bought down from the upper catchment caused due to heavy rainfall. In coastal areas, floods are caused by cyclones or typhoons. Flash floods occur in low lying areas near foothills. Some other causes of floods are backing up water in tributaries at their outfalls in the main river with landslides blocking the stream, resulting in backwater overflowing riverbanks. The leading cause of the flood is heavy or excessive rainfall that occurs mainly in monsoon months from July to September. Sometimes, floods are caused by Glacial Lake Outburst Floods (GLOFs), i.e., the surge which occurs when a dam consisting of a glacial lake fails to work.

Heavy rainfall, low capacity of rivers to carry extreme flood discharge, inadequate drainage to take away rainwater to streams or rivers, man-made factors like failure of dams are the major causes of flood. Also, ice jams or landslides blocking streams, backwater, debris flow, and cyclones cause the flood. Floods occur almost every year in some parts of the world or the other. Different regions have different climates or rainfall patterns in a country. Some regions suffer devastating floods, and some suffer drought. Due to varying rainfall, areas which are never prone to floods traditionally also experience it. Geomorphological, extreme rain, inflow, and outflow limits of sewerage also contribute to cascades. Indian Summer Monsoon (ISM) has different phases, which are—onset (mid-May to mid-July), peak rainfall (July to August), and withdrawal (mid-September to mid-October). Also, the shift of heat source over Northern India due to shifting of Intertropical Convergence Zone (ITCZ) generally stays between 20° and 30° North during peak rainfall months (July to August). Their shifting affects the monsoon due to which heavy rainfall occurs during this phase. Heavy rains are linked with heavy downpours, low pressure, and monsoon breaks. In the Himalayas, low pressure, Western Disturbances (WDs), and ISM lead to flood. For example, on 16–17 June 2013 Uttarakhand flood, GLOF from Mahatma Gandhi Sagar due to glacier/melt and glacial moraines led to an increase in overflow toward Kedarnath and downstream.

Deforestation also plays a vital role in the flooding equation. As trees prevent runoff, lower the number of trees, more is the water flow, leading to destruction. Therefore, the more is the forest cover, the lesser is the risk of flood.

Why Flooding Is a Problem?

Floods cause loss to both life and the economy to a large extent. According to Rashtriya Barh Ayog (National Commission on Floods), India has a geographical area of 329 Million hectares, out of which 40 million hectares (one-eighth of total area) are prone to flood. Every year, 7.5 Million hectares of land are affected, 1600 lives are lost, and other damages like crops, houses, and public utilities are of USD 250 Million. The highest loss of lives was 11,316 in 1977. Flood causes fear and insecurity in the minds of people residing in floodplains. The aftereffects of floods are suffering from people, the spread of some diseases, unavailability of essential commodities and medicines, etc. High rainfall causes a rise in water level, which leads to submergence of regions, landslides, waterborne diseases, etc. Floods during the Rabi and Kharif seasons affect the food security of India.

For example, on 16–17 June 2013, the Uttarakhand flood led to massive destruction of life and land. Heavy rainfall caused flashflood in the Kedarnath valley, Mandakini, and Saraswati rivers. Interaction between West-Northwest moving monsoon, low pressure, and eastward-moving mid-latitude WD leads to extreme rainfall. During the same time, a monsoon low developed over the north Bay of Bengal and moved westnorthwest across northern India. Low pressure formed on the Gangetic plain caused high moisture over the northwestern part of India.

Due to floods, salt in seawater contaminates land and reduces crop yield, electricity supply cuts, increased traffic congestion, increased costs of emergency services, loss of exports, etc.

To manage floods, the water level should be controlled, done by dams/reservoirs storing floodwater, to be leveled without exceeding in downstream. The lower the level of the dam, the lower is the risk of flood. Another method is levees, which consist of earthen dams built between rivers and the areas to be protected. When these methods fail, sandbags or portable inflation tubes are used. Another technique is dike; it lowers the risk of flood and protects land naturally underwater most of the time. The weir is also constructed across the river to change its flow, which acts as an obstruction for water flow.

How Can Algorithmic Solution Help?

A dataset with monthly rainfall amounts for each year from 1900 to 2015 for each state has the potential to explore the rainfall patterns, with which a prototype has been developed shown in Appendix B. The basic approach for the problem is that of a binary classification. Dataset also has the data of the duration of 3 months. Using the dataset, first data preprocessing is performed, like removing null values, which are zero in the dataset. Next, the average rainfall for every ten days is calculated. This intermediate data is given as an input to the machine learning model, which provides output labels as 0 or 1 (whether flood will occur or not). Next, the model is trained depending on a threshold value of average rainfall in the dataset. Giving the average data of 10 days to the model as input, the model predicts whether there are chances of flooding or not by setting a threshold value in the training data.

There is an official website of government called cwc.gov.in, which updates itself regularly, telling whether an area's water level is (i) normal flood, i.e., the situation at any flood forecasting sites when the water level of the river is below the warning level; (ii) above normal flood, i.e., if the river's water level at the flood forecasting site touches or crosses the warning level but remains under the site's danger level. This category is assigned a yellow color; (iii) severe flood, i.e., if the river's water level at the forecasting site touches or crosses danger level but below the highest flood level of forecasting. Orange color is assigned to this category; and (iv) extreme flood, i.e., when the water level of river touches or crosses the highest flood level recorded by any forecasting site so far. This category is assigned a red color.

Which Analytical Techniques to Use?

The technique used for flood forecasting is logistic regression. This is because the overall aim was to get 0 or 1 labels as output, i.e., binary outcome, 0 for no severe risk of flood, and 1 for severe risk of flood. Linear regression can also be used for binary outcomes. But if it is used, it is possible to have fitted regression where predicted values for some individuals are outside 0 or 1 range of probability. For a binary outcome, logistic regression is used to model the log odds as a linear combination of parameters and regressors. Logistic regression is the most popular technique for classification and regression. It is used when probabilities between the two classes are required. In linear regression, the outcome can be any continuous value, making it difficult to classify, whereas logistic gives only binary value that is biased and with low variance. Various research papers show how logistic regression is better than linear regression for binary outcomes. V. V. Srinivas shows how fuzzy means clustering can be worked upon for flood prediction. A. Mosavi describes different machine learning models for flood prediction. Trace Smith also reveals that logistic regression is better than random forest classification for binary outcomes.

Can There Be an Impact of Technology?

The approach can be used to identify whether an area may flood or not, given the region's rainfall data. The solution can be augmented with the existing solutions of dividing an area into different zones based on the severity of the floods or being used for alert predictors. If accessed, the database can be used to send a red alert warning to mobile phones of people living in the affected area using a free online text message sending portal. The people in the affected area can migrate to some other area so as for their protection. The government can take steps to protect the animal species too. Early warning systems can help a lot. Lives can be protected, and essential commodities can be collected at times by those who cannot migrate. Automated demand predictions and supply chain management can be done on the basis of flood predictions in advance.

7.3   EDUCATION & ASSESSMENT

The Problem of Transforming to Online Education

Online learning may have been on the rise in recent years. However, it has become a necessity and a temporary substitute in many places, which are still under extended lockdowns amid the COVID-19 pandemic. As education has undergone a tremendous transformation with the emerging technologies enabling digital learning, a key aspect may be to explore the potential of a segment that has not found large-scale adoption yet, i.e., the virtual exams. Exams are a crucial component of any educational program or a system, and online education programs are no exception. Given any exam, there is a possibility of cheating, and therefore its detection and prevention play a critical role. With several exams being postponed or conducted amid immense health risks to students, remote proctoring systems can enable them to take exams in the safety of their homes. What adds to this is, with AI-based invigilation technologies ensuring that they do not cheat or indulge in unfair means during the assessment, educational institutions can also benefit from this arrangement. The most critical factor among faculty and student concerns are student privacy and increasing test anxiety via a sense of being surveilled. Some experts might also argue that the whole premise of asking students to recall information under pressure without access to their course materials is flawed.

Online human monitoring is a common approach for proctoring online exams. Still, the main downside is that it is very costly in requiring many employees to monitor the test takers. With AI being able to tackle the offline model's challenges, especially amid such crucial times, it can prove to be a gamechanger and prepare students and educators for the post-pandemic world. Online exam conduction with AI-based proctoring can significantly reduce the human efforts and efficiently conduct the examinations online and proper monitoring of any suspicious actions or movements of the students. The main goal is to develop a proctoring system and eliminate the need for human proctors, reducing the cost, time, and the chances of any human errors in detecting any suspicious activities. The AI-based proctoring system is a real-time system that can completely manage the conduction of exams, from verifying the student's identity to notice any unnecessary movements and generating warnings till the end of the exam.

The conduction of exams through an online mode and using AI-based systems used for proctoring would be an emerging trend, which can be quickly adopted in the times of a pandemic like COVID-19. This advancement in technology can prove to be a boon to any country throughout the world and to any institution or body, which cannot follow the traditional trend of taking the exams physically. Cutting the labor costs would prove to be technological advancement with higher reliability and accuracy than the conventional method of taking exams. While the challenge could be of the prerequisites for implementing this new advancement, of the laptop and a good internet connection, but once met, it can be of immense importance to certify or test any student taking an exam for his/her skills.

Importance of Online Assessments

Online learning is growing at a rapid rate. Due to lockdown and health crisis in the current situation, it is the need for the hour to build a system that makes our education system up and running. Online Exam conducting using AI proctoring system has become so comfortable using this. It is such an efficient and cost-effective way to conduct exams. Since assessments are a crucial component of any education system, it is necessary to conduct exams, and AI proctoring system can help to continue the exam process. The main concern when conducting online exams is whether the exams will be done without cheating and monitoring students. So, to solve this problem, the AI proctoring system keeps the camera switched on, and using artificial intelligence, each student can be controlled individually. Moreover, to add functionality to this system, the system can give warnings, and after a specific number of warnings, the artificial proctor will cancel out the exam.

This system provides easy management for the institutions and reduces human error and effort. The labor cost is reduced using this remote AI proctor. AI proctor will itself see any suspicious activity and raise a warning on such a situation. AI proctor will minimize human error, and continuous monitoring of each student is not possible with physical invigilators' help, but AI proctor manages and handles them with ease. AI proctoring is a scalable solution and can be implemented at various stages and a variety of platforms. AI proctoring system has been a technological boom to the education system, with such advancements in technology. This is very useful for the education system's future, which is to set up its foot in the online education system. This solution helps those scenarios where the individual cannot reach the destination of the exam center. Using AI proctoring technology, students can give their exams online sitting at their home. Institutions need not worry about cheating or suspicious stuff as the system itself will manage that. This system is a convenient way to conduct exams in such a health crisis where leaving homes will jeopardize thousands of lives. Seeing the current situation and analyzing the fact that conducting exams is a necessity AI proctoring system seems to be the most feasible and reliable solution.

Understanding the health and education AI proctoring system's concern bridges the gap between the two without compromising with anyone of them. This solution could result in a drastic and better change in the future. This system can set up an example for future how online exams can be conducted and changes that are required for the betterment of this system. Machine learning and Artificial Intelligence provide a platform to build such a scalable solution for this complex problem. AI proctoring system will reduce the cheating and analyze the marks accordingly based on the evaluation. The candidates capable of qualifying will only qualify using the AI proctor.

Algorithmic Solution to Proctoring

The AI proctoring system is built to solve remotely conducting exams, such as health crises, and managing those exams free from any cheating and continuous monitoring.

The examination problem to conduct at remote places online was a challenge. This system performs the exam remotely and online and ensures there are the least chances of the candidate using fraud methods to pass an exam.

Figure 7.2 shows the AI proctoring system overview, which starts using object detection, counting the number of persons, and tracking eyes and mouth to avoid cheating. If the mouth is opened, alerts are displayed on the screen, and analysis is done using the behavior of fraud of the candidate. Detect the eyes, mouth, and face of the person giving the exam. AI proctoring system tracks the movement of eyes, mouth, and face simultaneously. Using the analysis of the face's parts, one can raise a warning for suspicious activity.

Figure 7.3 displays the face detection algorithm and overview of the prototype solution present in Appendix C. YOLO face detection first detects the persons given a frame of the image and find whether there is any person in the image or not. The probability of the face is calculated, and using anchor boxes, the person's face will be outlined using a rectangular table. It then calculates if any other person is there in the frame. Using a sliding window algorithm, it then alerts the screen more than one person detected and displays an alert.

The algorithm, after detecting the face, now captures the points on the eyes and mouth, as per the given process in Fig. 7.4. Using those points on the eyes, it analyzes the movement of the eyes' pupil. It displays the eye's position wherever it moves, i.e., either left, right, or upwards if it detects any suspicious movement of the eye.

Fig. 7.2 Flow diagram of AI proctoring solution (*Source* Author creation)

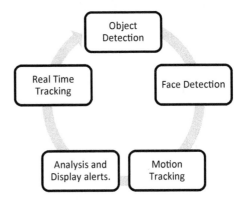

Fig. 7.3 Face detection YOLO algorithm (*Source* Author creation)

Fig. 7.4 Motion tracking of eyes and mouth (*Source* Author creation)

Next up, it captures the position of the mouth. The data points obtained during face detection, the aspects of the mouth are analyzed. If the mouth is open to a certain threshold, it displays that the person has opened mouth, indicating the person talking to someone, saying this message on the screen, and sending an alert.

Analysis and display of alerts: The algorithm detects the person's face and tracks the eyes and mouth. After all the detection and recognition, the alerts must be displayed. So, any suspicious activity including more than one person on screen or detection of remote or mobile phone on the screen, movement of eyes where the eyes move will be captured, and alerts will be displayed on the screen in real-time. If the person opens his/her mouth, the message is displayed as a proctor finds this as a way of cheating. The statement above is displayed on the screen.

The solution presented for conducting exams is a model that is ready to use in real-time environments while facing all the challenges that are offered toward it. It is robust to handle such situations.

Analytical Techniques for AI Proctoring

Object Detection: The principal technique used in the AI proctoring system is object detection and recognition. Object detection plays an important role when it comes to analyzing real-time data. An Online AI proctor needs to detect a person's identity; it needs object detection. It should ensure that human is only giving the test and not any robot. Secondly, it must provide the status of the person passing an exam. Object detection includes this. It must also detect any object that is brought during the exam, which is not allowed. For example, a mobile phone, earphones, and other such devices are not permitted during the exams. Object detection, for the solution in this book, seemed to work well. The reason behind selecting such a technique was to ensure the person's real identity and use of any suspicious object that is not allowed during examinations. Object detection algorithm can detect many other things in the image in real-time that can be counted as suspicious.

Face Detection: This technique plays a significant role in detecting faces and the number of persons in the screen frame. As AI proctoring system uses the camera of the course being used, it must recognize that remotely some other person is not helping the candidate. So, our model needed to detect the number of persons. For the face detection algorithm, we used the YOLO algorithm. Using this, we counted the number of faces shown on the image, and a warning is indicated if more than a single person is detected in the camera. The face detection algorithm technique was our choice to discover the number of faces given a frame quickly. In face detection, we noticed two parts of the face—eyes and mouth. The discovery of the pupil of the eyes will tell whether the individual is looking on the screen or somewhere else. The mouth part detection will help in finding whether he opened his mouth for saying something or not. If the algorithm detects whether the person is opening his/her mouth, the algorithm will display a message on the screen. Using the detection of eyes and mouth, we can make sure that the person is not involved in any suspicious activity or cheating.

Object Tracking: this technique helps in measuring and tracking the objects we detected earlier. The eye-tracking or pupil tracking will track the area where the pupil of eyes moved, and accordingly, the proctor will display a message on the screen whether the individual is looking toward the left-right, bottom, or up. Next up for tracking, we use mouth tracking and lips tracking. If the lips are apart from each other, the tracking algorithm tells if the person is speaking or not. That can be used to verify if the person is involved in cheating. Object tracking algorithm helps detect and analyze the candidate's cheating behavior, and that can be used in the marking scheme. We chose object tracking as this is the best way to solve our problem and conduct exams remotely.

Impact of AI Proctoring on Online Education

With this lockdown period growth of online education is quite a trend. So, conducting online exams is quite a challenging task. The solution above is going to have a considerable impact on the education system. The online conduction of exams based on the AI proctoring system is both beneficial and efficient. Building such a model is advantageous and robust as well. AI proctoring system can replace physical teachers, and cheating can be reduced to minimal. The quality of education will tend to improve as those students who are capable will qualify.

This system can detect the number of persons given a frame. If a person uses a cell phone, it will see that, and if a person is looking somewhere else apart from the screen, it will display the message and alert accordingly.

There is a significant variation in proctored and physical conduction of exams. It is challenging for a single teacher to look at all students, while this problem is easily solved using the proctor. The AI proctor will automatically recognize the person's identity. There is a chance of fraud in the case of physical exams. The AI proctor system will also have a mechanism to detect the person's voice, whether he is saying something or not. If the students are cheating, their behavior can be observed, and marks can be given accordingly. With less labor cost, this will be a tremendous technological advancement with higher accuracy, reliability, and adaptive than traditional conduction of exams. This system is built to reduce human error and save time. AI proctoring system will cut short the human error, and the detection of any suspicious activity is more likely to be caught by this rather than a physical teacher. Also, in this health crisis, where the need of the hour is to conduct exams remotely, AI proctoring system is the most viable and reliable solution. This system also allows the institutions to benefit from removing AI proctoring and disallowing students to engage or indulge in unfair means to pass the exams. Also, the online proctoring through AI can automatically scan and verify the student's identity, and if it doesn't match, he/she will not be eligible to give the exam. The system can also monitor competitive exams for those students who need to travel across cities for exams. This system can be helpful in these situations.

AI proctoring system can be a boon to the education system at a minimal cost. During exams, we hear about cheating news on media. Using AI proctoring system, these will be reduced. Also, in this health crisis, where the need of the hour to conduct exams remotely, AI proctoring system is the most viable and reliable source. AI proctoring in the education department will play a significant role shortly, and it can remove the traditional approach of conducting exams. Due to any situation, the students cannot reach their destined locations for exams can give their exams online remotely. This AI proctoring system later can replace competitive exams where students need to travel cities to pass exams using the AI proctoring system; they can easily give exams sitting at their home. So, AI proctoring system will prove to be significant technological advancement in the education system.

7.4   Entrance Exams and Admissions

Problem of Admissions to Educational Institutions

University education has become a necessary part of people's preparation for working life. Admission to the university is an important issue. How the student must choose the university and how the university must select a student on so many applicants. The success of both sides is determined through education. The students' enrollment has increased in past years, which leads to more applications, more paperwork, and processing challenges. Every applicant's forms are routed through different departments for evaluation and manual processing, which causes difficulty in the admission process. In today's time, despite technological advancement still, the admission process at college or school admission is being carried out manually, which is very time-consuming. An automated student admission system's development is the best solution to speed up and simplify the admission process and remove manual processing. The development of science and technology has immensely contributed to the growth of the internet, which has increased the need to develop an automated student admission process. The problems associated with the current system are that they publish multiple merit lists, leading to double work for the university executive and even for applicants to visit again to check the list. The manual admission process leads to the high cost of the application process because the colleges' paperwork and admission fees are high. Even for the institute, they have to do all the manual work of handling the papers. With the advancement in technology, the process of admission can be done in an automated way by taking the data from previous year students, which are given admission to train a model that can predict new applicants' selection possibility. It will be beneficial for both the applicants and university admission cell to provide a better deserving candidate admission into the university program. This model will increase the process and accuracy to select the applicant. Before the entrance, every university considers a general aptitude; it can be GMAT, GRE, CAT, GATE, and others, but all these exams are conducted at centers to have a check on the identity of the person who has appeared for the exam. There are problems associated with this procedure. Every year millions of students give entrance test which leads to rush at the exam center and even on the roads many times leads to traffic jam because of this, students sometimes reach late, and they can't appear for the test and miss the opportunity. To make this process completely automated, we can conduct the exams at home for students.

Requirement of the Online Entrance Process

In today's world, the number of students who go for higher education has gradually increased. Based on data analysis from the UNESCO Institute of Statistics 2016, more than 300,000 Indian students have been gone out for higher studies. There is an annual growth rate of 22% in 16 years. The shift in trend for higher education has led to so many applications every year to the universities, making it difficult for them to decide which requests should be granted admission. This has become a major problem nowadays and till now the decision is taken by the admission cell on the manual basis which is time-consuming. Let's look at the traditional admission method that was informing the students and applicants was done by putting up the notices on notice board and advertisements in the newspaper. The application form was a hard copy style where physically you have to go to the university to submit, and then evaluation is being carried out by the staff. With advancements in technology, the application form gets turned into a digital way, but the assessment is still done manually. The problem statement has brought a new change from paperwork to digital format, standing in a queue, and submitting the application form to submit the form online with just one click of a button. There is a need for a shift in the admission process for graduate education. Technological advancement can help to solve the problem of manual evaluation of each applicant's form. According to the report Artificial Intelligence Market in the US Education Sector, AI will grow at a compound annual rate of 47.7 percent from 2018 to 2022. AI has the potential to change how the admission process of domestic and international students can be changed by creating algorithms and models to predict the most likely applicant to be selected. Machine learning, the subset of AI, helps the computers analyze and learn from the university data, which factors are essential for admission. According to the Enrolment Management Report, AI can change the entry for small and prominent universities in both the public and private sectors.

Algorithmic Solution

With the advancement in technology, now, we can automate the whole process of admission through machines. From the entrance exam conduction to the result generation, document verification, and admission selection, all can be done with a machine's help. The solution which is used to automate the entrance exam process is that while the applicant submits his identity card details, we can use face verification to check the identity of the person who is sitting in front of the computer to check that same applicant is giving the exam, or there is some cheating happening so we can easily terminate the exam of such faulty applicants. As shown in Fig. 7.5, the block diagram depicts the applicant's real-time face verification at the time of giving the entrance test. The prototype code is shown in Appendix D.

After the entrance exam, the selected applicants apply for the document submission process. In the letter of recommendation, we can use sentimental analysis using natural language processing techniques to quickly get to know about positive or negative results about the person based on the advice given in the letter. The block diagram, as shown in Fig. 7.6, depicts the working of sentimental analysis.

After passing through the document verification stage, we can feed the data to the system to evaluate that the applicant has the chance of getting selected or not. Admission officers have a rich dataset of information of the past applicants, including the decision. Using this data, we employ supervised machine learning techniques to classify applicants.

For the classification problem, the information which has been taken is shown in Table 7.1. The dataset attributes will be pre-processed, and the missing values and outliers will be checked. After that, we will pass on the dataset to the classification models to train the model, and testing data will help verify the accuracy of the model. The classification model block diagram is shown in Fig. 7.7.

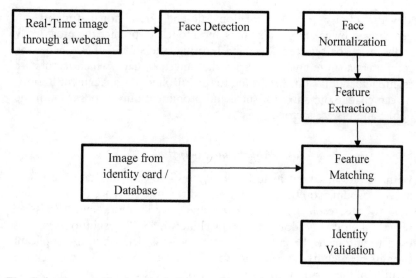

Fig. 7.5   Face verification block diagram (*Source* Author creation)

Analytical Techniques Used for Solution

Artificial Neural Network: Artificial neural networks (ANN) mimic the human body system's biological brain. They are modeled after biological neurons, learn by the training given to them. The structure of ANN has three components input layer, hidden layer, and output layer. We use activation functions to convert the weighted sum of a neuron's input signals into the output signal. In ANN, we use two methods, feedforward, and backpropagation, to tune the desired output model. In feed-forward, the input layer sends the input values to the hidden layer, which processes the signals and sends them to the output layer through an activation function. In the backpropagation method of supervised learning, the difference between desired and output result is measured. Then, the weights' values are modified to obtain the nearest possible output value compared to the desired result.

Figure 7.8 shows the structure of ANN where we have taken all the variable from dataset, i.e., age, board, 12th%, GRE score, CGPA, and others as input variables. They are then passed on to the hidden layer using the sigmoid activation function, which is used in a binary classification where small change occurs in x, resulting in a large change in y. The

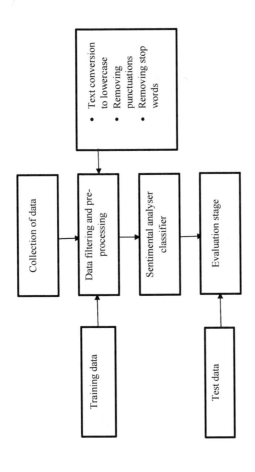

Fig. 7.6 Sentiment analysis block diagram (*Source* Author creation)

Table 7.1 Dataset attributes considered for Prototyping

Variable name	Description	Category
Age	Age of applicant	Quantitative
Board	CBSE/ISCE/State	Categorical
12th %	Percentage in 12th class	Quantitative
GRE score	GRE marks	Quantitative
Category	Gen/OBC/ST/SC	Categorical
SOP	Statement of purpose	Quantitative
LOR	Letter of recommendation	Quantitative
CGPA	Undergraduate CGPA	Quantitative
Research	Research experience	Quantitative
Chances of admit	Chances of admission (0–1)	Quantitative

function is defined as shown in Eq. 7.3

$$S(x) = \frac{1}{1 + e^{(-x)}} \tag{7.3}$$

After the hidden layer processing, the result is sent to the output layer.

Logistic Regression: Logistic regression is a popular technique used in classification problems because it results in a value between 0 and 1. On the other hand, linear regression results can be positive or negative in cost, which cannot distinguish between an applicant's application for higher education to be accepted or rejected, so we use logistic regression as the first method in most cases. The admission decision function is as follows.

Admission prediction $= f$(GRE score, Research experience, 12th %, and other variables)

Decision Tree: A decision tree is a supervised machine learning algorithm used for classification problems. The decision tree comprises several branches, root nodes, and leaf nodes. It generated a tree-like structure by splitting the data according to specified parameters. Feature selection is based on the most significant information gain of features, and then the

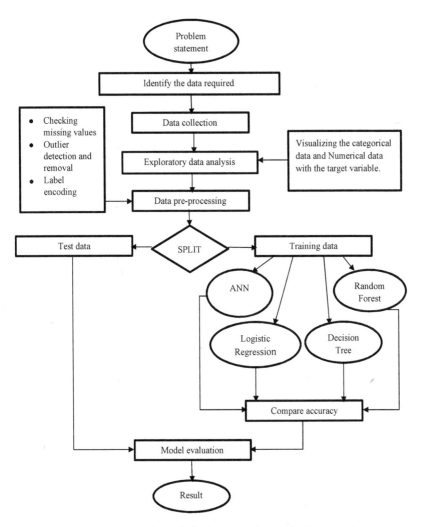

Fig. 7.7 Classification analysis block diagram (*Source* Author creation)

iterative process repeats itself until it reaches the leaves. In our case, we have a feature like age, GRE score, 12th percentage, LOR, and other variables according to which the decision tree is formed. The root node contains the element with the most significant information gain of them

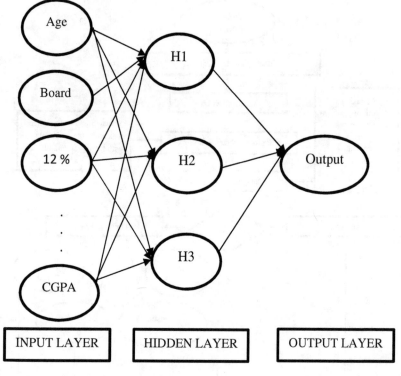

Fig. 7.8 ANN block diagram (*Source* Author creation)

all. According to the problem statement, let's see an example of a decision tree, as shown in Fig. 7.9.

In Fig. 7.9, an example illustrating the decision tree for a candidate's admission prediction is shown. If a candidate has a CGPA of above 9.0, and either has done some research work or is having a GRE score of more than 320, has more chances of getting selected for admission to the university.

Random Forest: Random forest classification belongs to a supervised learning algorithm, an ensemble learning method for classification that operates by constructing a multitude of decision trees at training time and outputting the class that is the mode of the categories or means prediction of the individual trees. It smoothes the error which exists in a single tree,

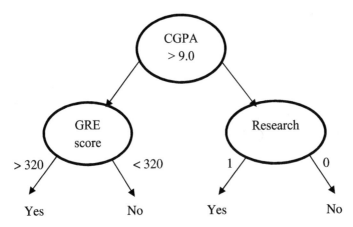

Fig. 7.9   Decision tree block diagram (*Source* Author creation)

and it increases the overall performance and accuracy of the model and provides explainable scores. The random forest provides us with an intuitive way to look at our features by listing individual feature importance, which gives us the importance of each factor affecting the loan approval. As compared with the decision tree, random forest works very fast, accurate, and robust. It can be used for both classifications and the regression problem

Impact of Algorithmic Solution

The automated entrance exams and admission process will positively affect the system because the current system of manual exams and admission process is very hectic, time-consuming, and includes paperwork. With the automation of the whole process from entrance exams to admission, we can eliminate all the current system's disadvantages. The solution will change the entire process of admission process in the higher education system. In the entrance exams, instead of going to the exam centers, we can automate the exams, and students can give them while sitting at home. It will save the applicant's travel cost who will be traveling from a remote area to appear for the exam at the center. We can make a big bank of question pool through this process so that there will be no chances of cheating. With the microphone and webcam on, we can keep a check on the applicant. The face verification model will continuously track the applicants' face to know that there is no cheating happening while giving the exam. With the auto-grade procedure, we will save the applicant and the university's time because the result will be given to the applicants within few hours, and then they can move to the next stage of the admission process. Even in the job aptitude exams, we can use these automated entrance exams, and the applicant can easily give it from their home.

At the time of document identification and submission of papers, we can easily use the natural language processing model to evaluate them. In the letter of recommendation (LOR), which is submitted by the applicant for higher education, we can assess the message by sentimental analysis technique. We can rate the student's feedback as positive or negative, which is considered an essential factor at the time of evaluation of an applicant because it tells about the applicant's personality and past work history. With such an admission system, the applicant can have a real-time check on the status of his/her application to a university. After all, the data from documents are verified and collected is stored in the database.

With the help of supervised classification learning, we can evaluate the applicant's data. This will help the admission officers quickly and accurately judge a student's application without any manual evaluation done by a human. The classification model will easily predict the chances of an individual in the university. This will make the workload of the admission cell lighter and more accurate. This automated system will create a positive impression on students and engage the students with clear and transparent information in students' selection. It will help to select the best talent from the pool of applicants. Students prefer to interact via the website and mobile devices with the hyper-growth of digital technologies, which increases student satisfaction.

7.5   Funding & Loans

The Problem of Loan Frauds

In the banking industry, the distribution of loans is the core business of every bank. The central bank's asset directly came from the profit earned from loan distribution by the bank. The prime objective in the banking industry is to invest its assets into safe hands. Banks and financial companies approve a loan after the validation and verification process, but still, there is no guarantee that the selected applicant is a deserving applicant or not. Due to insufficient credit history, many people face loan rejection.

These people are students or unemployed adults because they do not have enough knowledge to justify their credibility. For example, an employed adult has an income source, which turns out to be a significant factor in repayment of the loan. There are many factors like real estate, marriage, city of residence, and others, which play a credit score history for loan approval.

In today's world, the banks struggle to gain the upper hand over each other to enhance their business. Retaining customers and fraud detection are the two critical goals in the banks. There are many risks for the bank, as well as those who get the loan. Stake in the bank involves credit risk, i.e., the loan won't be returned in time or at all, the interest rate may be too low that the bank won't be able to earn adequate money. Risk management is widely used in the banking sector, and the executives need to know the credibility of the customer they are dealing with. Offering the customer's credit card or loan is always a risky job.

With the advancement in technology, the banks focus on the automation process of fraud detection in the loan approval or credit card. Manual processing of the loan lacks consistency and accuracy; above all, it is time-consuming. Automation in loan approval processing facilitates faster and more accurate loan applications, which make the whole process seem less dreadful, faster, and more reliable. More rapid loan processing is always a competitive advantage for them. The availability of a vast amount of data helps the banks to enhance their loan lending operation by implementing the loan lending prediction. The bank's historic data plays a crucial role in training the model to predict loan approval. The loan prediction is helpful for the banks and applicants because the main goal is to provide the loan to the right applicant as fast as possible. The loan prediction system helps the executives directly jump to a specific application without wasting time on other apps, and it can be checked on a priority basis. The close monitoring of why one applicant's loan was approved and others were rejected such data is beneficial to the customers and the banks.

Importance of Detecting Fraudulent

Credit scoring is a process of evaluation before the credit score is sanctioned. This process is called credit evaluation, which concludes the approval or rejection. Credit scoring plays a vital role in evaluating the applicant's loan approval or denial in the banking sector. There are 5C's involved in the process in credit evaluation, which are character, credit report, capacity, cash flow, and collateral. A person who sounds financially stable is likely granted a loan very quickly. Credit history is another critical feature to approve the credit application. The credit report includes the person's past transactions, borrowing, and other functions. If the person has a good cash flow, then the chances of getting credit approval are much higher.

As per a study, more than 50% of the first-time loan applicants get rejected from the banks and financial institutions because the existing predicting system works on credit scores and paperwork. Due to the high demand and the reliability of the banks and financial institutions on loan lending, there is a demand for further improvement of the credit scoring model. As per the study conducted by the National Business Research Institute and Narrative Science, around 32% of financial service providers in the country have already begun using AI tech. As the world is changing, the model for evaluating the credit score has to changes. In India, 80% of the population doesn't have a credit score, which leads to the rejection of the loan approval request. If, with the help of Artificial Intelligence, we can build creditworthiness, it will open a big business portal for the banks and financial institutes. Nowadays, fintech companies are taking the data from the person's transaction, like how much he/she spends on food, travel, clothing, and more. All this data can be used to create a person's creditworthiness rather than relying on old factors like credit history and credit score.

The importance of the existing problem in the banking sector helps find new fields in the world to make the current system more robust and refined. As discussed earlier new system will open large business portals for the banking sector. From the expert's point of view, the AI can help lenders, banks, and financial institutions to reach over 300 million new first-time loan applicants, which will boost the economy. According to a report by the Boston Consulting Group, the use of AI in loan assessment can help digital lending to grow to USD 100 Billion business by 2023 in India.

Algorithmic Approach

The above problem statement can be solved using the machine learning methodology. We can use the bank's historical data from the loan applications and all the documents attached to the application for loan approval. The process of loan evaluation is a sequence of steps taken to grant

Fig. 7.10 Process diagram for loans & funding (*Source* Author creation)

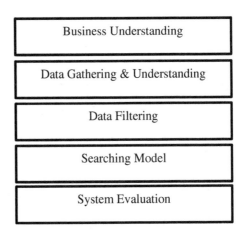

the loan to the right applicant. The proposed model for the problem statement is shown in Fig. 7.10.

Business Understanding: The initial phase focuses on understanding the project objective and the required business perspective forms. In the banking sector, we need knowledge about the loan approval process, essential documents required, criteria on which decision is made for the approval and rejection.

Data Gathering & Understanding: The process of gathering the data depends on the problem statement we can choose for the real-time data or collecting the data from various files or databases. There are free datasets available on the website, like Kaggle and machine learning repositories. The data understanding phase focuses on familiarizing data, identifying the relation of features with the target value, and getting to know more about the data. Generally, we apply an 80:20 split to the data for the training and testing process, respectively. A collection of data from the bank sector has been selected for the prototype shown in Appendix E. Table 7.2 indicates the name of attributes, description, and category which are used to train the model.

Data Filtering: The bank dataset attributes are filtered, and the relevant attributes needed for prediction are selected. The process of cleaning the raw data is termed data preprocessing. The handling of missing values, outliers, and human errors is corrected before passing the model's inputs. The preprocessing is done because noisy data leads to inconsistency. Handling noisy data improves the efficiency of the algorithm.

Table 7.2   Dataset attributes for the Prototyping

Variable name	Description	Category
Loan ID	Unique loan ID	Qualitative
Age	Age of the applicant	Qualitative
Gender	Male/Female	Categorical
Married	Marital status	Categorical
Dependents	Number of dependents	Qualitative
Education qualification	Graduate/Not graduate	Categorical
Housing	Own/Free/Rent	Categorical
Self employed	Yes/No	Categorical
Credit card	Applicant credit card (0/1)	Qualitative
Existing client	Applicant is an existing client (0/1)	Qualitative
Applicant income	Income	Qualitative
Co-applicant income	Income	Qualitative
Payment delay	Is there any payment delay (0/1)	Qualitative
Average house spend	Household spend monthly	Qualitative
Existing loan	Is there any existing loan (0/1)	Qualitative
Average travel	Traveling expense	Qualitative
Present account balance	Account balance	Qualitative
Minimum balance	Minimum balance in 6 months	Qualitative
Loan amount	Amount	Qualitative
Loan amount term	Term of the loan in months	Qualitative
Credit history	credit history meets guidelines	Qualitative
Property area	Urban/Semi-urban/Rural	Categorical
Loan status	Loan approved (Y/N)	Categorical

Searching Model: Our main goal is to train the best-performing model using the filtered data. In our case, we have the target variable, that applicant should get loan approval or rejection based on the model's input features. We will use the classification problem because we want the output to be true or false, yes or no. The most commonly used classification algorithms are K-nearest neighbor, logistic regression, decision tree, and random forest.

System Evaluation: The best-performing models are evaluated during the model development process, finding the best-performing model on the filtered data. Then we apply that model to the test data to check the performance.

The block diagram for the solution is shown in Fig. 7.11.

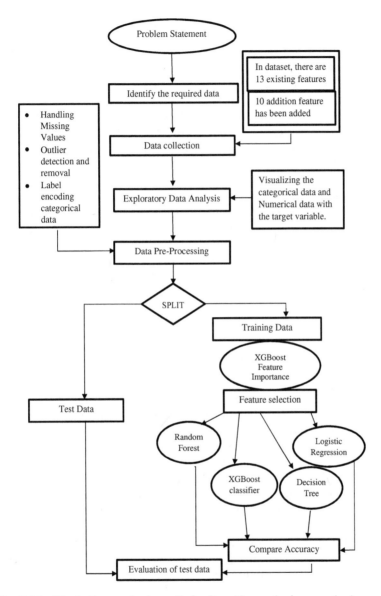

Fig. 7.11 Block diagram for loans & funding (*Source* Author creation)

Techniques Used for Algorithmic Solution

Logistic Regression: Logistic regression technique is the most popular statistical technique in the financial sector world, especially for the credit risk assessment or loan approval prediction. As compared to linear regression, it overcomes multiple issues, such as in linear regression, and we can get a negative or positive output, which is not possible in probability. In contrast, logistic regression provides a continuous range of values between 0 and 1. We can assume that the likelihood of loan approval follows the logistic distribution; it follows the function of loan approval, which is written as follows.

Loan approval = f(credit history, applicant Income, Education qualification, Employment status, and other dummy variables)

Where the Loan approval decision is 1, and the rejection is 0.

In logistic regression, to map the predicted values to probability, the sigmoid function is used to map them. The sigmoid function is shown in Eq. 7.4

$$f(x) = \frac{1}{1 + e^{(-x)}} \tag{7.4}$$

In the case of a classification problem, it is a great model to try as the first step because it outputs conditional probability value; however, we find predicted value in regression.

Decision Tree: A decision tree is a supervised machine learning algorithm used for classification problems. The banking industry is widely used for credit risk assessment as the decision tree comprises several branches, root nodes, and leaf nodes. It generated a tree-like structure by splitting the data according to specific parameters. Feature selection is based on the most significant information gain of features, and then the iterative process repeats itself until it reaches the leaves. An example of a decision tree is depicted in Fig. 7.12 related to the banks and financial institutions' loan approval process.

In the decision tree, there is a set of rules which are trained using the training data. It ignores the irrelevant features which are not required. Figure 7.12 shows that if an applicant who applies for the loan application has an excellent credit rating gets a loan approval very quickly. The

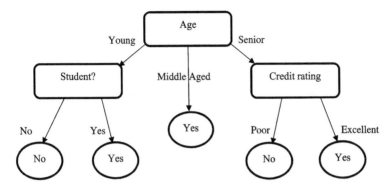

Fig. 7.12 Decision tree structure (*Source* Author creation)

decision tree model is suitable for small and straightforward datasets as it is easy to interpret the tree. Still, when the data gets more complicated, its accuracy decreases and gets challenging to interpret.

Random Forest: Random forest classification belongs to a supervised learning algorithm, an ensemble learning method for classification that operates by constructing a multitude of decision trees at training time and outputting the class that is the mode of the categories or means prediction of the individual trees. It smoothes the error which exists in a single tree, and it increases the overall performance and accuracy of the model and provides explainable scores. The random forest provides us with an intuitive way to look at our features by listing individual feature importance, which gives us the importance of each factor affecting the loan approval. As compared with the decision tree, random forest works very fast, accurate, and robust, and it can work on large datasets and deal with the unbalanced dataset. It can be used for both classifications and the regression problem.

XGBoost: XGBoost stands for extreme gradient boosting is a scalable and highly efficient boosting system. It is an ensemble of decision trees algorithm where trees are added until no further improvements can be made to the model. The benefit of using XGBoost is that it helps determine the critical feature in the dataset and helps to evaluate the model on them for better results. It provides a score that indicates how useful a feature is in the construction of the model. In the solution, we have used XGBoost for feature selection and classification.

Impact of Algorithmic Solution

Automation in the loan approval processing has distinct advantages over the existing system. In a week, banks and financial institutions received thousands of loan applications, and only a few percentages of them are approved. But with automated loan approval processing gives the ability to quickly evaluate the thousands of applications and find the right applicants that meet the credibility criteria. Replacing the manual steps with automation and transferring the paperwork to a digital platform leads to a better user experience and improve the speed and accuracy of loan approval. As per the Federal Reserve survey in 2016, half of the applicants complained about the difficulty during the application process and the time taken to receive the credit decision. An automated lending system can dramatically change this perception by simplifying and accelerating the credit decision's entire operation. The digitalization of documents will make automation in the loan approval process quick because all the required information will be collected in no time and transferred to the system for the decision evaluation.

In today's auto credit lending market, a faster credit decision is a competitive advantage for both banks and financial institutions. Suppose a small bank has a much quick and automated decision system for loan approval. In that case, the applicants applying for the loan are much more satisfied, which helps the bank retain its customer, which is the bank's main objective, and the bank provided stiff competition to the others.

Automation in the banking sector will optimize all the operations. Most of the banks already have automated banking services, and automating the core services like loan approval will be another step in the industry. All the operations will be done online, producing more clear data, and enhancing the loan approval process model. Even the loan process's management visibility can easily be seen by the applicant, which makes it fairer to know the rejection of the application.

The automation process will reduce loan processing cost as the bank companies do not have to spend the money on training the employees for service loans. Even the automation process will save the time of the executive as time is money in every industry. The decrease in the paperwork will be an added advantage to companies' cost reduction in handling the paperwork, manually entering the customers' financial information to remove the paperwork from the process of credit lending.

7.6   ONLINE REPUTATION MANAGEMENT

The Problem of Online Reviews for Government

Many Governments across the world are trying to move closer to their citizens to achieve transparency and engagement. In recent years, there has been growing interest in mining the online sentiment to predict how a decision made by the Government is taken by the public, either positively or negatively. The explosion of social media is opening new opportunities to help the Government achieve it. People are continuously using social media daily to communicate and express their opinions about various subjects, products, and services. It has emerged as a precious resource for text mining and sentiment analysis. Social media communications include Facebook, Twitter, etc. Twitter is one of the most widely used social media sites used by citizens. In this use case, an attempt has been made to analyze the citizen sentiment in social media such as Twitter. Primary data was collected through Twitter API. An approach to a real-world problem and how Government agencies can benefit from it as described in this section.

A measure of the customer's attitude toward the aspects of a service or product which they describe in text or a computational study of opinions and emotions is called the sentiment analysis. Sentiment analysis is in demand nowadays because of its efficiency and ability to analyze even huge texts in minutes. The task of analyzing the sentiments typically involves taking a piece of writing, which can be either a sentence, a comment, or an entire document, and returning a 'score,' which is a measure of how positive, negative, or neutral the text is. This helps evaluate the Government's performance from the people's perspective instead of making people's surveys, which might be expensive and time-consuming. Sentiment analysis is also known as opinion mining, and subjectivity analysis determines the attitude or polarity of opinions given by humans for a particular scheme. Polarity is the quantification of sentiments with a negative or positive value. Sentiment analysis can be applied to any textual form of opinions such as reviews, blogs, and Microblogs. Microblogs are small text messages such as tweets or a short message with a limitation of 160 characters. In previous years, Twitter has gained more and more popularity and is used as a microblogging website. The messages in Twitter, or tweets, are a way to publicly share and express a defined group of users' interests. With the limitation of the tweets' size, it has challenged the users to express their emotions in one or two key lines or sentences, and hence, it gives a fair reflection of what is happening across the country and the world.

The complete process of identifying and extracting the subjective data from the available raw data is called sentiment analysis. Natural language processing, which describes the relationship between human language and machine, tries to narrow down the gap between humans and machines by extracting useful information from the natural language messages. In this case-study, the extraction of the sentiments from the tweets is studied.

Importance of Online Sentiments

Sentiment analysis is a technique to discover knowledge with the help of data mining. Also known as opinion mining, this can be applied to unstructured data sources and can cover various information on various topics related to politics and government. According to an estimate, 80% of the data is unstructured or unorganized. A considerable volume of data is in documents, emails, media conversations articles, and surveys created every day, which is very hard to analyze computationally very time-consuming. Sentiment analysis helps by tagging the unstructured data and sorting data. Sentiment analysis is considered a beneficial approach in predicting the current trends, interpreting the nation's reaction and nerve. Opinions of people can be evaluated, and suggestions can be implemented. The workflow of governance with sentiment analysis can result in better and efficient use of power and energy in the correct direction.

Sentiment analysis can identify critical issues and that too in real-time. Sentiment analysis helps government sites identify the reactions and sentiments of people on a program or policy created by them for the welfare of the citizens. Different government sites can analyze the response of the public on their strategy and work for the betterment. In 2013 US presidential elections sentiment analysis was used. Governments can use the data from the social media platforms to analyze for predicting and the opinion of the common public. News media has always been using sentiment analysis to predict trends. The project of the government, whether it was successful or not, is analyzed using sentiment analysis. Opinion polls of the Indian elections of 2019 were predicted using major news media platforms' sentiment analysis. Sentiment analysis on the above problem helps the governments prioritize work per the demands of the citizens and channelize the workflow of the government that puts the needs and services of the citizens rather than the governments themselves.

Extracting data and analyzing the reactions and based on the responses, the policies can be modified and created, keeping the citizens' view and opinion first.

Sentiment analysis is in trend already and is being used by most governments around the world to build a citizen-centric governance model. It is sensed to be quite a popular tool for the governments to analyze their policies and the workflow in which they work. In the coming decade, governments will have a tremendous amount of involvement from its citizens. Governments and citizens will work together in sync with the help of sentiment analysis. Governments can set up a criterion for its policy to pass or fail based on the review of the country's people. The new welfare programs for the citizens and what they require next can be analyzed, and based on that, knowledge gained can bring up new plans that cover up the needs and necessities of the people around the country. Governments will get a clear view of how people look forward to their policies and programs.

Algorithmic Solution

The approach used for solving the sentiment analysis problem that has been adopted for the prototype shown in Appendix F is presented in Fig. 7.13 and described below.

1. Data collection: The first step of sentiment analysis includes collecting data from blogs, social networks, and forums. The data is first scrapped from the official Government site. Based on the scraped information, the tweets from Twitter are extracted and saved into a CSV file. The data collected is unorganized and in different languages; therefore, text classification and natural language processing are used to extract and classify the data.
2. Data Preprocessing: The data preprocessing step comprises cleaning the noisy and incomplete data. The irrelevant and non-textual

Fig. 7.13 Sentiment analysis approach (*Source* Author creation)

content are identified and eliminated before analyzing the data. The preprocessing for the sentiment analysis includes the following tasks.

- Removing the URLs, punctuation, special characters, etc.
- Removing the Stopwords.
- Removing Retweets.
- Stemming.
- Tokenization.

3. Sentiment detection: Sentiment detection is a fundamental work in various sentiment analysis and opinion mining applications, such as tweets mining and tweet classification. The extracted sentences of the reviews and opinions are examined, and the sentences with subjective expressions such as opinions, beliefs, or views are retained. Sentences with external communication like facts or factual information are discarded. The words for the sentiment words can be classified into positive, negative, and neutral words.

4. Sentiment polarity: TextBlob is a Python library for processing textual data. TextBlob provides an API for diving into standard natural language processing (NLP) tasks such as part-of-speech tagging, sentiment analysis, classification, translation. Here, TextBlob is used for calculating the polarity as well as classifying into sentiments. Polarity is a float value within the range $[-1.0$ to $1.0]$ where 0 depicts neutral, $+1$ depicts a very positive sentiment, and -1 represents a negative sentiment. Subjectivity is a float value within the range $[0.0$ to $1.0]$ where 0.0 is hugely objective, and 1.0 is exceptionally subjective. The subjective sentence expresses some personal feelings, views, beliefs, opinions, allegations, desires, and beliefs, whereas objective sentences are factual.

5. Sentiment classification: based on the previous step's polarity, subjective sentences are classified in positive, negative, good, bad, like-dislike, but classification can be made by using multiple points. The sentiments derived from the sentences can be divided into three categories, as shown in Fig. 7.14.

6. Analysis of tweets: The main objective of performing sentiment analysis is to convert unstructured text into meaningful information. So, the analysis of results is vital to decide by the government. In the case of government schemes announced by the central government, if more tweets result is positive, then people support that particular scheme. Analysis can be used to take feedback on specific plans with

Fig. 7.14 Sentiment classification (*Source* Author creation)

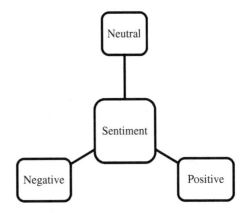

appropriate discussions in public and decide for proper implementation of government schemes. This can also be visually plotted on graphs like a pie chart, bar chart, and line graphs. When the analysis is finished, the results are displayed with the percentage of positive, negative, or neutral tweets.

Analytical Techniques for Sentiments

The solution to this problem requires the application of a few of the following analytical techniques.

1. Web Scraping: Web scraping is also known as web data extraction. It refers to the process of retrieving or 'scraping' data from a website. Unlike the regular operation of manually extracting data, web scraping makes use of intelligent automation to retrieve data points from the internet. It is a technique used to pull large amounts of data from websites whereby the data is extracted and saved to a local file on a computer or PC. Web scraping can be used for sentiment analysis to obtain the data from any Government site or organization. First, the web scraper will be given one or more URLs to load the page before scraping. The scraper would then load the entire HTML code for the page. In this project, web scraping has been used to extract the data from the official Government website, mygov.in. The scraper would either remove all the data on the page. The views of the people are obtained from the discussion forum on

a particular topic. Lastly, the scrapper would output all the data it has extracted from the website.

2. Natural Language Processing and Information extraction: After web scraping the data from the Government site, natural language processing was applied to get the most frequent words and extract the Twitter data related to the most frequently occurring word. The information was then stored in a CSV file. Natural language processing libraries were used for the preprocessing of the text. The data collected from the government websites was used to find out the frequent word discussed and accordingly found the tweets for Twitter and analyzing those tweets for sentiment analysis. The tweets selected were preprocessed using a natural language processing tool kit, and different sentiments were analyzed. We used the natural language processing technique as this is best suited for the preprocessing of the text data and was feasible for our problem statement.

3. Text analysis and classification: After applying the Natural language processing techniques and preprocessing the data, removing the URLs, hashtags, usernames, lemmatization, stemming, etc. TextBlob was used to calculate the polarity of sentiments and classify them into positive (if the polarity is greater than 0), negative (if the polarity is less than 0), or neutral views. TextBlob is based upon Pattern Analyzer and Naïve Bayes Analyzer. The columns for the calculated polarity and the classification of sentiments were added. For classification of the tweets and labeling them as positive and negative is done using classification techniques. TextBlob has an inbuilt library for classifying sentiments using the subjectivity and polarity of the text. Using that sentiment analysis of TextBlob, it is much easier to scale tweets and classify them according to the problem statement.

4. Visualizing the results: After the classification of sentiments, the percentage of the total number of positive, negative, or neutral tweets is calculated individually. These tweets can be visualized easily using matplotlib and pyplot libraries. Visualizing the results is much easy to analyze and depict what is happening in the entire code.

Impact of the Algorithmic Solution

In today's world, governments are moving toward citizen-centric governance where the priorities are services driven by the citizens instead of the government. Today analyzing and getting into the nerves of common people is the new form of governance. Every government wants to know the impact or the reaction of the citizens on any new policy or act or decision. Governments today wish to take the people's opinions and get to the real perspective of the country's people so, if they could analyze the citizens' reaction and further work more to improve the decision or law that could help a government stay in power and understand the real situation and work upon that.

This is the age of social media. Hashtags, mentions, and whatnot today's generation express themselves quite well on social media, so the best form of opinions reactions and suggestions can be gathered from that public sourced data. Governments have realized that social media is an excellent vehicle for getting closer to the citizens. The solution above will have a massive impact on the way governance will change to citizen-centric administration. This model will help the government understand the citizens, how they think, and how they can make changes to better the country and society. The above solution will take the discussions from the government sites initiated by ordinary people. The most common word on the discussion form will be selected and searched for on the social media platform and will analyze accordingly how citizens feel about that policy, law, or decision made by the government. Sentiment analysis is a useful tool for the governments and can help determine whether a particular program initiated by them was successful or a complete failure. This solution's impact is that this will create a bridge between the government and the citizens' opinion. With the help of sentiment analysis, governments can reprioritize their policies and reallocate their funds on how citizens can gain from those funds. All this sentiment analysis activity can be done at a minimal cost while also getting the common people's trends and reactions. Measuring the customer's attitude toward the aspects of a service or product described in the text or a computational study of opinions and emotions can help the government. Governments can study the sentiments and accordingly modify or make changes in the policies and laws. This type of sentiment analysis on the public's views can be used to segregate different sections of society. It can be used to predict the average percentage of supporters of the government. Harsh comments can be directly eliminated to maintain the balance between the sentiments and get accurate results. The repeated Retweets by a person can be removed so that accuracy is calculated based on all the persons' views and not affected very much by a single person.

Although these are the early stages of this in the future with the amount of data increasing and getting such a massive volume of opinions and suggestions can make the governance more robust and flexible at the same time. Citizens never were so crucial in the country's progress, but this will help in betterment due to the sentiment analysis. People can openly express and judge the government's initiatives, and the government can make the necessary changes required as per the demands of the people.

FURTHER READINGS

Alessia, D., Ferri, F., Grifoni, P., & Guzzo, T. (2015). Approaches, tools and applications for sentiment analysis implementation. *International Journal of Computer Applications, 125*(3).

Alessio, H. M., Malay, N., Maurer, K., Bailer, A. J., & Rubin, B. (2017). Examining the effect of proctoring on online test scores. *Online Learning, 21*(1), 146–161.

Arun, K., Ishan, G., & Sanmeet, K. (2016). Loan approval prediction based on machine learning approach. *IOSR Journal of Computer Engineering, 18*(3), 18–21.

Arunachalam, R., & Sarkar, S. (2013, October). The new eye of government: Citizen sentiment analysis in social media. In *Proceedings of the IJCNLP 2013 workshop on natural language processing for social media (SocialNLP)* (pp. 23–28).

Aslam, U., Tariq Aziz, H. I., Sohail, A., & Batcha, N. K. (2019). An empirical study on loan default prediction models. *Journal of Computational and Theoretical Nanoscience, 16*(8), 3483–3488.

Bakliwal, A., Foster, J., van der Puil, J., O'Brien, R., Tounsi, L., & Hughes, M. (2013, June). *Sentiment analysis of political tweets: Towards an accurate classifier.* Association for Computational Linguistics.

Basu, B., & Srinivas, V. V. (2016). Regional flood frequency analysis using entropy-based clustering approach. *Journal of Hydrologic Engineering, 21*(8), 04016020.

Bramer, M. (Ed.). (2006). *Artificial intelligence in theory and practice: IFIP 19th World Computer Congress, TC 12: IFIP AI 2006 Stream, August 21–24, 2006, Santiago, Chile* (Vol. 217). Springer Science & Business Media.

Bryant, P., & Ruello, J. (2019). One system to examine them all: Defining the complexities of implementing an institution wide online exam model. *Personalised Learning. Diverse Goals. One Heart.*, 370.

Corallo, A., Fortunato, L., Matera, M., Alessi, M., Camillò, A., Chetta, V., …, Storelli, D. (2015, July). Sentiment analysis for government: An optimized approach. In *International Workshop on Machine Learning and Data Mining in Pattern Recognition* (pp. 98–112). Cham: Springer.

Coşer, A., Maer-matei, M. M., & Albu, C. (2019). Predictive models for loan default risk assessment. *Economic Computation & Economic Cybernetics Studies & Research, 53*(2).

Fong, S., & Biuk-Aghai, R. P. (2009, December). An automated university admission recommender system for secondary school students. In *The 6th International Conference on Information Technology and Applications* (p. 42).

Gao, X., Wen, J., & Zhang, C. (2019). An improved random forest algorithm for predicting employee turnover. *Mathematical Problems in Engineering, 2019.*

Goyal, A., & Kaur, R. (2016). A survey on ensemble model for loan prediction. *International Journal of Engineering Trends and Applications (IJETA), 3*(1), 32–37.

Gupta, M., Iyer, K. K., Singh, M. R., & Kadam, A. K. (2017). Automated online college admission management system. *International Journal of Computer Science Trends and Technology, 5*(3).

Hamid, A. J., & Ahmed, T. M. (2016). Developing prediction model of loan risk in banks using data mining. *Machine Learning and Applications: An International Journal (MLAIJ), 3*(1).

Hubert, R. B., Estevez, E., Maguitman, A., & Janowski, T. (2018, May). Examining government-citizen interactions on Twitter using visual and sentiment analysis. In *Proceedings of the 19th Annual International Conference on Digital Government Research: Governance in the Data Age* (pp. 1–10).

Kaur, A., & Hasija, S. (2015). A conceptual model of admission system and performance evaluation for a university. *International Journal of Computer Applications, 125*(4).

Li, M., Sikdar, S., Xia, L., & Wang, G. (2020). *Anti-cheating online exams by minimizing the cheating gain.*

Liang, Y., Jin, X., & Wang, Z. (2019). *Loanliness: Predicting loan repayment ability by using machine learning methods.*

Lux, T., Pittman, R., Shende, M., & Shende, A. (2016, May). Applications of supervised learning techniques on undergraduate admissions data. In *Proceedings of the ACM International Conference on Computing Frontiers* (pp. 412–417).

Madane, N. (2019). Loan prediction analysis using decision tree. *Journal of the Gujarat Research Society, 21*(14s), 214–221.

Mirza, M. M. Q., Dixit, A., & Nishat, A. (Eds.). (2003). *Flood problem and management in South Asia*. Kluwer Academic.

Purohit, S., & Kulkarni, A. (2011, December). Credit evaluation model of loan proposals for Indian Banks. In *2011 World Congress on Information and Communication Technologies* (pp. 868–873). IEEE.

Sankarasubramanian, B., Rathinakumar, M., Balakrishnan, B., & Bharathwajan, R. (2014). An automated implementation of Indian university admission system using artificial neural networks. *ICTACT Journal on Soft Computing, 4*(3), 767–771.

Sebastiani, F. (2002). Machine learning in automated text categorization. *ACM Computing Surveys (CSUR), 34*(1), 1–47.

Sivasree, M. S., & Rekha Sunny, T. (2015). Loan credibility prediction system based on decision tree algorithm. *International Journal of Engineering Research & Technology (IJERT), 4*(9).

Syaifudin, Y. W., & Puspitasari, D. (2017). Twitter data mining for sentiment analysis on peoples feedback against government public policy. *MATTER: International Journal of Science and Technology, 3*(1).

Takahashi, M., Moro, A., Ji, Y., & Umeda, K. (2020). *Expandable YOLO: 3D object detection from RGB-D images*. arXiv preprint arXiv:2006.14837.

Vargiu, E., & Urru, M. (2013). Exploiting web scraping in a collaborative filtering-based approach to web advertising. *Journal of Artificial Intelligence Research, 2*(1), 44–54.

Walczak, S., & Sincich, T. (1999). A comparative analysis of regression and neural networks for university admissions. *Information Sciences, 119*(1–2), 1–20.

Waldrop, M. M. (2017). News feature: The genuine problem of fake news. *Proceedings of the National Academy of Sciences, 114*(48), 12631–12634.

Wang, M., Yu, J., & Ji, Z. (2018). *Credit fraud risk detection based on XGBoost-LR hybrid model*.

Waters, A., & Miikkulainen, R. (2014). Grade: Machine learning support for graduate admissions. *AI Magazine, 35*(1), 64.

Zhou, L., & Wang, H. (2012). Loan default prediction on large imbalanced data using random forests. *TELKOMNIKA Indonesian Journal of Electrical Engineering, 10*(6), 1519–1525.

Zhu, L., Qiu, D., Ergu, D., Ying, C., & Liu, K. (2019). A study on predicting loan default based on the random forest algorithm. *Procedia Computer Science, 162*, 503–513.

Appendix A: Python Code for Use Case 1—Media

Prototyping

Fake News Detection can be implemented using python as shown in the code below.

```
1.  #Importing relevant libraries
2.  import pandas as pd

3.  #Importing the dataset
4.  REAL_df= pd.read_csv("C:/Users/Desktop/fakenews/True.csv")
5.  FAKE_df= pd.read_csv("C:/Users/Desktop/fakenews/Fake.csv")
6.  FAKE_df.head(2)
```

	title	text	subject	date
0	Donald Trump Sends Out Embarrassing New Year'...	Donald Trump just couldn t wish all Americans ...	News	December 31, 2017
1	Drunk Bragging Trump Staffer Started Russian ...	House Intelligence Committee Chairman Devin Nu...	News	December 31, 2017

```
7.  REAL_df.head(2)
```

	title	text	subject	date
0	As U.S. budget fight looms, Republicans flip t...	WASHINGTON (Reuters) - The head of a conservat...	politicsNews	December 31, 2017
1	U.S. military to accept transgender recruits o...	WASHINGTON (Reuters) - Transgender people will...	politicsNews	December 29, 2017

```
8.  #Creating 'label' in both dataframes which is the target feature so as to identify the fake and real
    news
9.  REAL_df['label'] = 'TRUE'
10. FAKE_df['label'] = 'FAKE'
11. REAL_df.head(2)
```

	title	text	subject	date	label
0	As U.S. budget fight looms, Republicans flip t...	WASHINGTON (Reuters) - The head of a conservat...	politicsNews	December 31, 2017	TRUE
1	U.S. military to accept transgender recruits o...	WASHINGTON (Reuters) - Transgender people will...	politicsNews	December 29, 2017	TRUE

© The Editor(s) (if applicable) and The Author(s), under exclusive license to Springer Nature Singapore Pte Ltd. 2021
R. Gupta and S. K. Pal, *Introduction to Algorithmic Government*,
https://doi.org/10.1007/978-981-16-0282-5

```
12. #Combining both the data frames
13. TOTAL_NEWS_df = pd.concat([REAL_df,FAKE_df])
14. TOTAL_NEWS_df.shape()
```

```
                              (44898,5)
```

```
15. TOTAL_NEWS_df.to_excel("Fakenews.xlsx")
```

```
16. #Searching null values
17. TOTAL_NEWS_df.isna().sum()
```

```
                    title      0
                    text       0
                    subject    0
                       date     0
                       label    0
                       dtype: int64
```

```
18. #Removing urls
19. pattern_Delete = "http"
20. filter1 = TOTAL_NEWS_df['date'].str.contains(pattern_Delete)
21. TOTAL_NEWS_df = TOTAL_NEWS_df[~filter1]
22. pattern = "Jan|Feb|Mar|Apr|May|Jun|Jul|Aug|Sep|Oct|Nov|Dec"
23. filter2 = TOTAL_NEWS_df['date'].str.contains(pattern)
24. TOTAL_NEWS_df=TOTAL_NEWS_df[filter2]
```

```
25. #Grouping data by subject and label
26. TOTAL_NEWS_df_sub=TOTAL_NEWS_df.groupby(['subject', 'label'])['text'].count()
27. TOTAL_NEWS_df_sub
```

```
                subject          label
        Government News     FAKE       1568
           Middle-east      FAKE        778
                 News       FAKE       9050
            US_News         FAKE        783
             left-news      FAKE       4456
              politics      FAKE       6836
          politicsNews     TRUE       11272
            worldnews      TRUE       10145
                   Name: text, dtype: int64
```

```
28. TOTAL_NEWS_df_sub = TOTAL_NEWS_df_sub.unstack().fillna(0)
29. TOTAL_NEWS_df_sub
```

label	FAKE	TRUE
subject		
Government News	1568.0	0.0	0.0
Middle-east	778.0	0.0	0.0
News	9050.0	0.0	0.0
US_News	783.0	0.0	0.0

label	FAKE	TRUE	
subject			
left-news	4456.0	0.0	0.0
politics	6836.0	0.0	0.0
politicsNews	0.0	11272.0	0.0
worldnews	0.0	10145.0	0.0
Count	0.0	0.0	21417.0

```
30. #Visualising the data
31. import matplotlib.pyplot as plt
32. ax = (TOTAL_NEWS_df_sub).plot(kind='bar',figsize=(10, 7),grid=True)
33. ax.set_ylabel('Count')
34. plt.show()
```
The generated bar plot shows the count of each type of news in the dataset.

```
35. TOTAL_NEWS_df_sub['Count']=TOTAL_NEWS_df_sub['FAKE']+TOTAL_NEWS_df_sub['TR
    UE']
36. import plotly.graph_objects as go
37. labels = TOTAL_NEWS_df_sub.index
38. values = TOTAL_NEWS_df_sub['Count']
39. fig = go.Figure(data=[go.Pie(labels=labels, values=values)])
40. fig.show()
```
The generated pie chart shows the different types of news in the dataset along with their percentage.

```
41. #Combining 'title', 'text' and 'subject' into 'article' feature
42. TO
    TAL_NEWS_df['article']=TOTAL_NEWS_df['title']+""+TOTAL_NEWS_df['text']+""+['subject'
    ]
```

```
43. #Creating final data frame with only 'article' and 'label' feature
44. df_final = TOTAL_NEWS_df[['article','label']]
45. df_final(2)
```

	article	label
0	As U.S. budget fight looms, Republicans flip t...	TRUE
1	U.S. military to accept transgender recruits o...	TRUE

```
46. #Converting data to lower case
47. df_final['article'] = df_final['article'].apply(lambda x: x.lower())
48. df_final['article'].head()
```

```
0    as u.s. budget fight looms, republicans flip t...
1    u.s. military to accept transgender recruits o...
2    senior u.s. republican senator: 'let mr. muell...
3    fbi russia probe helped by australian diplomat...
4    trump wants postal service to charge 'much mor...
Name: article, dtype: object
```

```
49. #Removing punctuation
50. import string
51. def punctuation_removal(messy_str):
52.    clean_list = [char for char in messy_str if char not in string.punctuation]
53.    clean_str = ''.join(clean_list)
54.    return clean_str
55. df_final['article'] = df_final['article'].apply(punctuation_removal)
56. df_final['article'].head()
```

```
0    as us budget fight looms republicans flip thei...
1    us military to accept transgender recruits on ...
2    senior us republican senator let mr mueller do...
3    fbi russia probe helped by australian diplomat...
4    trump wants postal service to charge much more...
Name: article, dtype: object
```

```
57. #Removing stopwords
58. import nltk
59. nltk.download('stopwords')
60. from nltk.corpus import stopwords
61. stop = stopwords.words('english')
62. df_final['article'].apply(lambda x: [item for item in x if item not in stop])
```

```
0        [ , u,  , b, u, g, e,  , f, g, h,  , l,  , r, ...
1        [u,  , l, r,  ,  , c, c, e, p,  , r, n, g, e, ...
2        [e, n, r,  , u,  , r, e, p, u, b, l, c, n,  , ...
3        [f, b,  , r, u,  , p, r, b, e,  , h, e, l, p, ...
4        [r, u, p,  , w, n,  , p, l,  , e, r, v, c, e, ...
5        [w, h, e,  , h, u, e,  , c, n, g, r, e,  , p, ...
23479    [h, w,  ,  , b, l, w,  , 7, 0, 0,  , l, l, n, ...
23480    [1, 0,  , u,  , n, v,  , l, r,  , h, e, l,  , ...
Name: article, Length: 44898, dtype: object
```

```
63. #Visualising the data using wordcloud
64. %matplotlib inline
65. from wordcloud import WordCloud
66. words = ' '.join([text for text in df_final.article])
67. wordcloud = WordCloud(width= 800, height= 500, max_font_size = 110,collocations =
    False).generate(words)
68. import matplotlib.pyplot as plt
69. plt.figure(figsize=(10,7))
70. plt.imshow(wordcloud, interpolation='bilinear')
71. plt.axis("off")
72. plt.show()
```

The generated tag cloud or word cloud is a visual representation of text data, used to depict the tags. Tags are mainly single words and their importance is shown with their font size or color.

```
73. #Plotting the pareto chart for visualizing frequencies of words
74. from nltk import tokenize
75. token_space = tokenize.WhitespaceTokenizer()
76. import seaborn as sns
77. import nltk
78. def pareto(text, column_text, quantity):
79.     all_words = ' '.join([text for text in text[column_text]])
80.     token_phrase = token_space.tokenize(all_words)
81.     frequency = nltk.FreqDist(token_phrase)
82.     df_frequency = pd.DataFrame({"Word": list(frequency.keys()),
83.                         "Frequency": list(frequency.values())})
84.     df_frequency = df_frequency.nlargest(columns = "Frequency", n = quantity)
85.     plt.figure(figsize=(12,8))
86.     ax = sns.barplot(data = df_frequency, x = "Word", y = "Frequency")
87.     ax.set(ylabel = "Count")
88.     plt.show()
89. pareto(df_final, "article", 15)
```
The generated pareto chart shows the top 15 most frequently occurring words in the dataset.

```
90. #Creating bag of words and TF-IDF
91. from sklearn.feature_extraction.text import CountVectorizer
92. bow_article = CountVectorizer().fit(df_final['article'])
93. article_vect = bow_article.transform(df_final['article'])

94. #TF-IDF
95. from sklearn.feature_extraction.text import TfidfTransformer
96. tfidf_transformer = TfidfTransformer().fit(article_vect)
97. news_tfidf = tfidf_transformer.transform(article_vect)
98. print(news_tfidf.shape)
```

$$(44898, 248247)$$

```
99. #Using 20% of the data to train the models.
100.from sklearn.model_selection import train_test_split
101.X = news_tfidf
102.y = df_final['label']
103.X_train, X_test, Y_train,Y_test= train_test_split(X, y, test_size=0.2)

104.#Naive Bayes classifier
105.from sklearn.naive_bayes import MultinomialNB
106.fakenews_detector = MultinomialNB().fit(X_train, Y_train)
107.predictions = fakenews_detector.predict(X_test)
108.print(predictions)
109.final=pd.DataFrame(columns=["article","check"])
```

$$['TRUE' \ 'FAKE' \ 'TRUE' \ ... \ 'FAKE' \ 'FAKE' \ 'FAKE']$$

```
110.#Model Evaluation
111.from sklearn import metrics
112.from sklearn.metrics import classification_report
113.print (classification_report(Y_test, predictions))
114.print("Accuracy:", metrics.accuracy_score(Y_test, predictions))
```

	precision	recall	f1-score	support
FAKE	0.93	0.96	0.94	4671
TRUE	0.95	0.92	0.94	4309
micro avg	0.94	0.94	0.94	8980
macro avg	0.94	0.94	0.94	8980
weighted avg	0.94	0.94	0.94	8980

Accuracy: 0.9413140311804009

```
115.#Stochastic Gradient Descent classifier
116.from sklearn.linear_model import SGDClassifier
117.fake_detector_svc = SGDClassifier().fit(X_train, Y_train)
118.prediction_svc = fake_detector_svc.predict(X_test)

119.#Model Evaluation
120.print (classification_report(Y_test, prediction_svc))
121.print("Accuracy:", metrics.accuracy_score(Y_test, prediction_svc))
```

	precision	recall	f1-score	support
FAKE	0.99	0.99	0.99	4671
TRUE	0.99	0.99	0.99	4309
micro avg	0.99	0.99	0.99	8980
macro avg	0.99	0.99	0.99	8980
weighted avg	0.99	0.99	0.99	8980

Accuracy: 0.9913140311804008

```
122.#Logistic Regression model
123.from sklearn.linear_model import LogisticRegression
124.fake_detector_logistic = LogisticRegression().fit(X_train, Y_train)
125.predictions_log_reg = fake_detector_logistic.predict(X_test)

126.#Model Evaluation
127.print (classification_report(Y_test, predictions_log_reg))
128.print("Accuracy:", metrics.accuracy_score(Y_test, predictions_log_reg))
```

	precision	recall	f1-score	support
FAKE	0.99	0.99	0.99	4671
TRUE	0.99	0.99	0.99	4309
micro avg	0.99	0.99	0.99	8980
macro avg	0.99	0.99	0.99	8980
weighted avg	0.99	0.99	0.99	8980

Accuracy: 0.9885300668151448

```
129.#Passive Aggressive classifier
130.from sklearn.linear_model import PassiveAggressiveClassifier
131.PA = PassiveAggressiveClassifier().fit(X_train, Y_train)
```

```
132.prediction = PA.predict(X_test)

133.#Model Evaluation
134.print (classification_report(Y_test, prediction))
```

	precision	recall	f1-score	support
FAKE	0.99	1.00	1.00	4671
TRUE	1.00	0.99	0.99	4309
micro avg	1.00	1.00	1.00	8980
macro avg	1.00	1.00	1.00	8980
weighted avg	1.00	1.00	1.00	8980

Accuracy: 0.9951002227171493

```
135.#Random Forest classifier
136.print("Accuracy:", metrics.accuracy_score(Y_test, prediction))
137.from sklearn.ensemble import RandomForestClassifier
138.RF=RandomForestClassifier().fit(X_train, Y_train)
139.prediction_rf = RF.predict(X_test)

140.#Model Evaluation
141.print (classification_report(Y_test, prediction_rf))
142.print("Accuracy:", metrics.accuracy_score(Y_test, prediction_rf))
```

	precision	recall	f1-score	support
FAKE	0.95	0.99	0.97	4671
TRUE	0.98	0.94	0.96	4309
micro avg	0.96	0.96	0.96	8980
macro avg	0.97	0.96	0.96	8980
weighted avg	0.96	0.96	0.96	8980

Accuracy: 0.9636971046770602

```
143.#K- nearest neighbors classifier
144.from sklearn.neighbors import KNeighborsClassifier
145.KN=KNeighborsClassifier().fit(X_train, Y_train)
146.prediction_kn = RF.predict(X_test)
147.#Model Evaluation
148.print (classification_report(Y_test, prediction_kn))
149.print("Accuracy:", metrics.accuracy_score(Y_test, prediction_kn))
```

	precision	recall	f1-score	support
FAKE	0.95	0.99	0.97	4671
TRUE	0.98	0.94	0.96	4309
micro avg	0.96	0.96	0.96	8980
macro avg	0.97	0.96	0.96	8980
weighted avg	0.96	0.96	0.96	8980

Accuracy: 0.9636971046770602

APPENDIX B: PYTHON CODE FOR USE CASE 2—DISASTER MANAGEMENT

Prototyping

Flood Prediction can be implemented using Python as shown in the code below.

```
1.  #Importing relevant libraries
2.  import pandas as pd
3.  import matplotlib.pyplot as plt
4.  import numpy as np
5.  import scipy
6.  from scipy.stats import spearmanr
7.  from sklearn.ensemble import RandomForestClassifier
8.  from sklearn.preprocessing import scale
9.  from sklearn.linear_model import LogisticRegression
10. from sklearn.model_selection import train_test_split
11. from sklearn import preprocessing

12. #Importing the dataset
13. x=pd.read_csv("C:/Users/Desktop/kerala.csv")

14. #Plotting scatter plot showing monsoon rainfall amount from year 1900 to 2015 as in India monsoon
    belt is from June to September
15. y1=list(x["YEAR"])
16. x1=list(x["Jun-Sep"])
17. z1=list(x["JUN"])
18. w1=list(x["MAY"])
19. plt.plot(y1, x1,'*')
20. plt.show()
    #The output shows rainfall amount from June to September in Kerala

21. flood=[]
22. june=[]
23. sub=[]
24. #Creating a new column with binary classification depending on whether that year had flooded or
    not, using rainfall of that year as threshold.
25. print(x1[114])
26. for i in range(0,len(x1)):
27.     if x1[i]>2400:
28.         flood.append('1')
29.     else:
30.         flood.append('0')
31. print(len(x1))

32. #Finding approximate rainfall data for 10 days for month of June every year from 1901-2015
33. for k in range(0,len(x1)):
34.     june.append(z1[k]/3)
```

© The Editor(s) (if applicable) and The Author(s), under exclusive
license to Springer Nature Singapore Pte Ltd. 2021
R. Gupta and S. K. Pal, *Introduction to Algorithmic Government*,
https://doi.org/10.1007/978-981-16-0282-5

```
35. #Finding increase in rainfall from month of May to Month of June every year from 1901-2015
36. for k in range(0,len(x1)):
37.     sub.append(abs(w1[k]-z1[k]))

38. print(len(flood),len(x1))
39. df = pd.DataFrame({'flood':flood})
40. df1=pd.DataFrame({'per_10_days':june})
41. x["flood"]=flood
42. x["avgjune"]=june
43. x["sub"]=sub

44. #Saving new columns in the new CSV file.
45. x.to_csv("out1.csv")
46. print((x))

47. #Taking the columns which are to be used for training in the model.
48. #16(Mar-May)
49. #20(Average of first 10 days of June)
50. #21(Difference of rainfall from May to June)
51. #19(Binary classification of flood 0 or 1)
52. #Using Logistic Regression model
53. X = x.ix[:,{16,20,21}].values
54. y1=x.ix[:,19].values
55. (X_train, X_test, Y_train, Y_test) = train_test_split(X, y1, random_state=0)
56. X1= scale(X)
57. print(X1)
58. Lr=LogisticRegression()
59. Lr.fit(X,y1)

60. #Printing the accuracy
61. print(Lr.score(X,y1))
62. ypred=Lr.score(X_test,Y_test)
63. print(ypred)
```

                                0.8608695652173913

```
64. q1=275 # present years march to may rainfall data on average
65. w1=130 #average rainfall in past 10 days of june
66. e1=260 #average increase  in rainfall from may to june
67. q2=200 # present years march to may rainfall data on average
68. w2=400 #average rainfall in past 10 days of june
69. e2=300 #average increase  in rainfall from may to june
70. l=[[q1,w1,e1],[q2,w2,e2],[50,300,205]]
71. print(X)
72. ypred=Lr.predict(X)
73. f1=Lr.predict(l)
74. for i in range(len(f1)):
75.   if (int(f1[i])==1):
76.       print(f1[i],"- possibility of  severe flood")
77.   else:
78.       print(f1[i],"- no chance of severe flood")
```

                        0 - no chance of severe flood
                        1 - possibility of severe flood

1 - possibility of severe flood

```
79.  Y1=list(x["YEAR"])
80.  X1=list(x["Jun-Sep"])
81.  Z1=list(x["JUN"])
82.  W1=list(x["MAY"])

83.  #Plotting scatter plot showing monsoon rainfall amount from year 1900 to 2015 as in India monsoon
     belt is from June to September
84.  plt.plot(Y1, X1,'*')
85.  plt.show()

     #The output shows rainfall amount from June to September in Kerala

86.  flood=[]
87.  june=[]
88.  sub=[]
89.
90.  #Creating a new column with binary classification depending on whether that year had flooded or
     not, using rainfall of that year as threshold.
91.  print(x1[114])
92.  for i in range(0,len(X1)):
93.      if X1[i]>2400:
94.          flood.append('1')
95.      else:
96.          flood.append('0')
97.  print(len(X1))

98.  #Finding approximate rainfall data for 10 days for month of June every year from 1901-2015
99.  for k in range(0,len(X1)):
100.     june.append(Z1[k]/3)

101. #Finding increase in rainfall from month of May to Month of June every year from 1901-2015
102. for k in range(0,len(X1)):
103.     sub.append(abs(W1[k]-Z1[k]))
104. print(len(flood),len(x1))
105. df = pd.DataFrame({'flood':flood})
106. df1=pd.DataFrame({'per_10_days':june})

107. Y["flood"]=flood
108. Y["avgjune"]=june
109. Y["sub"]=sub

110. #Saving new columns in the new CSV file.
111. Y.to_csv("out2.csv")
112. print((Y))
113. #Taking the columns which are to be used for training in the model.
114. #16(Mar-May)
115. #20(Average of first 10 days of June)
116. #21(Difference of rainfall from May to June)
117. #19(Binary classification of flood 0 or 1)

118. #Using Logistic Regression model
119. X1 = Y.ix[:,{16,20,21}].values
```

```
120.Y1=Y.ix[:,19].values
121.(X_train, X_test, Y_train, Y_test) = train_test_split(X1, y1, random_state=0)
122.X1= scale(X)
123.print(X1)
124.Lr=LogisticRegression()
125.Lr.fit(X1,Y1)

126.#Printing the accuracy
127.print(Lr.score(X1,Y1))
128.ypred=Lr.score(X_test,Y_test)
129.print(ypred)
```

                                    0.8695652173913043

```
130.q1=275 # present years march to may rainfall data on average
131.w1=130 #average rainfall in past 10 days of june
132.e1=260 #average increase  in rainfall from may to june
133.q2=200 # present years march to may rainfall data on average
134.w2=400 #average rainfall in past 10 days of june
135.e2=300 #average increase  in rainfall from may to june
136.l=[[q1,w1,e1],[q2,w2,e2],[50,300,205]]
137.print(X)
138.#ypred=Lr.predict(X)
139.f1=Lr.predict(l)
140.for i in range(len(f1)):
141.    if (int(f1[i])==1):
142.        print(f1[i],"- possibility of  severe flood")
143.    else:
144.        print(f1[i],"- no chance of severe flood")
```

                        0- no chance of severe flood
                        1 - possibility of severe flood
                        0 - no chance of severe flood

Appendix C: Python Code for Use Case 3—Education & Assessment

Prototype

Online Exam Conduction using AI proctor can be implemented using Python as shown in the code below.

```
1.   #download YOLOV3 weights from https://pjreddie.com/media/files/yolov3.weights
2.   #download        the        file        for        dlib        model        from
     https://github.com/antoinelame/GazeTracking/tree/master/gaze_tracking/trained_models and save
     it as shape_68.dat
3.   #Keep all the files in the same folder.

4.   #Create a yolo_helper.py file and paste the code given below.

5.   #Importing relevant libraries
6.   import tensorflow as tf
7.   import numpy as np
8.   import cv2
9.   from tensorflow.keras import Model
10.  from tensorflow.keras.layers import (
11.      Add,
12.      Concatenate,
13.      Conv2D,
14.      Input,
15.      Lambda,
16.      LeakyReLU,
17.      UpSampling2D,
18.      ZeroPadding2D,
19.      BatchNormalization
20.  )
21.  from tensorflow.keras.regularizers import l2

22.  #Loading darknet weights for yolo
23.  def load_darknet_weights(model, weights_file):
24.      #Open the weights file
25.      wf = open(weights_file, 'rb')
26.      major, minor, revision, seen, _ = np.fromfile(wf, dtype=np.int32, count=5)

27.      #Define names of the Yolo layers
28.      layers = ['yolo_darknet',
29.          'yolo_conv_0',
30.          'yolo_output_0',
31.          'yolo_conv_1',
32.          'yolo_output_1',
33.          'yolo_conv_2',
34.          'yolo_output_2']
35.      for layer_name in layers:
```

R. Gupta and S. K. Pal, *Introduction to Algorithmic Government*,
https://doi.org/10.1007/978-981-16-0282-5

```
36.    sub_model = model.get_layer(layer_name)
37.    for i, layer in enumerate(sub_model.layers):
38.        if not layer.name.startswith('conv2d'):
39.            continue
40.      # for custom Batch normalization layer
41.        batch_norm = None
42.        if i + 1 < len(sub_model.layers) and \
43.            sub_model.layers[i + 1].name.startswith('batch_norm'):
44.            batch_norm = sub_model.layers[i + 1]
45.        filters = layer.filters
46.        size = layer.kernel_size[0]
47.        in_dim = layer.input_shape[-1]
48.        if batch_norm is None:
49.            conv_bias = np.fromfile(wf, dtype=np.float32, count=filters)
50.        else:
51.            bn_weights = np.fromfile(
52.                wf, dtype=np.float32, count=4 * filters)
53.            bn_weights = bn_weights.reshape((4, filters))[[1, 0, 2, 3]]
54.        conv_shape = (filters, in_dim, size, size)
55.        conv_weights = np.fromfile(
56.            wf, dtype=np.float32, count=np.product(conv_shape))
57.        conv_weights = conv_weights.reshape(
58.            conv_shape).transpose([2, 3, 1, 0])
59.        if batch_norm is None:
60.            layer.set_weights([conv_weights, conv_bias])
61.        else:
62.            layer.set_weights([conv_weights])
63.            batch_norm.set_weights(bn_weights)
64.    assert len(wf.read()) == 0, 'failed to read all data'
65.    wf.close()

66. #function to draw predictions on image
67. def draw_outputs(img, outputs, class_names):
68.    objectness, classes, nums = outputs
69.    boxes, objectness, classes, nums = boxes[0], objectness[0], classes[0], nums[0]
70.    wh = np.flip(img.shape[0:2])
71.    for i in range(nums):
72.        x1y1 = tuple((np.array(boxes[i][0:2]) * wh).astype(np.int32))
73.        x2y2 = tuple((np.array(boxes[i][2:4]) * wh).astype(np.int32))
74.        img = cv2.rectangle(img, x1y1, x2y2, (255, 0, 0), 2)
75.        img = cv2.putText(img, '{} {:.4f}'.format(
76.            class_names[int(classes[i])], objectness[i]),
77.            x1y1, cv2.FONT_HERSHEY_COMPLEX_SMALL, 1, (0, 0, 255), 2)
78.    return img

79. # define anchor boxes shapes
80. yolo_anchors = np.array([(10, 13), (16, 30), (33, 23), (30, 61), (62, 45),
81.                  (59, 119), (116, 90), (156, 198), (373, 326)],
82.                  np.float32) / 416
83. yolo_anchor_masks = np.array([[6, 7, 8], [3, 4, 5], [0, 1, 2]])

84.  # function to define a single Darknet convolutional layer
85. def DarknetConv(x, filters, kernel_size, strides=1, batch_norm=True):
86.    #Image padding
```

```
87.    if strides == 1:
88.        padding = 'same'
89.    else:
90.        x = ZeroPadding2D(((1, 0), (1, 0)))(x)  # top left half-padding
91.        padding = 'valid'
92.    #Defining the Conv layer
93.    x = Conv2D(filters=filters, kernel_size=kernel_size,
94.            strides=strides, padding=padding,
95.            use_bias=not batch_norm, kernel_regularizer=l2(0.0005))(x)
96.    if batch_norm:
97.        x = BatchNormalization()(x)
98.        x = LeakyReLU(alpha=0.1)(x)
99.    return x


100.#function to define a single DarkNet Residual layer
101.def DarknetResidual(x, filters):
102.    prev = x
103.    x = DarknetConv(x, filters // 2, 1)
104.    x = DarknetConv(x, filters, 3)
105.    x = Add()([prev, x])
106.    return x


107.# function to define a single DarkNet Block (made of multiple Residual layers)
108.def DarknetBlock(x, filters, blocks):
109.    x = DarknetConv(x, filters, 3, strides=2)
110.    for _ in range(blocks):
111.        x = DarknetResidual(x, filters)
112.    return x


113.#function that creates the whole DarkNet
114.def Darknet(name=None):
115.    x = inputs = Input([None, None, 3])
116.    x = DarknetConv(x, 32, 3)
117.    x = DarknetBlock(x, 64, 1)
118.    x = DarknetBlock(x, 128, 2)  # skip connection
119.    x = x_36 = DarknetBlock(x, 256, 8)  # skip connection
120.    x = x_61 = DarknetBlock(x, 512, 8)
121.    x = DarknetBlock(x, 1024, 4)
122.    return tf.keras.Model(inputs, (x_36, x_61, x), name=name)


123.#function to define the Yolo Conv layer.
124.def YoloConv(filters, name=None):
125.    def yolo_conv(x_in):
126.        if isinstance(x_in, tuple):
127.            inputs = Input(x_in[0].shape[1:]), Input(x_in[1].shape[1:])
128.            x, x_skip = inputs
129.            # concat with skip connection
130.            x = DarknetConv(x, filters, 1)
131.            x = UpSampling2D(2)(x)
132.            x = Concatenate()([x, x_skip])
133.        else:
134.            x = inputs = Input(x_in.shape[1:])
135.        x = DarknetConv(x, filters, 1)
136.        x = DarknetConv(x, filters * 2, 3)
```

```
137.      x = DarknetConv(x, filters, 1)
138.      x = DarknetConv(x, filters * 2, 3)
139.      x = DarknetConv(x, filters, 1)
140.      return Model(inputs, x, name=name)(x_in)
141.    return yolo_conv

142.#function for yolo v3 output
143.def YoloOutput(filters, anchors, classes, name=None):
144.    def yolo_output(x_in):
145.      x = inputs = Input(x_in.shape[1:])
146.      x = DarknetConv(x, filters * 2, 3)
147.      x = DarknetConv(x, anchors * (classes + 5), 1, batch_norm=False)
148.      x = Lambda(lambda x: tf.reshape(x, (-1, tf.shape(x)[1], tf.shape(x)[2],
149.                          anchors, classes + 5)))(x)
150.      return tf.keras.Model(inputs, x, name=name)(x_in)
151.    return yolo_output

152.#function to get bounding boxes from network predictions
153.def yolo_boxes(pred, anchors, classes):
154.    grid_size = tf.shape(pred)[1]
155.    #Extracting box coortinates from prediction vectors
156.    box_xy, box_wh, objectness, class_probs = tf.split(
157.        pred, (2, 2, 1, classes), axis=-1)
158.    #Normalize coordinates
159.    box_xy = tf.sigmoid(box_xy)
160.    objectness = tf.sigmoid(objectness)
161.    class_probs = tf.sigmoid(class_probs)
162.    pred_box = tf.concat((box_xy, box_wh), axis=-1)  # original xywh for loss
163.    grid = tf.meshgrid(tf.range(grid_size), tf.range(grid_size))
164.    grid = tf.expand_dims(tf.stack(grid, axis=-1), axis=2)  # [gx, gy, 1, 2]
165.    box_xy = (box_xy + tf.cast(grid, tf.float32)) / \
166.        tf.cast(grid_size, tf.float32)
167.    box_wh = tf.exp(box_wh) * anchors
168.    box_x1y1 = box_xy - box_wh / 2
169.    box_x2y2 = box_xy + box_wh / 2
170.    bbox = tf.concat([box_x1y1, box_x2y2], axis=-1)
171.    return bbox, objectness, class_probs, pred_box
172.def yolo_nms(outputs, anchors, masks, classes):
173.    # boxes, conf, type
174.    b, c, t = [], [], []
175.    for o in outputs:
176.      b.append(tf.reshape(o[0], (tf.shape(o[0])[0], -1, tf.shape(o[0])[-1])))
177.      c.append(tf.reshape(o[1], (tf.shape(o[1])[0], -1, tf.shape(o[1])[-1])))
178.      t.append(tf.reshape(o[2], (tf.shape(o[2])[0], -1, tf.shape(o[2])[-1])))
179.    bbox = tf.concat(b, axis=1)
180.    confidence = tf.concat(c, axis=1)
181.    class_probs = tf.concat(t, axis=1)
182.    scores = confidence * class_probs
183.    boxes, scores, classes, valid_detections = tf.image.combined_non_max_suppression(
184.        boxes=tf.reshape(bbox, (tf.shape(bbox)[0], -1, 1, 4)),
185.        scores=tf.reshape(
186.        scores, (tf.shape(scores)[0], -1, tf.shape(scores)[-1])),
187.        max_output_size_per_class=100,
188.        max_total_size=100,
```

```
189.     iou_threshold=0.5,
190.     score_threshold=0.6
191.   )
192.   return boxes, scores, classes, valid_detections

193.#define YoloV3 function
194.def YoloV3(size=None, channels=3, anchors=yolo_anchors,
195.         masks=yolo_anchor_masks, classes=80):
196.   x = inputs = Input([size, size, channels], name='input')
197.   x_36, x_61, x = Darknet(name='yolo_darknet')(x)
198.   x = YoloConv(512, name='yolo_conv_0')(x)
199.   output_0 = YoloOutput(512, len(masks[0]), classes, name='yolo_output_0')(x)
200.   x = YoloConv(256, name='yolo_conv_1')((x, x_61))
201.   output_1 = YoloOutput(256, len(masks[1]), classes, name='yolo_output_1')(x)
202.   x = YoloConv(128, name='yolo_conv_2')((x, x_36))
203.   output_2 = YoloOutput(128, len(masks[2]), classes, name='yolo_output_2')(x)
204.   boxes_0 = Lambda(lambda x: yolo_boxes(x, anchors[masks[0]], classes),
205.             name='yolo_boxes_0')(output_0)
206.   boxes_1 = Lambda(lambda x: yolo_boxes(x, anchors[masks[1]], classes),
207.             name='yolo_boxes_1')(output_1)
208.   boxes_2 = Lambda(lambda x: yolo_boxes(x, anchors[masks[2]], classes),
209.             name='yolo_boxes_2')(output_2)
210.   outputs = Lambda(lambda x: yolo_nms(x, anchors, masks, classes),
211.             name='yolo_nms')((boxes_0[:3], boxes_1[:3], boxes_2[:3]))
212.   return Model(inputs, outputs, name='yolov3')
213.#output

      #the output recognizes and predicts faces

214.#Create a dlib_helper.py file and paste the below code.

215.#import the necessary libraries
216.import cv2
217.import numpy as np

218.#define a function for marking points on face
219.def shape_to_np(shape, dtype="int"):
220.       # initialize the list of (x, y)-coordinates
221.   coords = np.zeros((68, 2), dtype=dtype)
222.       # loop over the 68 facial landmarks and convert them
223.       # to a 2-tuple of (x, y)-coordinates
224.   for i in range(0, 68):
225.       coords[i] = (shape.part(i).x, shape.part(i).y)
226.       # return the list of (x, y)-coordinates
227.   return coords

228.# function to create mask
229.def eye_on_mask(mask, side, shape):
230.   points = [shape[i] for i in side]
231.   points = np.array(points, dtype=np.int32)
232.   mask = cv2.fillConvexPoly(mask, points, 255)
233.   l = points[0][0]
234.   t = (points[1][1]+points[2][1])//2
235.   r = points[3][0]
```

```
236.    b = (points[4][1]+points[5][1])//2
237.    return mask, [l, t, r, b]


238.#function to find eyeball position
239.def find_eyeball_position(end_points, cx, cy):
240.    x_ratio = (end_points[0] - cx)/(cx - end_points[2])
241.    y_ratio = (cy - end_points[1])/(end_points[3] - cy)
242.    if x_ratio > 3:
243.        return 1
244.    elif x_ratio < 0.33:
245.        return 2
246.    elif y_ratio < 0.33:
247.        return 3
248.    else:
249.        return 0


250.#deine contours
251.def contouring(thresh, mid, img, end_points, right=False):
252.cnts,_=cv2.findContours(thresh,cv2.RETR_EXTERNAL,cv2.CHAIN_APPROX_NONE)[-2:]
253.    try:
254.        cnt = max(cnts, key=cv2.contourArea)
255.        M = cv2.moments(cnt)
256.        cx = int(M['m10']/M['m00'])
257.        cy = int(M['m01']/M['m00'])
258.        if right:
259.            cx += mid
260.        cv2.circle(img, (cx, cy), 4, (0, 0, 255), 2)
261.        return find_eyeball_position(end_points, cx, cy)
262.    except:
263.        Pass


264.#function to set up threshold
265.def process_thresh(thresh):
266.    thresh = cv2.erode(thresh, None, iterations=2)
267.    thresh = cv2.dilate(thresh, None, iterations=4)
268.    thresh = cv2.medianBlur(thresh, 3)
269.    thresh = cv2.bitwise_not(thresh)
270.    return thresh


271.#print position of eye
272.def print_eye_pos(left, right):
273.    if left == right:
274.        if left == 1:
275.            print('Looking left')
276.        elif left == 2:
277.            print('Looking right')
278.        elif left == 3:
279.            print('Looking up')
280.def nothing(x):
281.    pass
282.#output

    #output marks the points on eyes and mouth
```

```
283.#Create a define_mouth_distances.py file and paste the below code.
284.#importing necessary libraries
285.import cv2
286.from dlib_helper import shape_to_np

287.# show the output image with the face detections + facial landmarks
288.def return_distances(detector, predictor):
289.    outer_points = [[49, 59], [50, 58], [51, 57], [52, 56], [53, 55]]
290.    d_outer = [0]*5
291.    inner_points = [[61, 67], [62, 66], [63, 65]]
292.    d_inner = [0]*3

293.#capturing video and predicting in each frame.
294.    cap = cv2.VideoCapture(0)
295.    while(True):
296.        ret, img = cap.read()

297.#convert to grayscale
298.        gray = cv2.cvtColor(img, cv2.COLOR_BGR2GRAY)
299.        rects = detector(gray, 1)
300.        for rect in rects:
301.            shape = predictor(gray, rect)
302.            shape = shape_to_np(shape)
303.            for (x, y) in shape:
304.                cv2.circle(img, (x, y), 2, (0, 0, 255), -1)
305.            cv2.putText(img,    'Press    r    to    record    mouth    distance',    (30,    30),
     cv2.FONT_HERSHEY_SIMPLEX, 1, (0, 255, 255), 2)
306.            cv2.imshow("Output", img)
307.            if cv2.waitKey(1) & 0xFF == ord('r'):

308.#define outer boundary of mouth
309.                for i in range(100):
310.                    for i, (p1, p2) in enumerate(outer_points):
311.                        d_outer[i] += shape[p2][1] - shape[p1][1]
312.                    for i, (p1, p2) in enumerate(inner_points):
313.                        d_inner[i] += shape[p2][1] - shape[p1][1]
314.                    break
315.        cv2.destroyAllWindows()
316.    d_outer[:] = [x / 100 for x in d_outer]
317.    d_inner[:] = [x / 100 for x in d_inner]
318.    return d_outer, d_inner
319.#output

    #output measures the outer boundary of mouth.

320.#create a main.py file the paste the below code

321.#importing libraries
322.import os
323.import threading
324.import cv2
325.import dlib
326.import numpy as np
```

```
327.#importing weights and functions from yolo_helper.py and dlib_helper.py
328.from yolo_helper import YoloV3, load_darknet_weights, draw_outputs
329.from dlib_helper import (shape_to_np,
330.                          eye_on_mask,
331.                          contouring,
332.                          process_thresh,
333.                          print_eye_pos,
334.                          nothing)

335.#call define_mouth_distances.py file
336.from define_mouth_distances import return_distances
337.os.environ['TF_CPP_MIN_LOG_LEVEL'] = '2'
338.yolo = YoloV3()
339.load_darknet_weights(yolo, 'yolov3.weights')
340.detector = dlib.get_frontal_face_detector()
341.predictor = dlib.shape_predictor('shape_68.dat')
342.d_outer, d_inner = return_distances(detector, predictor)

343.#capturing video and reading the image frame
344.cap = cv2.VideoCapture(0)
345._, frame_size = cap.read()

346.#create a function to print the results of eyes movement and mouth
347.def eyes_mouth():
348.    ret, img = cap.read()
349.    thresh = img.copy()
350.    w, h = img.shape[:2]
351.    outer_points = [[49, 59], [50, 58], [51, 57], [52, 56], [53, 55]]
352.    inner_points = [[61, 67], [62, 66], [63, 65]]
353.    left = [36, 37, 38, 39, 40, 41]
354.    right = [42, 43, 44, 45, 46, 47]
355.    kernel = np.ones((9, 9), np.uint8)

356.    #display the image window
357.    cv2.namedWindow('image')
358.    cv2.createTrackbar('threshold', 'image', 0, 255, nothing)
359.    while True:
360.        ret, img = cap.read()
361.        gray = cv2.cvtColor(img, cv2.COLOR_BGR2GRAY)
362.        rects = detector(gray, 1)
363.        for rect in rects:
364.            shape = predictor(gray, rect)
365.            shape = shape_to_np(shape)

366.            # capture mouth points predict if mouth is open
367.            cnt_outer = 0
368.            cnt_inner = 0
369.            for i, (p1, p2) in enumerate(outer_points):
370.                if d_outer[i] + 5 < shape[p2][1] - shape[p1][1]:
371.                    cnt_outer += 1
372.            for i, (p1, p2) in enumerate(inner_points):
373.                if d_inner[i] + 3 < shape[p2][1] - shape[p1][1]:
374.                    cnt_inner += 1
375.            if cnt_outer > 3 or cnt_inner > 2:
```

```
376.          print('Mouth open')
377.          for (x, y) in shape[48:]:
378.              cv2.circle(img, (x, y), 2, (0, 0, 255), -1)

379.          #capture eyes point and print the movement
380.          mask = np.zeros((w, h), dtype=np.uint8)
381.          mask, end_points_left = eye_on_mask(mask, left, shape)
382.          mask, end_points_right = eye_on_mask(mask, right, shape)
383.          mask = cv2.dilate(mask, kernel, 5)
384.          eyes = cv2.bitwise_and(img, img, mask=mask)
385.          mask = (eyes == [0, 0, 0]).all(axis=2)
386.          eyes[mask] = [255, 255, 255]
387.          mid = (shape[42][0] + shape[39][0]) // 2
388.          eyes_gray = cv2.cvtColor(eyes, cv2.COLOR_BGR2GRAY)
389.          threshold = cv2.getTrackbarPos('threshold', 'image')
390.          _, thresh = cv2.threshold(eyes_gray, threshold, 255, cv2.THRESH_BINARY)
391.          thresh = process_thresh(thresh)
392.          eyeball_pos_left = contouring(thresh[:, 0:mid], mid, img, end_points_left)
393.          eyeball_pos_right = contouring(thresh[:, mid:], mid, img, end_points_right, True)
394.
395.          # print_eye_pos(eyeball_pos_left, eyeball_pos_right)
396.          if eyeball_pos_left == eyeball_pos_right:
397.              if eyeball_pos_left == 1:
398.                  print('Looking left')
399.              elif eyeball_pos_left == 2:
400.                  print('Looking right')
401.              elif eyeball_pos_left == 3:
402.                  print('Looking up')
403.          cv2.imshow('result', img)
404.          cv2.imshow("image", thresh)
405.          if cv2.waitKey(1) & 0xFF == ord('q'):
406.              break

407. #function to count number of people and phone
408. def count_people_and_phones():
409.      font = cv2.FONT_HERSHEY_SIMPLEX
410.      while True:
411.          ret, image = cap.read()
412.          frame = cv2.cvtColor(image, cv2.COLOR_BGR2RGB)
413.          frame = cv2.resize(frame, (320, 320))
414.          frame = frame.astype(np.float32)
415.          frame = np.expand_dims(frame, 0)
416.          frame = frame / 255
417.          class_names = [c.strip() for c in open("classes.txt").readlines()]
418.          boxes, scores, classes, nums = yolo(frame)
419.          count = 0
420.          for i in range(nums[0]):
421.              if int(classes[0][i] == 0):
422.                  count += 1
423.              if int(classes[0][i] == 67):
424.                  # print("Mobile Phone Detected")
425.                  cv2.putText(image,'Mobile phone detected',(0,130), font, 1, (200,255,155), 2, cv2.LINE_AA)
426.          #printing the results
```

```
427.    if count == 0:
428.        print('No person detected')
429.    elif count > 1:
430.        print('More than one person detected')
431.    image = draw_outputs(image, (boxes, scores, classes, nums), class_names)
432.    cv2.imshow('Prediction', image)
433.    if cv2.waitKey(1) & 0xFF == ord('q'):
434.        break
435.t1 = threading.Thread(target=eyes_mouth)
436.t2 = threading.Thread(target=count_people_and_phones)
437.t1.start()
438.t2.start()
439.t1.join()
440.t2.join()
441.cap.release()
442.cv2.destroyAllWindows()
443.#output
```

```
Looking up
Mouth open
Mouth open
Mouth open
Mouth open
Looking left
Looking left
Looking right
Mouth open
Mouth open
Mouth open
Mobile Phone Detected
Mobile Phone Detected
```

```
#the output detects cell phone, movement of eyes and mouth open.
```

Appendix D: Python Code for Use Case 4—Entrance Exams & Admissions

Prototyping

Exams and Admissions can be implemented using Python as shown in the code below.

```
1.  #Admission prediction classification model

2.  #importing all the relevant libraries used in the classification model.
3.  import matplotlib.pyplot as plt
4.  import numpy as np
5.  import pandas as pd
6.  import os
7.  import seaborn as sns
8.  from sklearn.preprocessing import LabelEncoder
9.  import keras
10. from sklearn.model_selection import train_test_split
11. from sklearn.preprocessing import MinMaxScaler
12. import numpy as np
13. from keras.models import Sequential
14. from keras.layers.core import Dense, Dropout, Activation
15. from keras.optimizers import SGD
16. from keras.utils import np_utils
17. from sklearn.linear_model import LogisticRegression
18. from sklearn.tree import DecisionTreeClassifier
19. from sklearn.ensemble import RandomForestClassifier
20. from sklearn.metrics import accuracy_score,classification_report,confusion_matrix

21. #loading the dataset.
22. data = pd.read_csv(r'C:\Users\Admission.xlsx')
23. data.head(2)
```

	Serial No.	Age	Board	12th %	GRE Score	Category	SOP	LOR	CGPA	Research	Chance of Admit
0	1	22	CBSE	91.4	337	Gen	4.5	4.5	9.65	1	0.92
1	2	22	ISCE	79.0	324	OBC	4.0	4.5	8.87	1	0.76

The output shows the dataset, which is imported from the file.

```
24. #The data columns
25. data.columns
        Index(['Serial No.', 'Age', 'Board', '12th %', 'GRE Score', 'Category', 'SOP',
```

© The Editor(s) (if applicable) and The Author(s), under exclusive license to Springer Nature Singapore Pte Ltd. 2021
R. Gupta and S. K. Pal, *Introduction to Algorithmic Government*,
https://doi.org/10.1007/978-981-16-0282-5

'LOR ', 'CGPA', 'Research', 'Chance of Admit '],

dtype='object')

The output shows the name of data fields in dataset

26. data.info()

```
RangeIndex: 98 entries, 0 to 97
Data columns (total 11 columns):
 #   Column          Non-Null Count  Dtype
---  ------          --------------  -----
 0   Serial No.      98 non-null     int64
 1   Age             98 non-null     int64
 2   Board           98 non-null     object
 3   12th %          98 non-null     float64
 4   GRE Score       98 non-null     int64
 5   Category        98 non-null     object
 6   SOP             98 non-null     float64
 7   LOR             98 non-null     float64
 8   CGPA            98 non-null     float64
 9   Research        98 non-null     int64
 10  Chance of Admit 98 non-null     float64
dtypes: float64(5), int64(4), object(2)
Memory usage: 8.5+ KB
```

The output shows the dataset information about data containing any null values, memory usage and data types.

27. data.shape

(98, 11)

The output shows the shape of the dataset it contains 98 rows and 11 columns.

```
28. #Exploratory data analysis
29. print("Students with Research Exp: {}".format(len(data[data.Research == 1])))
30. print("Students without Research Exp: {}".format(len(data[data.Research == 0])))
31.
32. y = np.array([len(data[data.Research == 1]),len(data[data.Research == 0])])
33. x = ['With Res Exp','Without Res Exp']
34.
35. plt.bar(x,y)
36. plt.title("Research Exp Numbers")
37. plt.xlabel("Candidates")
38. plt.ylabel("Frequency")
39. plt.show()
```

Students with Research Exp: 58
Students without Research Exp: 40

The generated output shows that 58 candidates have research experience in their history which is beneficial to get selected for higher education.

40. sns.barplot(data['Research'] , data['GRE Score'])

The generated output shows that students with or without GRE has scored equally good marks in GRE exam.

41. sns.jointplot(x = 'CGPA', y = 'GRE Score', color = 'darkblue', data = data, kind='scatter')
42. plt.title("GRE Score vs CGPA")

The generated output shows that students who have high GRE marks have high CGPA also.

43. toppers=data[data['CGPA']>=9.5].sort_values(by=['CGPA'],ascending=False)
44. print('There are {} university toppers'.format(len(toppers)))
45. sns.barplot(x='CGPA',y='Chance of Admit ',data=toppers, linewidth=1.5,edgecolor="0.1")

There are 11 university toppers

The generated output shows that there only 11 students who have CGPA above 9.5 which be beneficial for them to get selected very easily.

46. sns.barplot(x='Category',y='Chance of Admit ',data=data, linewidth=1.0,edgecolor="0.2");

The generated output shows that General category students have more chances to get selected after that ST category.

47. GREtoppers=data[data['GRE Score']>=320].sort_values(by=['GRE Score'],ascending=False)
48. print('There are {} GRE toppers'.format(len(GREtoppers)))
49. sns.barplot(x='GRE Score',y='Chance of Admit ',data=GREtoppers, linewidth=1.5,edgecolor="0.1")

There are 45 GRE toppers

The generated output shows that there are 45 applicants who has more than 320 marks in GRE out of 340.

50. #comparing the GRE score and chances of admission.
51. sns.scatterplot(data['GRE Score'] , data['Chance of Admit '] , hue=data['Chance of Admit '])
52. plt.axvline(data['GRE Score'].mean())
53. #comparing the CGPA score and chances of admission.
54. sns.scatterplot(data['CGPA'] , data['Chance of Admit '] , hue=data['Chance of Admit '])
55. plt.axvline(data["CGPA"].mean())
56. #comparing the 12% and chances of admission.
57. sns.scatterplot(data['12th %'] , data['Chance of Admit '] , hue=data['Chance of Admit '])
58. plt.axvline(data["12th %"].mean())

The generated output shows that the students which high GRE score have more chances
The generated output shows that the students which high undergraduate CGPA have more chances to get admission
The generated output shows that the 12th percentage also matter for admission in the university.

59. sns.heatmap(data.corr(), annot = True, linewidths=0.05,fmt='.2f',cmap="magma")

The generated output shows the heat map displaying the correlation of the dataset variables with each other. Higher the value more they are correlated with each other.

60. #Data pre-processing
61. print(data.isnull().sum())

```
62. sns.heatmap(data.isnull(), cbar=0)
```

```
Serial No.        0
Age               0
Board             0
12th %            0
GRE Score         0
Category          0
SOP               0
LOR               0
CGPA              0
Research          0
Chance of Admit   0
```

The generated output shows that the dataset has no missing values.

```
63. #Label encoding for categorical values.
64. from sklearn.preprocessing import LabelEncoder
65. var_mod = ['Category', 'Board']
66. le = LabelEncoder()
67. for i in var_mod:
68.     data[i] = le.fit_transform(data[i])
69. data.head(3)
```

	Serial No.	Age	Board	12th %	GRE Score	Category	SOP	LOR	CGPA	Research	Chance of Admit
0	1	22	0	91.4	337	0	4.5	4.5	9.65	1	0.92
1	2	22	1	79.0	324	1	4.0	4.5	8.87	1	0.76
2	3	23	2	77.0	316	3	3.0	3.5	8.00	1	0.72

The output shows the dataset after the label encoding of categorical values.

```
70. data.loc[data['Chance of Admit ']>=0.8,['Chance of Admit ']]=1
71. #Assigning the 0 and 1 value to students who have chances above .80 or below .80
72. data.loc[data['Chance of Admit ']<0.8,['Chance of Admit ']]=0
73. scalerX = MinMaxScaler(feature_range = (0,1))
```

```
74. X=data[['Age', 'Board', '12th %', 'GRE Score', 'Category', 'SOP','LOR ', 'CGPA', 'Research']]
75. # labels y are one-hot encoded, so it appears as two classes
76. y = keras.utils.to_categorical(np.array(data['Chance of Admit ']))
77. X = scalerX.fit_transform(X[X.columns])
```

```
78. #Splitting the train and test data.
79. X_train,X_test,y_train,y_test=train_test_split(X,y,train_size=0.7,random_state=100)
```

```
80. #defining the ANN model
81. model = Sequential()
```

```
82. model.add(Dense(128, input_dim=9, activation='sigmoid'))
83. model.add(Dense(32, activation='sigmoid'))
84. model.add(Dense(2, activation='sigmoid'))
85. model.compile(loss = 'categorical_crossentropy', optimizer='adam', metrics=['accuracy'])
86. model.summary()
```

Model: "sequential_9"

Layer (type)	Output Shape	Param #
dense_23 (Dense)	(None, 128)	1280
dense_24 (Dense)	(None, 32)	4128
dense_25 (Dense)	(None, 2)	66

Total params: 5,474
Trainable params: 5,474
Non-trainable params: 0

The output shows the summary of the model.

```
87. model.fit(X_train, y_train, epochs=150, verbose=1)
```

Epoch 1/150
68/68 [==============================] - 0s 220us/step - loss: 0.1581 - accuracy: 0.9559
...
...
Epoch 150/150
68/68 [==============================] - 0s 161us/step - loss: 0.1087 - accuracy: 0.9559

The output shows the iteration occurring in the ANN model for training the model.

```
88. score = model.evaluate(X_train, y_train)
89. print("\n Training Accuracy:", score[1])
90. score = model.evaluate(X_test, y_test)
91. print("\n Testing Accuracy:", score[1])
```

68/68 [==============================] - 0s 73us/step

Training Accuracy: 0.9558823704719543

30/30 [==============================] - 0s 67us/step

Testing Accuracy: 0.8666666746139526

The output shows the accuracy on training and testing dataset.

```
92. #again splitting the data into X and y variable where y is the target variable.
93. X = data.drop(['Serial No.','Chance of Admit '],axis=1)
94. y = data['Chance of Admit ']

95. #splitting the data into test and train set.
96. X_train,X_test,y_train,y_test=train_test_split(X,y,test_size=0.20,random_state=0)

97. #Logistic Regression
98. model = LogisticRegression(random_state=1)
99. model.fit(X_train, y_train)
100.pred_log = model.predict(X_test)
101.print(confusion_matrix(y_test,pred_log))
102.print(classification_report(y_test,pred_log))
103.print(accuracy_score(y_test,pred_log))
```

[[11 2]
[2 5]]

	Precision	recall	f1-score	support
0.0	0.85	0.85	0.85	13
1.0	0.71	0.71	0.71	7
Accuracy			0.80	20
Macro avg	0.78	0.78	0.78	20
Weighted avg	0.80	0.80	0.80	20

0.8

The output shows the logistic regression has an accuracy of 80%.

```
104.#Decision Tree classifier
105.model2 = DecisionTreeClassifier(random_state=1)
106.model2.fit(X_train, y_train)
107.pred_DT = model2.predict(X_test)
108.print(confusion_matrix(y_test,pred_DT))
109.print(classification_report(y_test,pred_DT))
110.print(accuracy_score(y_test,pred_DT))
```
[[10 3]

[1 6]]

	Precision	recall	f1-score	support
0.0	0.91	0.77	0.83	13
1.0	0.67	0.86	0.75	7
Accuracy			0.80	20
Macro avg	0.79	0.81	0.79	20
Weighted avg	0.82	0.80	0.80	20

0.8

The output shows the decision tree classifier has an accuracy of 80%.

```
111.model3 = RandomForestClassifier(random_state=1)
112.model3.fit(X_train, y_train)
113.pred_RF = model3.predict(X_test)
114.print(confusion_matrix(y_test,pred_RF))
115.print(classification_report(y_test,pred_RF))
116.print(accuracy_score(y_test,pred_RF))
```

[[12 1]

[2 5]]

	Precision	recall	f1-score	support
0.0	0.86	0.92	0.89	13
1.0	0.83	0.71	0.77	7
Accuracy			0.85	20
Macro avg	0.85	0.82	0.83	20
Weighted avg	0.85	0.85	0.85	20

0.85

The output shows the random forest classifier has an accuracy of 85%.

117. #Sentimental analysis of the letter of recommendation to give ratings.

```
118.#Importing relevant libraries for text analysis
119.import pandas as pd
120.import nltk
121.nltk.download('vader_lexicon')
122.from nltk.sentiment.vader import SentimentIntensityAnalyzer
123.import nltk
124.from nltk.corpus import stopwords
125.from nltk.tokenize import word_tokenize, sent_tokenize
```

```
126.#Positive recommendation
127.text = "It is with much enthusiasm that I recommend Joe Bloom for inclusion in the College
```
Scholars Program at the University of Tennessee. I was Joe's instructor for multiple English classes during his four years at Morristown-Hamblen High School, including AP English his junior year. In our classes, Joe displayed a level of creativity, wit, and analytical thought that is quite rare among high school students. His writing and research skills are truly phenomenal – for his major essay project in AP English, he researched and wrote a remarkable study of visual imagery in the works of Edgar Allan Poe. Joe's wide-ranging intellect is such that he would be bored by a most freshman- and sophomore-level Liberal Arts courses. He is ready to assume and excel in upper-division classwork and possesses the self-motivation to successfully create and execute an independent course of honours study. Joe's academic strengths are complemented by his demonstrated leadership skills – he was our band's drum major for two years and served as Vice President of the Student Council and Editor of our high school yearbook. He is also very active in his church and in the Sierra Student Coalition. Please let me know if I can provide any more information to strengthen Joe's candidacy for the College Scholars Program. He has a very special spark, and I trust he will go far in making our world a better place."

```
128.stopWords = set(stopwords.words("english"))
129.words = word_tokenize(text)
130.#text summarization
131.freqTable = dict()
132.for word in words:
133.    word = word.lower()
134.    if word in stopWords:
135.        continue
136.    if word in freqTable:
137.        freqTable[word] += 1
138.    else:
139.        freqTable[word] = 1
140.sentences = sent_tokenize(text)
141.sentenceValue = dict()
142.for sentence in sentences:
143.    for word, freq in freqTable.items():
144.        if word in sentence.lower():
145.            if sentence in sentenceValue:
146.                sentenceValue[sentence] += freq
147.            else:
148.                sentenceValue[sentence] = freq
149.sumValues = 0
150.for sentence in sentenceValue:
151.    sumValues += sentenceValue[sentence]
152.
153.# Average value of a sentence from the original text
154.
155.average = int(sumValues / len(sentenceValue))
156.
157.#storing sentences into our summary.
158.summary = ''
159.for sentence in sentences:
160.    if (sentence in sentenceValue) and (sentenceValue[sentence] > (1.2 * average)):
161.        summary += " " + sentence
162.print(summary)
```

> I was Joe's instructor for multiple English classes during his four years at Morristown-Hamblen High School, including AP English his junior year. His writing and research skills are truly phenomenal – for his major essay project in AP English, he researched and wrote a remarkable study of visual imagery in the works of Edgar Allan Poe. Joe's academic strengths are complemented by his demonstrated leadership skills – he was our band's drum major for two years and served as Vice President of the Student Council and Editor of our high school yearbook.

The output shows the summarized text of the input letter.

```
163.sia = SentimentIntensityAnalyzer()
164.text_Sia = ["I was Joe's instructor for multiple English classes during his four years at
```
Morristown-Hamblen High School, including AP English his junior year. His writing and research skills are truly phenomenal – for his major essay project in AP English, he researched and wrote a remarkable study of visual imagery in the works of Edgar Allan Poe. Joe's academic strengths are complemented by his demonstrated leadership skills – he was our band's

drum major for two years and served as Vice President of the Student Council and Editor of our high school yearbook."]

```
165.for sentence in text_Sia:
166.   print(sentence)
167.   ss = sia.polarity_scores(sentence)
168.   for k in ss:
169.      print('{0}: {1}, '.format(k, ss[k]), end='')
170.   print()
```

Neg: 0.0,
Neu: 0.902,
Pos: 0.098,
Compound: 0.8481,

The output shows the polarity of the entered text.

```
171.#Face verification for the entrance test
```

```
172.#importing the relevant package to check the images are similar or not which will help to verify
      the candidate sitting in from of webcam.
173.Visit the link for package details. -  https://pypi.org/project/deepface/
```

```
174.#importing the libraries.
175.from deepface import DeepFace
              Using TensorFlow backend.
```

```
176.import matplotlib.pyplot as plt
177.import matplotlib.image as mpimg
```

```
178.#you can import any two photos of face to check the module is working.
```

```
179.Display the images which are being checked.
180.plt.imshow(mpimg.imread(r"C:\Users\img1.jpg"))
181.plt.imshow(mpimg.imread(r"C:\Users \img10.jpg"))
```

```
182.#calling the function.
183.result2 = DeepFace.verify(r"C:\Users \img10.jpg",r"C:\Users \img1.jpg")
184. print(result2)
```

{'verified': True, 'distance': 0.3363303542137146, 'max_threshold_to_verify': 0.4, 'model': 'VGG-Face', 'similarity_metric': 'cosine'}

The output shows that both images are verified and true.

APPENDIX E: PYTHON CODE FOR USE CASE 5—FUNDING & LOANS

Prototyping

Fraud Prediction can be implemented using Python as shown in the code below.

```
1.  #importing all the relevant libraries needed.
2.  import pandas as pd
3.  import numpy as np
4.  import matplotlib.pyplot as plt
5.  import seaborn as sns
6.  import sklearn
7.  from sklearn.linear_model import LogisticRegression
8.  from sklearn import tree
9.  from sklearn.tree import DecisionTreeClassifier
10. from sklearn.ensemble import RandomForestClassifier
11. from sklearn.model_selection import train_test_split
12. from xgboost import XGBClassifier
13. from xgboost import plot_importance
14. from sklearn.metrics import classification_report, confusion_matrix, accuracy_score
15. from sklearn.preprocessing import LabelEncoder

16. #reading the dataset file.
17. df = pd.read_csv(r"C:\Users\train.xlsx")
18. df.head(2)
```

Loan_ID	Age	Gender	Married	Dependents	...	Credit_History	Property_Area	Loan_Status
LP001002	30	Male	No	0	...	1	Urban	Y
LP001003	50	Male	Yes	1	...	1	Rural	N
LP001005	34	Male	Yes	0	...	1	Urban	Y

The output shows the dataset which is imported from the file. It has 23 attributes.

```
19. df.columns
```

Index (['Loan_ID', 'Age', 'Gender', 'Married', 'Dependents', 'Education',
        'Housing', 'Self_Employed', 'Credit card', 'Existing client',
        'ApplicantIncome', 'CoapplicantIncome', 'Payment delay',
        'Avg_house_spend', 'Existing Loan', 'Avg_travel_spend',
        'Present Account balance', 'Minimum balance ', 'LoanAmount',
        'Loan_Amount_Term', 'Credit_History', 'Property_Area', 'Loan_Status'],
        dtype='object')

The Output shows all the features that are in the dataset.

R. Gupta and S. K. Pal, *Introduction to Algorithmic Government*, https://doi.org/10.1007/978-981-16-0282-5

```
20.  #Exploratory Data Analysis

21.  categorical = ['Gender', 'Married', 'Dependents', 'Education',
     'Self_Employed','Housing','Existing client','Payment delay','Credit
     card','Property_Area','Loan_Amount_Term','Credit_History','Existing Loan','Loan_Status']
22.  fig,axes = plt.subplots(7,2,figsize=(15,20))
23.  for idx,cat_col in enumerate(categorical):
24.      row,col = idx//2,idx%2
25.      sns.countplot(x=cat_col,data=df,hue='Loan_Status',ax=axes[row,col],palette="prism_r")
26.  plt.subplots_adjust(hspace=1)
```

The generated output shows the comparison of the categorical field with the target field i.e. Loan_Status. In data, there is 80% male in which male 2/3rd male and females have approval status. Around 65% of the applicants are married and they are more likely to be granted the loan. Most of the applicants in the data have no dependents and they are granted loan very easily. In terms of education, 80% of people are graduated and have a higher proportion of loan approval. Only 15% of people are self-employed. Majority of applicants has their own home to live and likely to have more chances of getting a loan.

The generated output shows the exploratory Data Analysis. The field existing clients has approx. equal number in of people which are new or already existing clients. There around 400 people who have no payment delay history and they are more likely granted the loan. More number of people doesn't have a credit card in the data. Majority of the people lives in a semi-urban area and they get loan approval more as compared to people in the rural and urban area. People have opted for 360 months of the term in their application and they are more likely to get it. There above 400 people who have a good credit history which makes their chances of getting loan approval very high. Around 69% of people get their loan approved form the dataset.

```
27.  numerical = ['ApplicantIncome', 'CoapplicantIncome',
     'LoanAmount','Avg_house_spend','Avg_travel_spend',
28.                'Present Account balance','Minimum balance ']
29.  for col in (numerical):
30.      sns.boxplot(df[col], orient = 'o')
31.      plt.title(col)
32.      plt.show()
```

The generated output shows the numerical data visualization using boxplot to check if the data has outliers or not. In applicant income, we can see that there are outliers which needed to be removed in the data pre-processing. This can be attributed to the income disparity in the society it can be driven by the fact that people who are graduate earn more income as compared to the non-graduated. In the present account income, we can see that there is an outlier who has such extreme values.

```
33.  df.boxplot(column='ApplicantIncome', by = 'Education')
34.  plt.suptitle("")
```

The generated output shows the boxplot confirms that in society people who are educated earn more income as compared to the non-graduate.

```
35.  #Data Pre-processing
```

```
36. #checking for the null values.
37. df.isnull().sum()
38. sns.heatmap(df.isnull(), cbar=0)
```

The generated output shows the heat map showing that dataset has null values which are needed to be removed or filled. We will be filling the null values using mean and mode for numerical and categorical categories respectively.

```
39. #for categorical data we are using the mode method to replace null values.
40. for col in categorical:
41.     df[col] = df[col].fillna(df[col].mode()[0])
```

```
42. #for numerical data we are using mean method to replace null values.
43. df['LoanAmount'].fillna(df['LoanAmount'].mean(), inplace=True)
44. df['Age'].fillna(df['Age'].mean(), inplace=True)
45. df['Present Account balance'].fillna(df['Present Account balance'].mean(), inplace=True)
46. df['Minimum balance '].fillna(df['Minimum balance '].mean(), inplace=True)
47. df['Avg_travel_spend'].fillna(df['Avg_travel_spend'].mean(), inplace=True)
48. df['ApplicantIncome'].fillna(df['ApplicantIncome'].mean(), inplace=True)
49. df['CoapplicantIncome'].fillna(df['CoapplicantIncome'].mean(), inplace=True)
50. df['Avg_house_spend'].fillna(df['Avg_house_spend'].mean(), inplace=True)
```

```
51. #Cross checking with a heat map to see is there any null value left.
52. sns.heatmap(df.isnull(), cbar=0)
```
The generated output shows that there are no null values left in the dataset.

```
53. df[df['ApplicantIncome'] > 20000].sort_values(by = 'ApplicantIncome')
```

We see that there is one loan application in which the applicant income is around 80000 and his present balance is 812033 which shows it's an extreme value so we will drop it.

```
54. df = df.drop(409)
55. #we can feed string inputs to the machine learning models so we will use label encoding.
56. from sklearn.preprocessing import LabelEncoder
57. var_mod = ['Gender', 'Married', 'Dependents', 'Education',
    'Self_Employed','Housing','Existing client', 'Payment delay', 'Credit
    card','Property_Area','Loan_Amount_Term','Credit_History','Existing Loan', 'Loan_Status']
58. le = LabelEncoder()
59. for i in var_mod:
60.     df[i] = le.fit_transform(df[i])
61. df.head(1)
```

The generated output shows that all the categorical columns have been label encoded.

```
62. plt.figure(figsize=(12,12))
63. cor = df.corr()
64. sns.heatmap(cor, annot=True, cmap=plt.cm.Reds)
65. plt.show()
```

The generated output shows the heat map showing the correlation of the features with each other.

66. #splitting the dataset into the training set and test set.
67. df=df.drop('Loan_ID', axis=1)
68. #dropping the load ID field we don't need it in in training model.
69. X = df.drop(['Loan_Status'],1)
70. y = df.Loan_Status
71. #in y, we have our target variable.

72. #using the train test split from sklearn.
73. x_train, x_cv, y_train, y_cv = train_test_split(X,y, test_size =0.3,random_state=3)
74. x_train.shape, x_cv.shape, y_train.shape, y_cv.shape
       ((429, 21), (185, 21), (429,), (185,))

The output shows the shape of training and test dataset where x_train and y_train are training dataset x_cv and y_cv is test dataset.

75. #First we will check the accuracy of models without any feature selection.
76. #Logistic regression
77. model = LogisticRegression(random_state=0)
78. model.fit(x_train, y_train)
79. pred_log = model.predict(x_cv)
80. print(confusion_matrix(y_cv, pred_log))
81. print(classification_report(y_cv, pred_log))
82. print(accuracy_score(y_cv, pred_log))

```
[[0 49]
 [1 135]]
```

	Precision	recall	f1-score	support
0	0.00	0.00	0.00	49
1	0.73	0.99	0.84	136
Accuracy			0.73	185
Macro avg	0.37	0.50	0.42	185
Weighted avg	0.54	0.73	0.62	185

0.7297297297297297

The output shows that the accuracy of the logistic regression is 72.97%

83. #Decision Tree classifier
84. model2 = DecisionTreeClassifier(random_state=0)
85. model2.fit(x_train, y_train)
86. pred_DT = model2.predict(x_cv)
87. tree.plot_tree(model2.fit(x_train, y_train))
88. accuracy_score(y_cv,pred_DT)
89. print(confusion_matrix(y_cv,pred_DT))
90. print(classification_report(y_cv,pred_DT))
91. print(accuracy_score(y_cv,pred_DT))

```
[[27 22]
 [37 99]]
```

	Precision	recall	f1-score	support
0	0.42	0.55	0.48	49
1	0.82	0.73	0.77	136
Accuracy			0.68	185
Macro avg	0.62	0.64	0.62	185
Weighted avg	0.71	0.68	0.69	185

0.6810810810810811

The output shows that the accuracy of the Decision tree classifier is 68.108%

```
92. #Random Forest classifier
93. Model3 = RandomForestClassifier(random_state=0)
94. Model3.fit(x_train, y_train)
95. pred_RF = model3.predict(x_cv)
96. model3.score(x_cv, y_cv)
97. print(confusion_matrix(y_cv,pred_RF))
98. print(classification_report(y_cv,pred_RF))
99. print(accuracy_score(y_cv,pred_RF))
```

```
[[21 28]
 [7 129]]
```

	Precision	recall	f1-score	support
0	0.75	0.43	0.55	49
1	0.82	0.95	0.88	136
Accuracy			0.81	185
Macro avg	0.79	0.69	0.71	185
Weighted avg	0.80	0.81	0.79	185

0.8108108108108109

The output shows that the accuracy of the Random Forest classifier is 81.08%

```
100.model4=XGBClassifier(random_state=0)
101.model4.fit(x_train, y_train)
102.pred_XGB = model4.predict(x_cv)
103.print(confusion_matrix(y_cv,pred_XGB))
104.print(classification_report(y_cv,pred_XGB))
105.print(accuracy_score(y_cv,pred_XGB)
            [[26 21]

            [21 116]]
```

	Precision	recall	f1-score	support
0	0.55	0.55	0.55	47

	1	0.85	0.85		0.85	137
Accuracy					0.77	184
Macro avg		0.70	0.70		0.70	184
Weighted avg		0.77	0.77		0.77	184

0.7717391304347826

The output shows that the accuracy of the XGBoost classifier is 77.17%

106. #Now we will use the XGBoost for feature selection to see that is there is any change in the accuracy of their classifiers after selecting important features from the dataset.

107. model4=XGBClassifier(random_state=0)
108. model4.fit(X,y)
109. plot_importance(model4)
110. plt.show()

The generated output shows the feature importance value of the features in the dataset, now will remove some features from the dataset and again check the accuracy of classifiers.

111. selected_features=["Age","Credit_History","Property_Area","CoapplicantIncome","LoanAmount","Minimum balance ","ApplicantIncome","Present Account balance",'Avg_travel_spend','Avg_house_spend']
112. X=X[selected_features]

113. #splitting the data into training and testing set.
114. X_train,X_test,Y_train,Y_test=train_test_split(X,y,test_size=0.25,random_state=0)

115. #logistic regression
116. model.fit(X_train,Y_train)
117. print(model.score(X_test,Y_test)*100,"%")
118. p_log = model.predict(X_test)
119. print(confusion_matrix(Y_test,p_log))
120. print(classification_report(Y_test,p_log))

```
[[8 34]
 [4 108]]
```

	Precision	recall	f1-score	support
0	0.67	0.19	0.30	42
1	0.76	0.96	0.85	112
Accuracy			0.75	154
Macro avg	0.71	0.58	0.57	154
Weighted avg	0.73	0.75	0.70	154

The output shows the accuracy of the logistic regression after feature selection is 75.32%.

121. #Decision Tree classifier
122. model2.fit(X_train,Y_train)

```
123.tree.plot_tree(model2.fit(X_train,Y_train))
124.p_DT = model2.predict(X_test)
125.print(confusion_matrix(Y_test,p_DT))
126.print(classification_report(Y_test,p_DT))
127.print(accuracy_score(Y_test,p_DT))
```

```
         [[26 16]
          [34 78]]
                  Precision    recall    f1-score    support

             0      0.43       0.62        0.51        42
             1      0.83       0.70        0.76        112

        Accuracy                          0.68        154
       Macro avg     0.63      0.66       0.63        154
    Weighted avg     0.72      0.68       0.69        154
```

0.6753246753246753

The output shows the accuracy of the Decision tree classifier after feature selection is 67.53%.

```
128.#Random forest classifier
129.Model3.fit(X_train,Y_train)
130.print(model3.score(X_test,Y_test)*100,"%")
131.p_RF = model3.predict(X_test)
132.print(confusion_matrix(Y_test,p_RF))
133.print(classification_report(Y_test,p_RF))
134.print(accuracy_score(Y_test,p_RF))
```

```
         [[23 19]
          [7 105]]
                  Precision    recall    f1-score    support

             0      0.77       0.55        0.64        42
             1      0.85       0.94        0.89        112

        Accuracy                          0.83        154
       Macro avg     0.81      0.74       0.76        154
    Weighted avg     0.82      0.83       0.82        154
```

0.8311688311688312

The output shows the accuracy of the Random forest classifier after feature selection is 83.11%.

```
135.model4.fit(X_train,Y_train)
136.p_XGB = model4.predict(X_test)
137.print(confusion_matrix(Y_test,p_XGB))
138.print(classification_report(Y_test,p_XGB))
139.print(accuracy_score(Y_test,p_XGB))
```

```
[[23 19]
 [15 97]]
```

	Precision	recall	f1-score	support
0	0.61	0.55	0.57	42
1	0.84	0.87	0.85	112
Accuracy			0.78	154
Macro avg	0.72	0.71	0.71	154
Weighted avg	0.77	0.78	0.78	154

0.7792207792207793

The output shows the accuracy of the XGBoost classifier after feature selection is 77.92%.

Appendix F: Python Code for Use Case 6—Online Reputation Management

Prototyping

Public Sentiment analysis using social media can be implemented using Python as shown in the code below.

```
1.  #Importing relevant libraries
2.  import nltk
3.  import numpy as np
4.  import random
5.  import string
6.  import bs4 as bs
7.  import urllib.request
8.  import re
9.  import requests
10. from bs4 import BeautifulSoup
11. import nltk
12. from nltk.corpus import stopwords
13. import matplotlib.pyplot as plt

14. #scraping data from mygov.in for the union budget 2019-20
15. #accessing the discussion forum through URL
16. page    =    requests.get('https://www.mygov.in/group-issue/inviting-ideas-and-suggestions-union-
    budget-2020-2021/')
17. page.content

18. # Creating a BeautifulSoup object
19. soup = BeautifulSoup(page.text, 'html.parser')
20. comments_text = ''
21. main=soup.find_all('div', class_='comment_body')
22. for comments in main:
23.     names = comments.contents[0].text
24.     comments_text += names

25. #applying tokenization on scraped data
26. from nltk.tokenize import sent_tokenize
27. tokenized_text=sent_tokenize(comments_text)

28. #translating comments in different language to English, using google translator
29. from googletrans import Translator
30. translator = Translator()
31. translations = translator.translate(tokenized_text, dest='en')
32. # max1='budget'
33. a1=[]
```

```
34. for translation in translations:
35.    a1.append(translation.text)
36. print(a1)
37. #output
```

['130 crore trees of African bread fruit can produce 200 million tonnes of protein-rich food. But for this, this article will have to be published in the media and it has to be implemented and brought down on the experimental plane. The problem of malnutrition and unemployment can be solved by planned plantation. With this, the income of farmers can also be increased manifold. When a foreign entity announces to invest in India, a central government officer from the Ministry of Commerce must be appointed as a person-in-charge to assist the foreign entity with all the government related inclusion and tax compliance procedures and advising them with all legal matters, so that the proposed investment turns into real investment on ground benefitting the society as soon as possible !!!', 'Please take efforts to make this possible !!!', '#Employment #Finance #Others #Investment Respected Prime Minister, we can make our country a fully developed country in 15 years with planned plantation. Trees and shrubs providing thousands of fruits, vegetables, greens, edible oils, grains and medicines that can grow in different climatic regions of the country by planting roads, canals, railways, and rivers, along the rivers and drains of more than necessary Can be produced. 130 crore trees of Maya bread nuts can produce 400 million tons of food grains. 130 crore trees of safau fruit, 150 million tons of edible oil, African Prime Minister, if you publish our research papers in the media, we will create water and Can solve the energy problem forever. By insulating the plates with the help of insulated plates, separating the ions from the seawater will provide potable pure water. No special energy will be used in this process. By this process, unlimited energy can also be obtained by separating hydrogen ions and hydraxyl ions from pure water. If we get the facility, we will have many types of rotic plastic honorable Pm ji\nmy suggestions for union budget 2020 are attached in pdf plz do consider itLet entrepreneurs export Agri products to Western countries in micro quantities through websites.', 'For example: entrepreneurs should be able to sell 1 kg premium turmeric to US customer through their website.', 'Currently rules for such sales are not at all clear.', 'Please help entrepreneurs for this.Please see the pdfRespected members\n#education\nMy Suggestion to Improve literacy rate in indiaENTREPRENEURSHIPMy recommendations attached.']

```
    #the output represents the translated data

38. #tokenizing words
39. str1=str(a1)
40. from nltk.tokenize import word_tokenize
41. tokenized_word=word_tokenize(str1)
42. print(tokenized_word)
43. #output
```

[['[', "'130', 'crore', 'trees', 'of', 'African', 'bread', 'fruit', 'can', 'produce', '200', 'million', 'tonnes', 'of', 'protein-rich', 'food', '.', 'But', 'for', 'this', ',', 'this', 'article', 'will', 'have', 'to', 'be', 'published', 'in', 'the', 'media', 'and', 'it', 'has', 'to', 'be', 'implemented', 'and', 'brought', 'down', 'on', 'the', 'experimental', 'plane', '.', 'The', 'problem', 'of', 'malnutrition', 'and', 'unemployment', 'can', 'be', 'solved', 'by', 'planned', 'plantation', '.', 'With', 'this', ',', 'the', 'income', 'of', 'farmers', 'can', 'also', 'be', 'increased', 'manifold', '.', 'When', 'a', 'foreign', 'entity', 'announces', 'to', 'invest', 'in', 'India', ',', 'a', 'central', 'government', 'officer', 'from', 'the', 'Ministry', 'of', 'Commerce', 'must', 'be', 'appointed', 'as', 'a', 'person-in-charge', 'to', 'assist', 'the', 'foreign', 'entity', 'with', 'all', 'the', 'government', 'related', 'inclusion', 'and', 'tax', 'compliance', 'procedures', 'and', 'advising', 'them', 'with', 'all', 'legal', 'matters', ',', 'so', 'that', 'the', 'proposed', 'investment', 'turns', 'into', 'real', 'investment', 'on', 'ground', 'benefitting', 'the', 'society', 'as', 'soon', 'as', 'possible', '!', '!', '!', "''", ',', "''", '#', 'Employment', '#', 'Finance', '#', 'Others', '#', 'Investment', 'Respected', 'Prime', 'Minister', ',', 'we', 'can', 'make', 'our', 'country', 'a', 'fully', 'developed', 'country', 'in', '15', 'years', 'with', 'planned', 'plantation', '.', 'Trees', 'and', 'shrubs', 'providing', 'thousands', 'of', 'fruits', ',', 'vegetables', ',', 'greens', ',', 'edible', 'oils', ',', 'grains', 'and', 'medicines', 'that', 'can', 'grow', 'in', 'different', 'climatic', 'regions', 'of', 'the', 'country', 'by', 'planting', 'roads', ',', 'canals', ',', 'railways', ',', 'and', 'rivers', ',', 'along', 'the', 'rivers', 'and', 'drains', 'of', 'more', 'than', 'necessary', 'Can', 'be', 'produced', '.', '130', 'crore', 'trees', 'of', 'Maya', 'bread', 'nuts', 'can', 'produce', '400', 'million', 'tons', 'of', 'food', 'grains', '.', '130', 'crore', 'trees', 'of', 'safau', 'fruit', '.', '150', 'million', 'tons', 'of', 'edible', 'oil', ',', 'African', 'Prime', 'Minister', ',', 'if', 'you', 'publish', 'our', 'research', 'papers', 'in', 'the', 'media', '.', 'we', 'will', 'create', 'water', 'and', 'Can', 'solve', 'the', 'energy', 'problem', 'forever', '.', 'By', 'insulating', 'the', 'plates', 'with', 'the', 'help', 'of', 'insulated', 'plates', ',', 'separating', 'the', 'ions', 'from', 'the', 'seawater', 'will', 'provide', 'potable', 'pure', 'water', '.', 'No', 'special', 'energy', 'will', 'be', 'used', 'in', 'this', 'process', '.', 'By', 'this', 'process', ',', 'unlimited', 'energy', 'can', 'also', 'be', 'obtained', 'by', 'separating', 'hydrogen', 'ions', 'and', 'hydroxyl', 'ions', 'from', 'pure', 'water', '.', 'If', 'we', 'get', 'the', 'facility', ',', 'we', 'will', 'have', 'many', 'types', 'of', 'rotic', 'plastic', 'honorable', 'Pm', 'ji\\nmy', 'suggestions', 'for', 'union', 'budget', '2020', 'are', 'attached', 'in', 'pdf', 'plz', 'do', 'consider', 'itLet', 'entrepreneurs', 'export', 'Agri', 'products', 'to', 'Western', 'countries', 'in', 'micro', 'quantities', 'through', 'websites', '.', '"""', ',', '"\'For"', 'example', ':', 'entrepreneurs', 'should', 'be', 'able', 'to', 'sell', '1', 'kg', 'premium', 'turmeric', 'to', 'US', 'customer', 'through', 'their', 'website', '.', '"""', ',', '"\'Currently"', 'rules', 'for', 'such', 'sales', 'are', 'not', 'at', 'all', 'clear', '.', '"""', ',', '"\'Please"', 'help', 'entrepreneurs', 'for', 'this.Please', 'see', 'the', 'pdfRespected', 'members\\n', '#', 'education\\nMy', 'Suggestion', 'to', 'Improve', 'literacy', 'rate', 'in', 'indiaENTREPRENEURSHIPMy', 'recommendations', 'attached', '.', '"""', ']']

#the output represents the tokenization of sentence into words

```
44. #removing stopwords
45. from nltk.corpus import stopwords
46. stop_words=set(stopwords.words("english"))
47. filtered_sent=[]
48. keymax=max1
49. for w in tokenized_word:
50.    if w not in stop_words:
51.        filtered_sent.append(w)
52. # print("Tokenized Sentence:",tokenized_word)
53. print("Filterd Sentence:",filtered_sent)
54. #output
```

Filterd Sentence: ['[', "'130"', 'crore', 'trees', 'African', 'bread', 'fruit', 'produce', '200', 'million', 'tonnes', 'protein-rich', 'food', '.', 'But', ',', 'article', 'published', 'media', 'implemented', 'brought', 'experimental', 'plane', '.', 'The', 'problem', 'malnutrition', 'unemployment', 'solved', 'planned', 'plantation', '.', 'With', ',', 'income', 'farmers', 'also', 'increased', 'manifold', '.', 'When', 'foreign', 'entity', 'announces', 'invest', 'India', ',', 'central', 'government', 'officer', 'Ministry', 'Commerce', 'must', 'appointed', 'person-in-charge', 'assist', 'foreign', 'entity', 'government', 'related', 'inclusion', 'tax', 'compliance', 'procedures', 'advising', 'legal', 'matters', ',', 'proposed', 'investment', 'turns', 'real', 'investment', 'ground', 'benefitting', 'society', 'soon', 'possible', '!', '!', '!', '"""', ',', '"\'Please"', 'take', 'efforts', 'make', 'possible', '!', '!', '!', '"""', ',', '"""', '#', 'Employment', '#', 'Finance', '#', 'Others', '#', 'Investment', 'Respected', 'Prime', 'Minister', ',', 'make', 'country', 'fully', 'developed', 'country', '15', 'years', 'planned', 'plantation', '.', 'Trees', 'shrubs', 'providing', 'thousands', 'fruits', ',', 'vegetables', ',', 'greens', ',', 'edible', 'oils', ',', 'grains', 'medicines', 'grow', 'different', 'climatic', 'regions', 'country', 'planting', 'roads', ',', 'canals', ',', 'railways', ',', 'rivers', ',', 'along', 'rivers', 'drains', 'necessary', 'Can', 'produced', '.', '130', 'crore', 'trees', 'Maya', 'bread', 'nuts', 'produce', '400', 'million', 'tons', 'food', 'grains', '.', '130', 'crore', 'trees', 'safau', 'fruit', ',', '150', 'million', 'tons', 'edible', 'oil', ',', 'African', 'Prime', 'Minister', ',', 'publish', 'research', 'papers', 'media', ',', 'create', 'water', 'Can', 'solve', 'energy', 'problem', 'forever', '.', 'By', 'insulating', 'plates', 'help', 'insulated', 'plates', ',', 'separating', 'ions', 'seawater', 'provide', 'potable', 'pure', 'water', '.', 'No', 'special', 'energy', 'used', 'process', '.', 'By', 'process', ',', 'unlimited', 'energy', 'also', 'obtained', 'separating', 'hydrogen', 'ions', 'hydraxyl', 'ions', 'pure', 'water', '.', 'If', 'get', 'facility', ',', 'many', 'types', 'rotic', 'plastic', 'honorable', 'Pm', 'ji\\nmy', 'suggestions', 'union', 'budget', '2020', 'attached', 'pdf', 'plz', 'consider', 'itLet', 'entrepreneurs', 'export', 'Agri', 'products', 'Western', 'countries', 'micro', 'quantities', 'websites', '.', "''", ',', "'For", 'example', ':', 'entrepreneurs', 'able', 'sell', '1', 'kg', 'premium', 'turmeric', 'US', 'customer', 'website', '.', "''", ',', "'Currently", 'rules', 'sales', 'clear', ',', "''", ',', "'Please", 'help', 'entrepreneurs', 'this.Please', 'see', 'pdfRespected', 'members\\n', '#', 'education\\nMy', 'Suggestion', 'Improve', 'literacy', 'rate', 'indiaENTREPRENEURSHIPMy', 'recommendations', 'attached', '.', "''", ']']

#the output removes the stop words from english

55. #applying stemming
56. from nltk.stem import PorterStemmer
57. from nltk.tokenize import sent_tokenize, word_tokenize
58. ps = PorterStemmer()
59. stemmed_words=[]
60. for w in filtered_sent:
61.   stemmed_words.append(ps.stem(w))
62. print("Stemmed Sentence:",stemmed_words)
63. #output

Stemmed Sentence: ['[', "'130", 'crore', 'tree', 'african', 'bread', 'fruit', 'produc', '200', 'million', 'tonn', 'protein-rich', 'food', '.', 'but', ',', 'articl', 'publish', 'media', 'implement', 'brought', 'experiment', 'plane', '.', 'the', 'problem', 'malnutrit', 'unemploy', 'solv', 'plan', 'plantat', '.', 'with', ',', 'incom', 'farmer', 'also', 'increas', 'manifold', '.', 'when', 'foreign', 'entiti', 'announc', 'invest', 'india', ',', 'central', 'govern', 'offic', 'ministri', 'commerc', 'must', 'appoint', 'person-in-charg', 'assist', 'foreign', 'entiti', 'govern', 'relat', 'inclus', 'tax', 'complianc', 'procedur', 'advis', 'legal', 'matter', ',', 'propos', 'invest', 'turn', 'real', 'invest', 'ground', 'benefit', 'societi', 'soon', 'possibl', '!', '!', '!', "''", ',', "''", "'pleas", 'take', 'effort', 'make', 'possibl', '!', '!', '!', "''", ',', "''", '#', 'employ', '#', 'financ', '#', 'other', '#', 'invest', 'respect', 'prime', 'minist', ',', 'make', 'countri', 'fulli', 'develop', 'countri', '15', 'year', 'plan', 'plantat', '.', 'tree', 'shrub', 'provid', 'thousand', 'fruit', ',', 'veget', ',', 'green', ',', 'edibl', 'oil', ',', 'grain', 'medicin', 'grow', 'differ', 'climat', 'region', 'countri', 'plant', 'road', ',', 'canal', ',', 'railway', ',', 'river', ',', 'along', 'river', 'drain', 'necessari', 'can', 'produc', '.', '130', 'crore', 'tree', 'maya', 'bread', 'nut', 'produc', '400', 'million', 'ton', 'food', 'grain', '.', '130', 'crore', 'tree', 'safau', 'fruit', ',', '150', 'million', 'ton', 'edibl', 'oil', ',', 'african', 'prime', 'minist', '.', 'publish', 'research', 'paper', 'media', ',', 'creat', 'water', 'can', 'solv', 'energi', 'problem', 'forev', '.', 'By', 'insul', 'plate', 'help', 'insul', 'plate', '.', 'separ', 'ion', 'seawat', 'provid', 'potabl', 'pure', 'water', '.', 'No', 'special', 'energi', 'use', 'process', '.', 'By', 'process', ',', 'unlimit', 'energi', 'also', 'obtain', 'separ', 'hydrogen', 'ion', 'hydraxyl', 'ion', 'pure', 'water', '.', 'If', 'get', 'facil', ',', 'mani', 'type', 'rotic', 'plastic', 'honor', 'Pm', 'ji\\nmi', 'suggest', 'union', 'budget', '2020', 'attach', 'pdf', 'plz', 'consid', 'itlet', 'entrepreneur', 'export', 'agri', 'product', 'western', 'countri', 'micro', 'quantiti', 'websit', '.', "''", ',', "'for", 'exampl', ':', 'entrepreneur', 'abl', 'sell', '1', 'kg', 'premium', 'turmer', 'US', 'custom', 'websit', '.', "''", ',', "'current", 'rule', 'sale', 'clear', ',', "''", ',', "'pleas", 'help', 'entrepreneur', 'this.pleas', 'see', 'pdfrespect', 'members\\n', '#', 'education\\nmi', 'suggest', 'improv', 'literaci', 'rate', 'indiaentrepreneurshipmi', 'recommend', 'attach', '.', "''", ']']

#the output represents the stemmed words.

64. #removing numbers and converting to lowercase
65. words=[word for word in stemmed_words if word.isalpha()]
66. a2=[x.lower() for x in words]
67. print(a2)
68. #output

['crore', 'tree', 'african', 'bread', 'fruit', 'produc', 'million', 'tonn', 'food', 'but', 'articl', 'publish', 'media', 'implement', 'brought', 'experiment', 'plane', 'the', 'problem', 'malnutrit', 'unemploy', 'solv', 'plan', 'plantat', 'with', 'incom', 'farmer', 'also', 'increas', 'manifold', 'when', 'foreign', 'entiti', 'announc', 'invest', 'india', 'central', 'govern', 'offic', 'ministri', 'commerc', 'must', 'appoint', 'assist', 'foreign', 'entiti', 'govern', 'relat', 'inclus', 'tax', 'complianc', 'procedur', 'advis', 'legal', 'matter', 'propos', 'invest', 'turn', 'real', 'invest', 'ground', 'benefit', 'societi', 'soon', 'possibl', 'take', 'effort', 'make', 'possibl', 'employ', 'financ', 'other', 'invest', 'respect', 'prime', 'minist', 'make', 'countri', 'fulli', 'develop', 'countri', 'year', 'plan', 'plantat', 'tree', 'shrub', 'provid', 'thousand', 'fruit', 'veget', 'green', 'edibl', 'oil', 'grain', 'medicin', 'grow', 'differ', 'climat', 'region', 'countri', 'plant', 'road', 'canal', 'railway', 'river', 'along', 'river', 'drain', 'necessari', 'can', 'produc', 'crore', 'tree', 'maya', 'bread', 'nut', 'produc', 'million', 'ton', 'food', 'grain', 'crore', 'tree', 'safau', 'fruit', 'million', 'ton', 'edibl', 'oil', 'african', 'prime', 'minist', 'publish', 'research', 'paper', 'media', 'creat', 'water', 'can', 'solv', 'energi', 'problem', 'forev', 'by', 'insul', 'plate', 'help', 'insul', 'plate', 'separ', 'ion', 'seawat', 'provid', 'potabl', 'pure', 'water', 'no', 'special', 'energi', 'use', 'process', 'by', 'process', 'unlimit', 'energi', 'also', 'obtain', 'separ', 'hydrogen', 'ion', 'hydraxyl', 'ion', 'pure', 'water', 'if', 'get', 'facil', 'mani', 'type', 'rotic', 'plastic', 'honor', 'pm', 'suggest', 'union', 'budget', 'attach', 'pdf', 'plz', 'consid', 'itlet', 'entrepreneur', 'export', 'agri', 'product', 'western', 'countri', 'micro', 'quantiti', 'websit', 'exampl', 'entrepreneur', 'abl', 'sell', 'kg', 'premium', 'turmer', 'us', 'custom', 'websit', 'rule', 'sale', 'clear', 'help', 'entrepreneur', 'see', 'pdfrespect', 'suggest', 'improv', 'literaci', 'rate', 'indiaentrepreneurshipmi', 'recommend', 'attach']

#output represents removal of numbers and conversion to lower case character.

```
69.  #print word with max frequency
70.  from collections import Counter
71.  a2.remove('tree')
72.  counts = Counter(a2)
73.  print(counts)
74.  #ouput
```

Counter({'invest': 4, 'countri': 4, 'crore': 3, 'fruit': 3, 'produc': 3, 'million': 3, 'tree': 3, 'water': 3, 'energi': 3, 'ion': 3, 'entrepreneur': 3, 'african': 2, 'bread': 2, 'food': 2, 'publish': 2, 'media': 2, 'problem': 2, 'solv': 2, 'plan': 2, 'plantat': 2, 'also': 2, 'foreign': 2, 'entiti': 2, 'govern': 2, 'possibl': 2, 'make': 2, 'prime': 2, 'minist': 2, 'provid': 2, 'edibl': 2, 'oil': 2, 'grain': 2, 'river': 2, 'can': 2, 'ton': 2, 'by': 2, 'insul': 2, 'plate': 2, 'help': 2, 'separ': 2, 'pure': 2, 'process': 2, 'suggest': 2, 'attach': 2, 'websit': 2, 'articl': 1, 'implement': 1, 'brought': 1, 'experiment': 1, 'plane': 1, 'the': 1, 'malnutrit': 1, 'unemploy': 1, 'with': 1, 'incom': 1, 'farmer': 1, 'increas': 1, 'manifold': 1, 'when': 1, 'announc': 1, 'india': 1, 'central': 1, 'offic': 1, 'ministri': 1, 'commerc': 1, 'must': 1, 'appoint': 1, 'assist': 1, 'relat': 1, 'inclus': 1, 'tax': 1, 'complianc': 1, 'procedur': 1, 'advis': 1, 'legal': 1, 'matter': 1, 'propos': 1, 'turn': 1, 'real': 1, 'ground': 1, 'benefit': 1, 'societi': 1, 'soon': 1, 'take': 1, 'effort': 1, 'employ': 1, 'financ': 1, 'other': 1, 'respect': 1, 'fulli': 1, 'develop': 1, 'year': 1, 'shrub': 1, 'thousand': 1, 'veget': 1, 'green': 1, 'medicin': 1, 'grow': 1, 'differ': 1, 'climat': 1, 'region': 1, 'plant': 1, 'road': 1, 'canal': 1, 'railway': 1, 'along': 1, 'drain': 1, 'necessari': 1, 'maya': 1, 'nut': 1, 'safau': 1, 'research': 1, 'paper': 1, 'creat': 1, 'forev': 1, 'seawat': 1, 'potabl': 1, 'no': 1, 'special': 1, 'use': 1, 'unlimit': 1, 'obtain': 1, 'hydrogen': 1, 'hydraxyl': 1, 'if': 1, 'get': 1, 'facil': 1, 'mani': 1, 'type': 1, 'rotic': 1, 'plastic': 1, 'honor': 1, 'pm': 1, 'union': 1, 'budget': 1, 'pdf': 1, 'plz': 1, 'consid': 1, 'itlet': 1, 'export': 1, 'agri': 1, 'product': 1, 'western': 1, 'micro': 1, 'quantiti': 1, 'exampl': 1, 'abl': 1, 'sell': 1, 'kg': 1, 'premium': 1, 'turmer': 1, 'us': 1, 'custom': 1, 'rule': 1, 'sale': 1, 'clear': 1, 'see': 1, 'pdfrespect': 1, 'improv': 1, 'literaci': 1, 'rate': 1, 'indiaentrepreneurshipmi': 1, 'recommend': 1})

```
#the output represents frequency of words.

75. Keymax = max(counts, key=counts.get)
76. print(Keymax)
77. #ouput
```

invest

```
#output gives word with maximum frequency

78. #Import the necessary libraries
79. from tweepy.streaming import StreamListener
80. from tweepy import OAuthHandler
81. from tweepy import Stream
82. import tweepy
83. import json
84. import time
85. import pandas as pd
86. import preprocessor as p
87. from textblob import TextBlob, Word
88. from sklearn.externals import joblib
89. from gensim.parsing.preprocessing import remove_stopwords
90. #user credentials to access twitter API
91. access_token = '1278003838180421632-pRmvo6gkQDC65EaoH2UfUIngozjfJe'
92. access_secret = 'WQOEZiJiEcK2PTwBSlLaNodMFvyY0emahbwvEjlu6sKPF'
93. consumer_key = 'ek5otqDgVUUACYOk2WZ7SOmDK'
94. consumer_secret = 'CfyaZsTBa2PA9DLLyaeuzOLvuiAw2edLkwzZYKlWkeB1AUYmxk'
95. auth = OAuthHandler(consumer_key, consumer_secret)
96. auth.set_access_token(access_token, access_secret)
97. api = tweepy.API(auth, wait_on_rate_limit=True, wait_on_rate_limit_notify=True)
98. #search for query on twitter , word with max frequency
99. searchquery = Keymax
100.users =tweepy.Cursor(api.search,q=searchquery).items()
101.count = 0
102.start = 0
103.errorCount=0
104.waitquery = 100
105.waittime = 2.0
106.total_number = 1000
107.justincase = 1
108.text = [0] * total_number
109.secondcount = 0
110.idvalues = [1] * total_number
111.#save the data in csv file
112.while secondcount < total_number:
113.    try:
114.        user = next(users)
115.        count += 1
116.        if (count%waitquery == 0):
117.            time.sleep(waittime)
118.    except tweepy.TweepError:
```

```
119.      print ("sleeping....")
120.      time.sleep(60*justincase)
121.      user = next(users)
122.    except StopIteration:
123.      break
124.    try:
125.        text_value = user._json['text']
126.        language = user._json['lang']
127.      if "RT" not in text_value:
128.          if language == "en":
129.              text[secondcount] = text_value
130.              secondcount = secondcount + 1
131.    except UnicodeEncodeError:
132.        errorCount += 1
133.        print ("UnicodeEncodeError,errorCount ="+str(errorCount))
134.print("Creating dataframe:")
135.d = {"text": text, "id": idvalues}
136.df = pd.DataFrame(data = d)
137.df.to_csv('upset.csv', header=True, index=False, encoding='utf-8')
138.print ("completed")
139.#output

     Creating dataframe:
     completed

140.train_df = pd.read_csv('upset.csv')
141.train_df.count()
142.#output

     text    1000
     id      1000
     dtype: int64

143.#dropping duplicates and null values
144.train_df = train_df.dropna()
145.train_df = train_df.drop_duplicates()
146.train_df.head(10)
147.#output
```

	text	id
0	and whoever that dumb bitch @divahmoon is talk...	1
1	i love how confused aa twt is rn this is exact...	1
2	#Foxconn\n#Taiwanese Foxconn\n\nApple iPhone m...	1
3	If you had lots of money what would you do wit...	1
4	@quarantinebee Want to invest more in police t...	1
5	@boy_geezer @2cTwister Invest in air instead h...	1
6	Invest in ya kids man give that head start not...	1
7	@Tobygreen4040 @DanScavino You are welcome!! A...	1
8	@c_chiurayi @FaraiZaba ya True the TOURISM sec...	1
9	Apple's Contract Manufacturer Foxconn To Inves...	1

```
     #the output shows dataframe dropping duplicates and null values

148.#preprocessing text
```

```
149.def preprocess_tweet(row):
150.    text = row['text']
151.    text = p.clean(text)
152.    return text
153.train_df['text'] = train_df.apply(preprocess_tweet, axis=1)
154.train_df.head(10)
155.#output
```

	text	id
0	and whoever that dumb bitch is talkin about im...	1
1	i love how confused aa twt is rn this is exact...	1
2	FoxconnApple iPhone maker Foxconn a Taiwanese ...	1
3	If you had lots of money what would you do wit...	1
4	Want to invest more in police to retrain them....	1
5	Invest in air instead	1
6	Invest in ya kids man give that head start not...	1
7	You are welcome!! And you can deposit all the ...	1
8	ya True the TOURISM sector needs to invest in ...	1
9	Apple's Contract Manufacturer Foxconn To Inves...	1

#the ouput shows the text after preprocessing.

```
156.#removing stop words
157.def stopword_removal(row):
158.    text = row['text']
159.    text = remove_stopwords(text)
160.    return text
161.train_df['text'] = train_df.apply(stopword_removal, axis=1)
162.train_df['text'] = train_df['text'].str.lower().str.replace('[^\w\s]',' ').str.replace('\s\s+', ' ')
163.train_df.head(10)
164.#output
```

	text	id
0	dumb bitch talkin im gonna send trucks yge inv...	1
1	love confused aa twt rn exactly going for. im ...	1
2	FoxconnApple iPhone maker Foxconn Taiwanese co...	1
3	If lots money it? Visit bf invest sticker shop I	1
4	Want invest police retrain them. Nothing chang...	1

#the output depicts the removal of stopwords

```
165.#checking polarity of tweets and create a new column for polarity
166.sample_reviews = train_df.copy()
167.def detect_polarity(text):
168.    return TextBlob(text).sentiment.polarity
169.sample_reviews['polarity'] = sample_reviews.text.apply(detect_polarity)
170.sample_reviews.head(10)
171.#output
```

	text	id	polarity
0	dumb bitch talkin im gonna send trucks yge inv...	1	-0.062500
1	love confused aa twt rn exactly going for im g...	1	0.116667
2	foxconnapple iphone maker foxconn taiwanese co...	1	0.000000
3	if lots money it visit bf invest sticker shop i	1	0.000000

```
4       want invest police retrain them nothing change...    1     0.000000
5       invest air instead                                   1     0.000000
6       invest ya kids man head start nothings wrong         1     -0.500000
7       you welcome and deposit money youve trumps ama...    1          0.700000
8       ya true tourism sector needs invest reviving i...    1     0.350000
9       apple s contract manufacturer foxconn to inves...    1     0.136364
```

#the output shows the polarity of tweets

```
172.#classify sentiments and create a column for sentiments
173.def detect_sentiment(text):
174.    analysis = TextBlob(text)
175.    if analysis.sentiment.polarity > 0:
176.        return 'positive'
177.    elif analysis.sentiment.polarity == 0:
178.        return 'neutral'
179.    else:
180.        return 'negative'
181.sample_reviews['sentiments'] = sample_reviews.text.apply(detect_sentiment)
182.sample_reviews.head()
183.#output
```

```
    text    id                                                      polarity  sentiments
0       dumb bitch talkin im gonna send trucks yge inv...    1      -0.062500 negative
1       love confused aa twt rn exactly going for im g...    1      0.116667  positive
2       foxconnapple iphone maker foxconn taiwanese co...1        0.000000  neutral
3       if lots money it visit bf invest sticker shop i      1          0.000000  neutral
4       want invest police retrain them nothing change...    1      0.000000  neutral
```

#the output shows the sentiments of the tweets

```
184.#percentage of positive negative and neutral tweets
185.ptweets=0
186.ntweets=0
187.for i in range(len(sample_reviews)) :
188.    if i==754 or i==990:
189.        continue
190.    if (sample_reviews.loc[i, "sentiments"]=="positive"):
191.        ptweets+=1
192.    if(sample_reviews.loc[i, "sentiments"]=="negative"):
193.        ntweets+=1
194.print("Positive tweets percentage: {} %".format(100*(ptweets)/len(sample_reviews)))
195.print("Negative tweets percentage: {} %".format(100*(ntweets)/len(sample_reviews)))
196.check = len(sample_reviews) - ntweets- ptweets
197.print("Neutral tweets percentage: {} %".format(100*(check/len(sample_reviews))))
198.#output
```

```
Positive tweets percentage: 37.07414829659319 %
Negative tweets percentage: 15.130260521042084 %
Neutral tweets percentage: 47.795591182364724 %
```

#percentage of sentiment of tweets

199.#visualizing results

```
200.def percentage(part,whole):
201.    return 100*float(part)/float(whole)
202.positive = percentage(ptweets,(ptweets + ntweets + check))
203.negative = percentage(ntweets,(ptweets + ntweets + check))
204.neutral = percentage(check,(ptweets + ntweets + check))
205.positive = format(positive,'.2f')
206.negative = format(negative,'.2f')
207.neutral = format(neutral,'.2f')
208.
209.labels = ['Positive ['+str(positive)+'%]', 'Negative ['+str(negative)+'%]',
210.'Neutral ['+str(neutral)+'%]']
211.sizes = [positive, negative, neutral]
212.colors = ['blue','red','violet']
213.patches, texts = plt.pie(sizes, colors=colors, startangle=90)
214.plt.legend(patches,labels,loc="best")
215.plt.title("Sentiment Analysis ")
216.plt.axis('equal')
217.plt.tight_layout()
218.plt.show()
    #generated output shows distribution of sentiments
```

Bibliography

Abiteboul, S., & Dowek, G. (2020). *The age of algorithms*. Cambridge University Press.

AI Now. (2018). *Litigating algorithms: Challenging government use of algorithmic decision systems*. New York: AI Now Institute.

Badia, A. (2019). *The information manifold: Why computers can't solve algorithmic bias and fake news*. MIT Press.

Baer, T. (2019). *Understand, manage, and prevent algorithmic bias: A guide for business users and data scientists*. Apress.

Batarseh, F. A., & Yang, R. (Eds.). (2017). *Federal data science: Transforming government and agricultural policy using artificial intelligence*. Academic Press.

Christian, B., & Griffiths, T. (2016). *Algorithms to live by: The computer science of human decisions*. Macmillan.

Cummings, M. L. (2004). Automation bias in intelligent time critical decision support systems. *AIAA Intelligent Systems Technical Conference*. https://doi.org/10.2514/6.2004-6313.

Dietvorst, B. J., Simmons, J. P., & Massey, C. (2016). Overcoming algorithm aversion: People will use imperfect algorithms if they can (even slightly) modify them. *Management Science, 64*(3), 1155–1170.

Dressel, J., & Farid, H. (2018). The accuracy, fairness, and limits of predicting recidivism. *Science Advances, 4*, 1–5.

Ebers, M. (2020). *Algorithmic governance and governance of algorithms: Legal and ethical challenges*. Springer Nature.

Ebers, M., & Navas, S. (Eds.). (2020). *Algorithms and law*. Cambridge University Press.

Edwards, E., & Lees, F. P. (Eds.). (1974). *The human operator in process control*. London: Taylor and Francis.

Endsley, M. R. (2017). From here to autonomy: Lessons learned from human–automation research. *Human Factors, 59*(1), 5–27.

Gamito, M. C., & Ebers, M. (2021). Algorithmic governance and governance of algorithms: An introduction. In *Algorithmic governance and governance of algorithms* (pp. 1–22). Cham: Springer.

Gupta, R., & Muttoo, S. K. (2016). Internet traffic surveillance & network monitoring in India: Case Study of NETRA. *Netw. Protoc. Algorithms, 8*(4), 1–28.

Gupta, R., Muttoo, S. K., & Pal, S. K. (2016a). BAT algorithm for improving fuzzy c-means clustering for location allocation of rural kiosks in developing countries under e-governance. *Egyptian Computer Society Journal, 40*(2), 77–86.

Gupta, R., Muttoo, S. K., & Pal, S. K. (2016b). Binary division fuzzy c-means clustering and particle swarm optimization based efficient intrusion detection for e-governance systems. *International Review on Computers and Software, 11*(8), 672–681.

Gupta, R., Muttoo, S. K., & Pal, S. K. (2016c, September). Design & analysis of clustering based intrusion detection schemes for e-governance. In *The international symposium on intelligent systems technologies and applications* (pp. 461–471). Cham: Springer.

Gupta, R., Muttoo, S. K., & Pal, S. K. (2017a). Fuzzy c-means clustering and particle swarm optimization based scheme for common service center location allocation. *Applied Intelligence, 47*(3), 624–643.

Gupta, R., Muttoo, S. K., & Pal, S. K. (2017b). Web mining and analytics for improving e-government services in India. In *Web usage mining techniques and applications across industries* (pp. 223–247). IGI Global.

Gupta, R., Muttoo, S. K., & Pal, S. K. (2017c). *E-governance in emerging economy: Development et assessment*. Scholars World a division of Astral International Pvt. Limited.

Gupta, R., Muttoo, S. K., & Pal, S. K. (2017d, March). Development of e-governance in an emerging economy like India: Assessment and way ahead for key components. In *Proceedings of the 10th International Conference on Theory and Practice of Electronic Governance* (pp. 613–616).

Gupta, R., Muttoo, S. K., & Pal, S. K. (2017e, March). The need of a development assessment index for e-governance in India. In *Proceedings of the 10th International Conference on Theory and Practice of Electronic Governance* (pp. 414–422).

Gupta, R., Muttoo, S. K., & Pal, S. K. (2019). Meta-Heuristic algorithms to improve fuzzy c-means and k-means clustering for location allocation of tele-centers under e-governance in developing nations. *International Journal of Fuzzy Logic and Intelligent Systems, 19*(4), 290–298.

Gupta, R., Muttoo, S. K., & Pal, S. K. (2020). Regional e-governance development index for developing nations. *Digital Government: Research and Practice, 1*(3), 1–26.

Gupta, R., Pal, S. K., & Muttoo, S. K. (2020). Data analytics for better branding of e-governance and e-business systems: Case of "DIGITAl India" campaign. In *Leveraging digital innovation for governance, public administration, and citizen services: Emerging research and opportunities* (pp. 51–78). IGI Global.

Hatvany, J., & Guedj, R. A. (1982). Man-machine interaction in computer-aided design systems. In *Proceedings IFAC/IFIP/IFORS/IEA Conference Analysis, design and evaluation of man-machine systems*. Oxford: Pergamon Press.

Hosanagar, K. (2020). *A human's guide to machine intelligence: How algorithms are shaping our lives and how we can stay in control*. Penguin Books.

Johannsen, G. (1982, September). Man-machine systems: Introduction and background. In *Proceedings of IFAC/IFIP/IFORS/IEA Conference on Analysis, Design and Evaluation of Man-Machine Systems*, Baden-Baden. Oxford: Pergamon Press.

Kalpokas, I. (2019). *Algorithmic governance: Politics and law in the post-human era*. Springer Nature.

Kearns, M., & Roth, A. (2019). *The ethical algorithm: The science of socially aware algorithm design*. Oxford University Press.

Leinberg, J., Lakkaraju, H., Leskovec, J., Ludwig, J., & Mullainathan, S. (2018). Human decisions and machine predictions. *Quarterly Journal of Economics, 2018*, 237–293.

Maclaurin, J., Liddicoat, J., Gavighan, C., Knott, A., & Zerilli, J. (2019). *Government Use of Artificial Intelligence in New Zealand*.

Margulies, F., & Zemanek, H. (1982). Man's role in man-machine systems. In *Proceedings IFAC/IFIP/IFORS/IEA Conference Analysis, Design and Evaluation of Man-Machine Systems*. Oxford: Pergamon Press.

Newell, A., & Simon, H. A. (1972). *Human problem solving*. Englewood-Cliffs, NJ: Prentice Hall.

Osoba, O. A., & Welser IV, W. (2017). *An intelligence in our image: The risks of bias and errors in artificial intelligence*. Rand Corporation.

Pal, S. K. (2019). Changing technological trends for E-governance. In *E-governance in India* (pp. 79–105). Singapore: Palgrave Macmillan.

Parasuraman, R., & Manzey, D. H. (2010). Complacency and bias in human use of automation: An attentional integration. *Human Factors, 52*(3), 381–410.

Peeters, R., & Schuilenburg, M. (2018). Machine justice: Governing security through the bureaucracy of algorithms. *Information Polity, 23*(3), 267–280.

Pohl, J. (2008). Cognitive elements of human decision making. In G. Phillips-Wren, N. Ichalkaranje, & L. C. Jain (Eds.), *Intelligent decision making: An AI-based approach* (pp. 41–76). Berlin: Springer.

Schnoll, H. J. (2015). *E-government: information, technology, and transformation: Information, technology, and transformation.* Routledge.

Schultze, U., Aanestad, M., Mähring, M., Østerlund, C., & Riemer, K. (Eds.). (2018, December 11–12,). *Living with Monsters? Social Implications of Algorithmic Phenomena, Hybrid Agency, and the Performativity of Technology: IFIP WG 8.2 Working Conference on the Interaction of Information Systems and the Organization, IS&O 2018.* San Francisco, CA, USA. (Vol. 543). Springer.

Slack, J. D., & Hristova, S. (2020). Why we need the concept of algorithmic culture. *Algorithmic culture: How big data and artificial intelligence are transforming everyday life* (p. 15).

Surden, H. (2014). Machine learning and law. *Washington Law Review, 89,* 87.

Tolan, S. (2018). *Fair and unbiased algorithmic decision making: Current state and future challenges* (JRC Digital Economy Working Paper 2018—10). European Commission.

United States. Executive Office of the President. (2016). *Artificial intelligence, automation, and the economy.*

Yeung, K., & Lodge, M. (Eds.). (2019). *Algorithmic regulation.* Oxford University Press.

Zafar, M. B. (2019). *Discrimination in algorithmic decision making: From principles to measures and mechanisms.*

Zuiderveen Borgesius, F. (2018). *Discrimination, artificial intelligence, and algorithmic decision-making.*

INDEX

© The Editor(s) (if applicable) and The Author(s), under exclusive license to Springer Nature Singapore Pte Ltd. 2021
R. Gupta and S. K. Pal, *Introduction to Algorithmic Government*,
https://doi.org/10.1007/978-981-16-0282-5

GPSR Compliance
The European Union's (EU) General Product Safety Regulation (GPSR) is a set
of rules that requires consumer products to be safe and our obligations to
ensure this.

If you have any concerns about our products, you can contact us on

ProductSafety@springernature.com

In case Publisher is established outside the EU, the EU authorized
representative is:

Springer Nature Customer Service Center GmbH
Europaplatz 3
69115 Heidelberg, Germany